D0528477

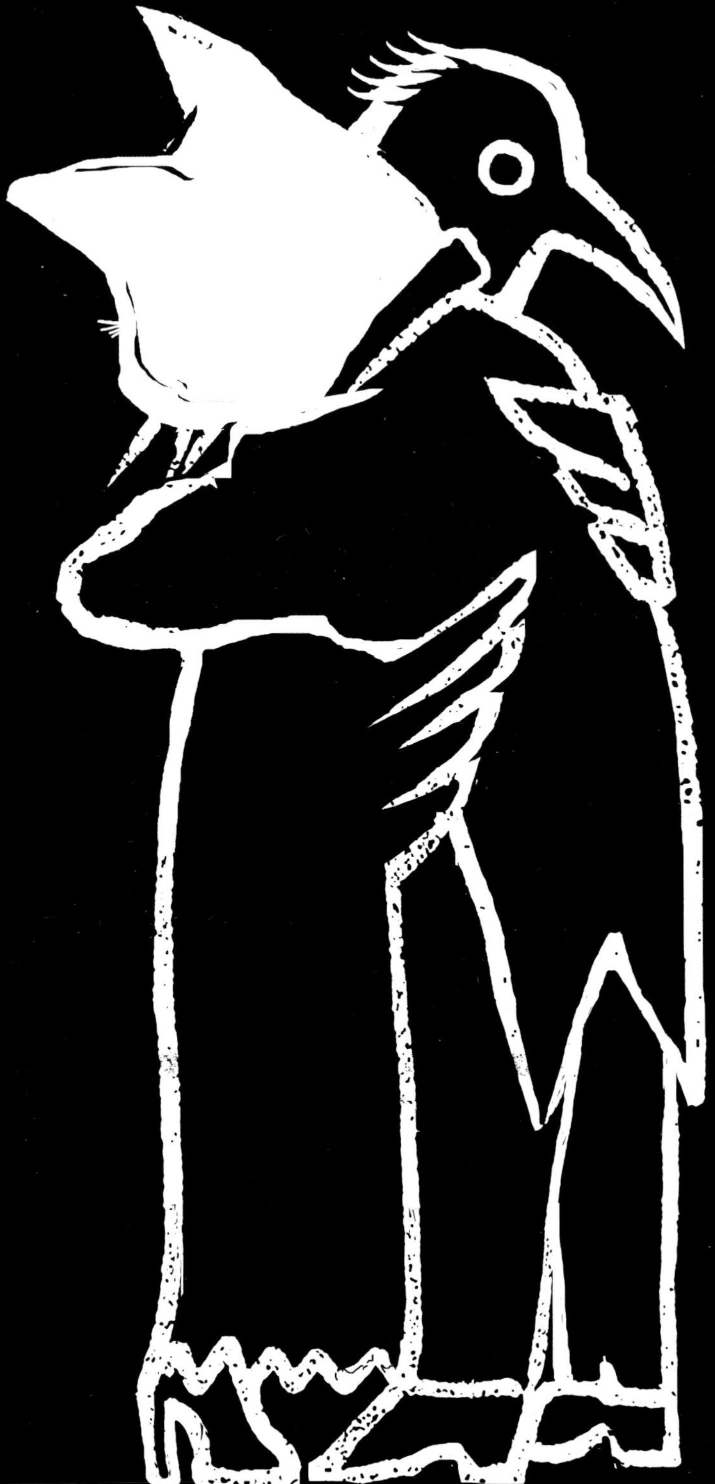

BIZARRE ROMANCE

STORIES BY
Audrey Niffenegger

ILLUSTRATED BY
Eddie Campbell

Waterford City and County Libraries

WITHDRAWN

Jonathan Cape

Contents

Introduction

Art is like love. It's impossible to will it into being; it won't come when called or leave when the party's over. Love and art manifest themselves through the most unlikely people, attract opposites, and defy expectations. Love and art are often unlovely, but when they are real, that doesn't matter so much. Disappointments and happy accidents alike can lead to new ways of seeing and happily ever after. Love and art require us to take risks.

A few months ago, Eddie Campbell and I got married. We had been conducting a *very* long-distance courtship: He lived in Brisbane, Australia, and I lived in Chicago, USA, two cities that are almost exactly opposite each other on the globe. After a number of "dates" that each lasted several weeks, we took the big plunge and applied for a K-1 visa from the US government. Eight months later, we stood together in front of a judge in the basement of Chicago City Hall and said, "I do."

Now we are living happily ever after. When I was small, I always wondered what that would mean; it was never specified, as though it was too marvelous or too boring to mention. I am pleased to report that in our case, living happily ever after includes working together on this book, *Bizarre Romance*.

These thirteen stories are sometimes romantic, sometimes star-crossed, or merely discombobulated, but all are at least a tiny bit bizarre. We embarked on the first of them when the *Guardian* invited us to collaborate for their special section, "Novelists Do Comics," wherein novel-writing persons and comics-drawing persons got together to produce comics. The result was "Thursdays, Six to Eight p.m." It amused us to make a twisted, twenty-first-century romance comic while pursuing our own romance from distant corners of the globe. We worked on the comic over email and by phone, mingling discussions about it with conversations about daily life in Brisbane (walks with Monty the dog, drinks at JoJo's pub) and Chicago (weird weather and politics, opera). Afterward we were pleased and relieved. *That wasn't so bad,* we thought. When the editors of *Shadow Show* invited us to turn my story "Backwards in Seville" into a comic, we realized that we had a good thing going, in more ways than one.

Some of these stories are new, and some have been published before, sans pictures. In the past I have been my own illustrator, and it has been a whole new crazy different wild thing to give the stories over to Eddie and to see his ideas take form and grow on the lattice each story provides. His art expands and comments upon the text, inflects and gently lampoons it, and sometimes moves sideways from the text, shakes it up a little. There are places where the words did not specify, and the images have moved into that empty space with form, color, a bustle of activity, a soft mood, or a jolt of realism; it has been interesting to find out what certain characters look like and to watch the interplay of words and images yield a more complete world for each story.

Taking risks is always surprising and often uncomfortable. We had to figure out new ways of working while we were figuring out how to reconfigure our lives after closing all that distance between us. We now live in the same house and work in adjoining rooms. We have learned things about art making and about each other. The result has been a book that neither of us would have made alone—a book that is ours.

Thursdays, Six to Eight p.m.

When Charles Walters finally proposed to Ellen Tripp, he held up a hand to stop the yes that was about to pop out of her mouth.

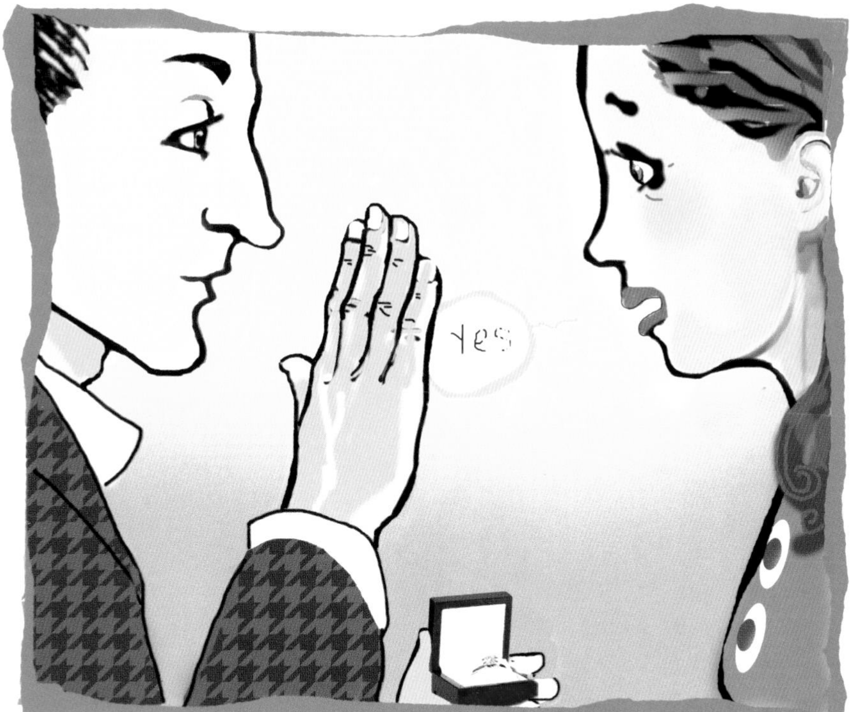
Yes

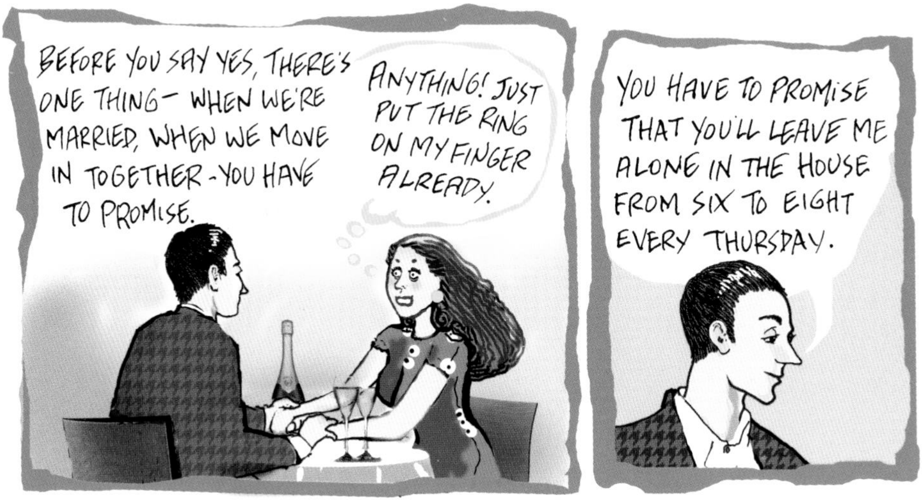
BEFORE YOU SAY YES, THERE'S ONE THING— WHEN WE'RE MARRIED, WHEN WE MOVE IN TOGETHER - YOU HAVE TO PROMISE.
ANYTHING! JUST PUT THE RING ON MY FINGER ALREADY.
YOU HAVE TO PROMISE THAT YOU'LL LEAVE ME ALONE IN THE HOUSE FROM SIX TO EIGHT EVERY THURSDAY.

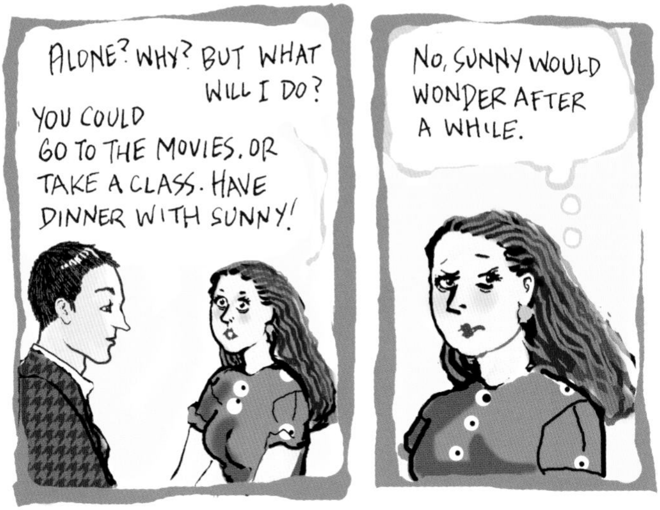
ALONE? WHY? BUT WHAT WILL I DO?
YOU COULD GO TO THE MOVIES. OR TAKE A CLASS. HAVE DINNER WITH SUNNY!
NO, SUNNY WOULD WONDER AFTER A WHILE.

She wondered, herself, for a moment, but then her thoughts skipped ahead to the things she'd been lusting after the whole seven years she and Charles had been dating. She tried to recollect whether they'd ever gone out together on a Thursday night.

Charles had been married before, had been married, in fact, when they began to see each other. But she was thirty-seven. This was no time to balk at small details.

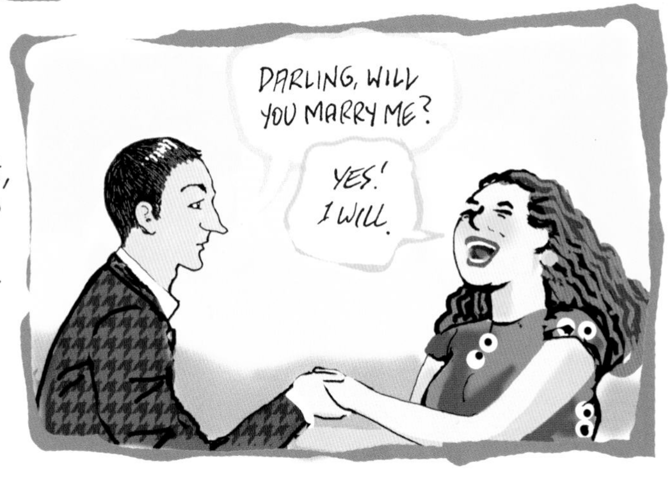
DARLING, WILL YOU MARRY ME?
YES! I WILL.

I n the subsequent sweetness of victory she forgot all about her concession. Ellen flaunted her large engagement ring, registered at Crate & Barrel, Barneys, and Macy's.

She happily endured her mother's bullying over the dress, the band, the flowers, the guest list.

Charles was co-operative, patient, and amused by her obsessive attention to minutiae.

He occasionally expressed a preference (for carrot cake over white, plain Ikea china over Limoges, tango over disco) but allowed himself to be overruled without fuss by Mrs. Tripp and Ellen.

The wedding happened with all the usual little snafus and inexplicable moments of genuine delight.

Charles was tender and serene in his tux; Ellen was, as they say, radiant (and later rather tipsy)

So they married and went off to the Bahamas, got sunburned and satiated with each other...

and returned to Chicago on a gray Saturday in March to their brand-new condo in Wicker Park.

They established a routine. Each morning Charles took the Blue Line downtown to the Board of Trade, where he bought and sold pork bellies and corn and other useful things he would never actually set eyes upon.

Damen
cta Blue Lin

Ellen walked a few blocks to North Avenue, where she had a job selling expensive shoes that looked as though dissolute medieval elves made them.

Most of her customers were middle-aged single women, and Ellen had to resist the urge to explain to them that heterosexual men would shun them if they wore these shoes. Ellen believed in the power of high heels and wore them to work even though she was supposed to wear the product.

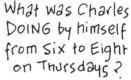

The first few Thursdays went by without incident. Ellen spent the hours at the café next to the shoe store.

But as the weeks went by, and the months, and after their anniversary came and went, Ellen was sick of Thursday Nights.

What was Charles DOING by himself from six to eight on Thursdays?

POPCORN

She made a list:

Porn?

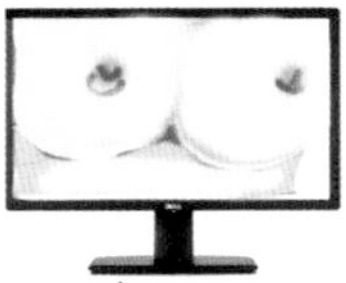

cross-dressing?

really weird Porn?

He's seeing someone else.

She had been his other woman herself and didn't have to imagine very hard to see him with someone younger.

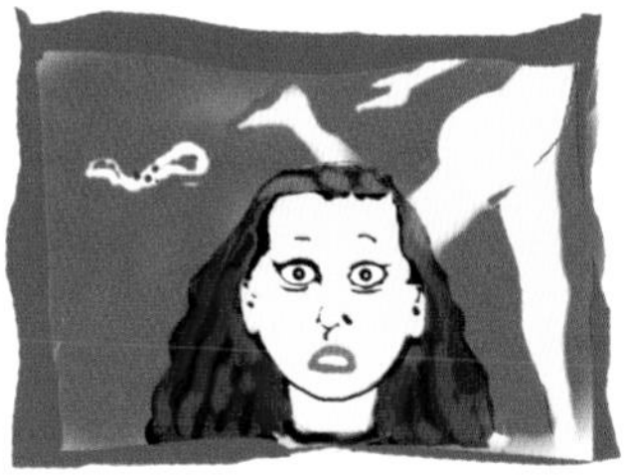

She decided at last to see if anyone came to the house on Thursday night. She arrived well before six.

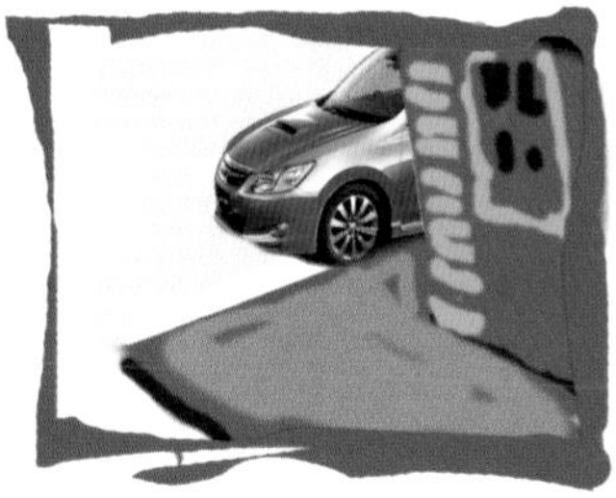

She sat in the car eating M&Ms, drinking bottled water, and watching the condo.

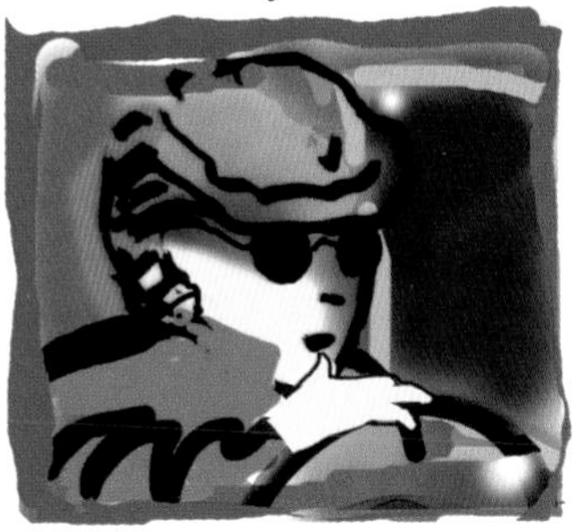

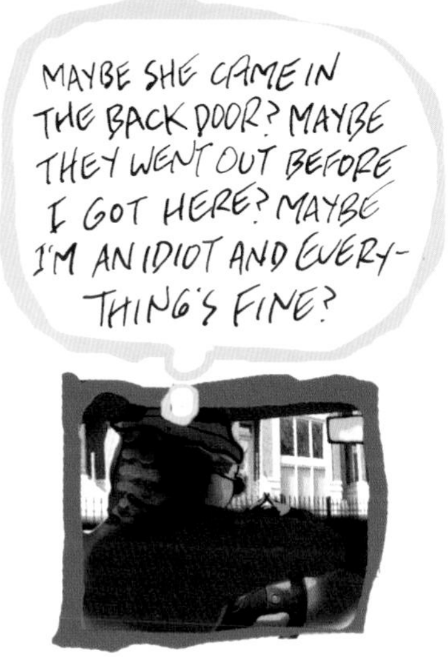
MAYBE SHE CAME IN THE BACK DOOR? MAYBE THEY WENT OUT BEFORE I GOT HERE? MAYBE I'M AN IDIOT AND EVERYTHING'S FINE?

She wished she hadn't drunk all that water. At 8:05 she let herself into the condo.

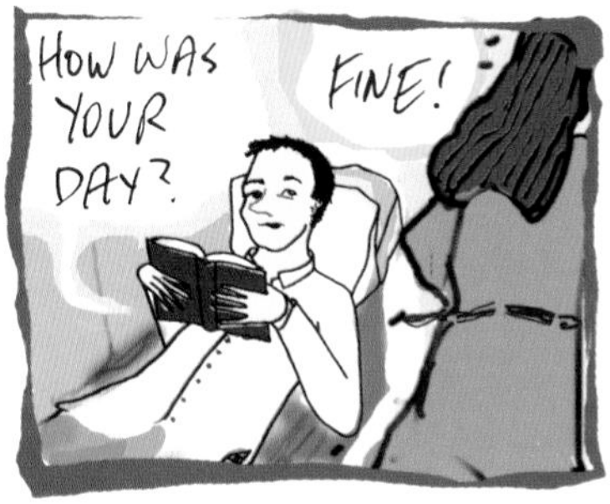
HOW WAS YOUR DAY?
FINE!

She realized she would need professional help.

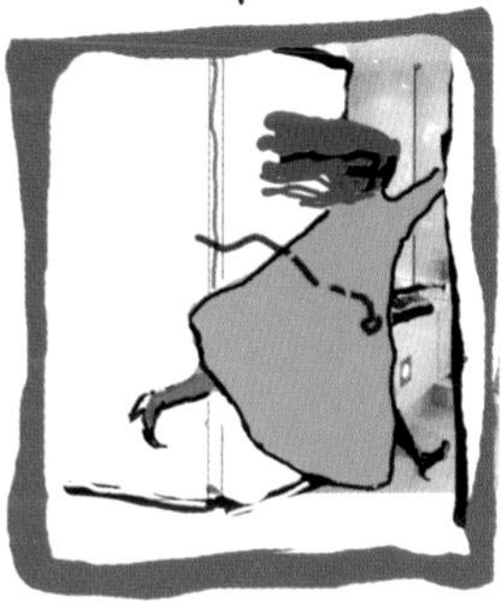

Her urge to find out was like a bad case of poison ivy.

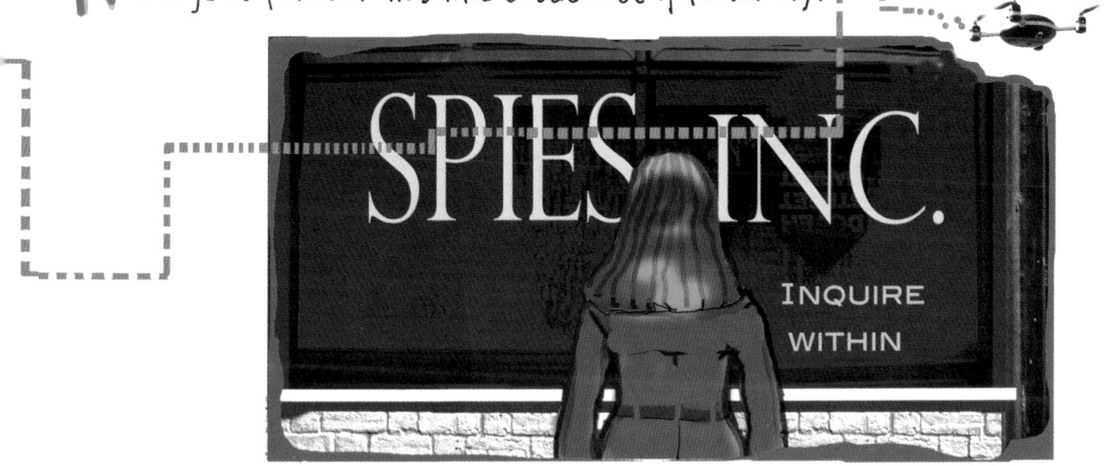
SPIES INC.
INQUIRE WITHIN

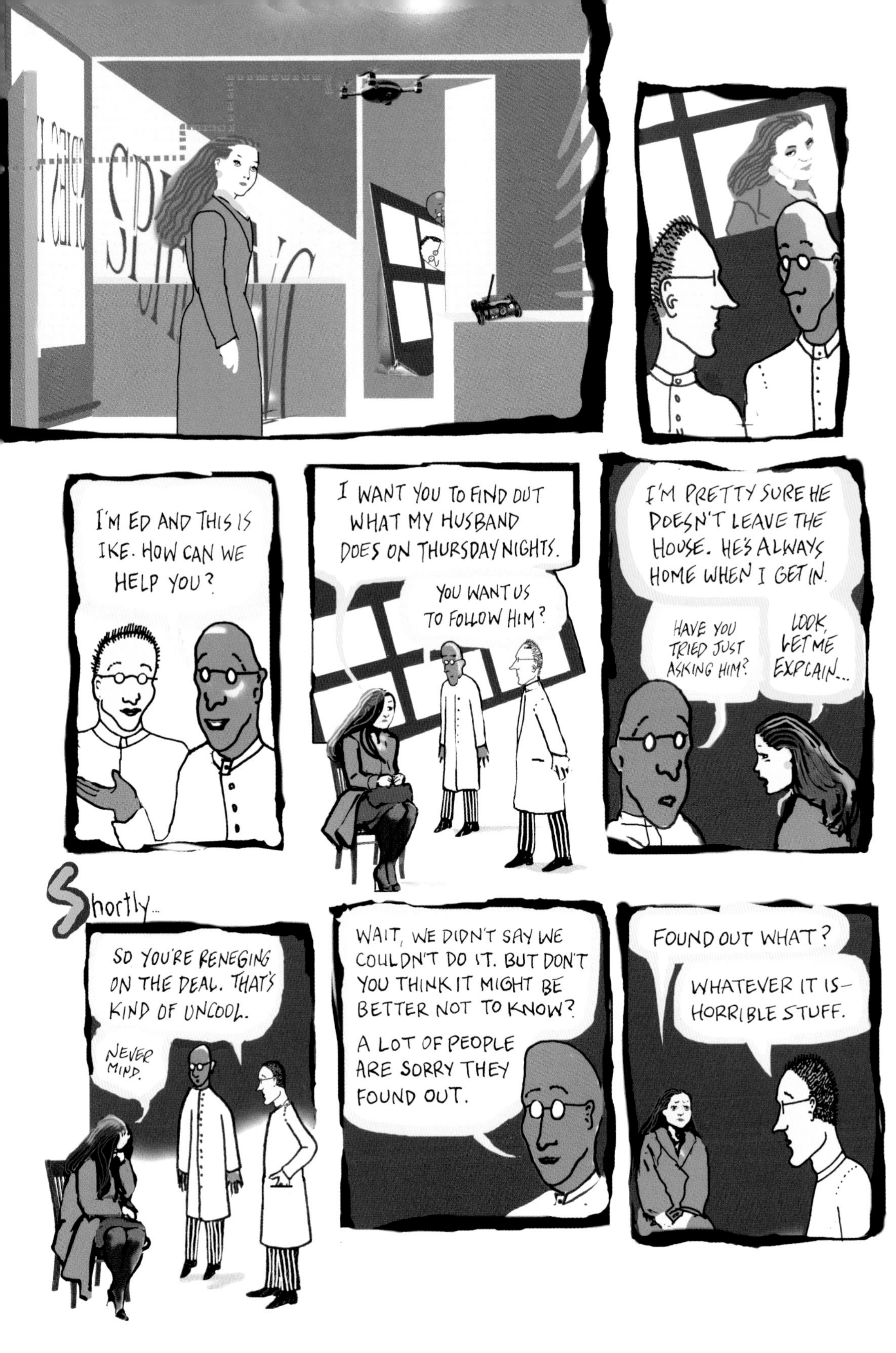
I'M ED AND THIS IS IKE. HOW CAN WE HELP YOU?
I WANT YOU TO FIND OUT WHAT MY HUSBAND DOES ON THURSDAY NIGHTS.
YOU WANT US TO FOLLOW HIM?
I'M PRETTY SURE HE DOESN'T LEAVE THE HOUSE. HE'S ALWAYS HOME WHEN I GET IN.
HAVE YOU TRIED JUST ASKING HIM?
LOOK, LET ME EXPLAIN...
Shortly...
SO YOU'RE RENEGING ON THE DEAL. THAT'S KIND OF UNCOOL.
NEVER MIND.
WAIT, WE DIDN'T SAY WE COULDN'T DO IT. BUT DON'T YOU THINK IT MIGHT BE BETTER NOT TO KNOW?
A LOT OF PEOPLE ARE SORRY THEY FOUND OUT.
FOUND OUT WHAT?
WHATEVER IT IS-HORRIBLE STUFF.

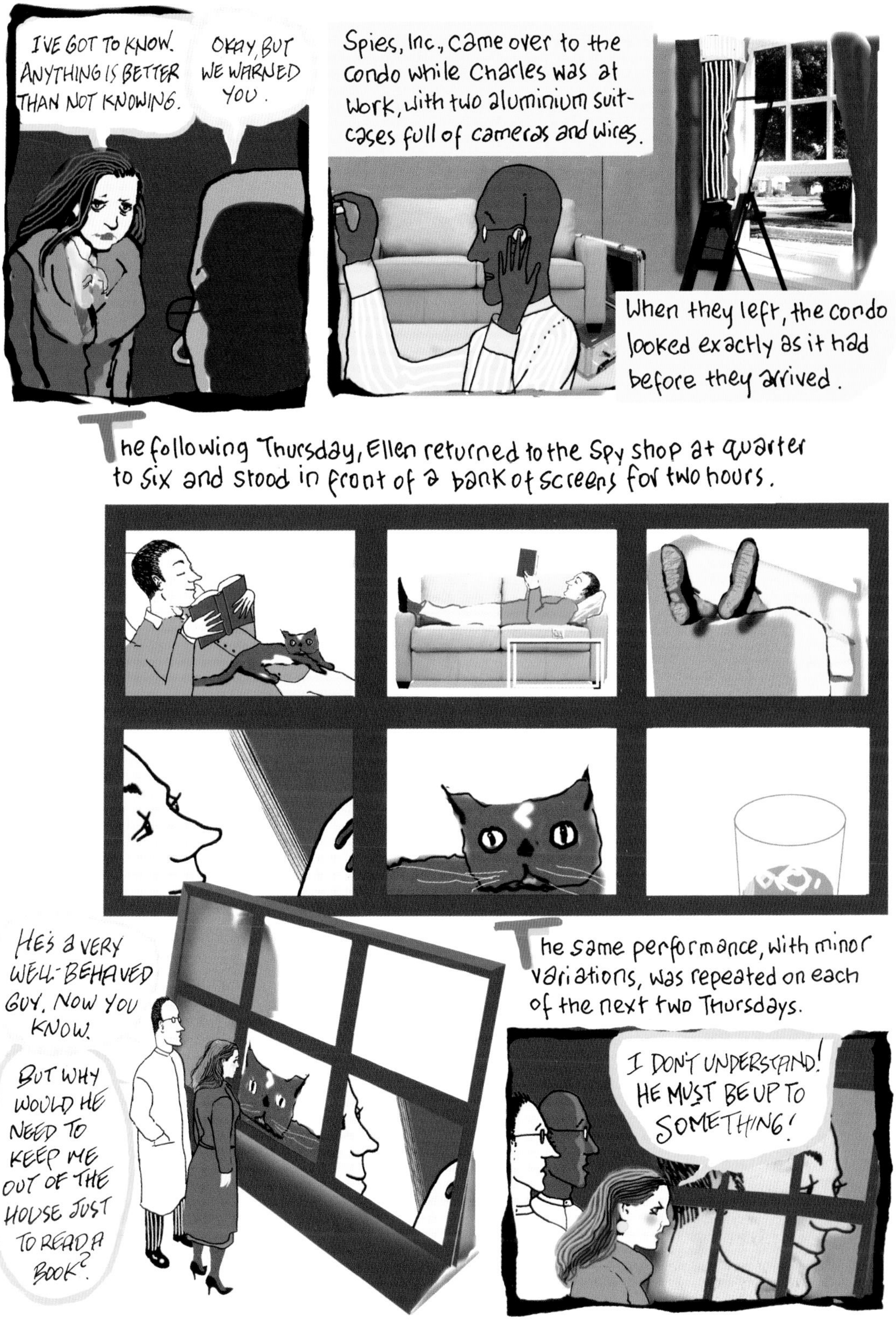
I'VE GOT TO KNOW. ANYTHING IS BETTER THAN NOT KNOWING.
OKAY, BUT WE WARNED YOU.
Spies, Inc., came over to the condo while Charles was at work, with two aluminium suitcases full of cameras and wires.
When they left, the condo looked exactly as it had before they arrived.
The following Thursday, Ellen returned to the Spy shop at quarter to six and stood in front of a bank of screens for two hours.
HE'S A VERY WELL-BEHAVED GUY. NOW YOU KNOW.
BUT WHY WOULD HE NEED TO KEEP ME OUT OF THE HOUSE JUST TO READ A BOOK?
The same performance, with minor variations, was repeated on each of the next two Thursdays.
I DON'T UNDERSTAND! HE MUST BE UP TO SOMETHING!

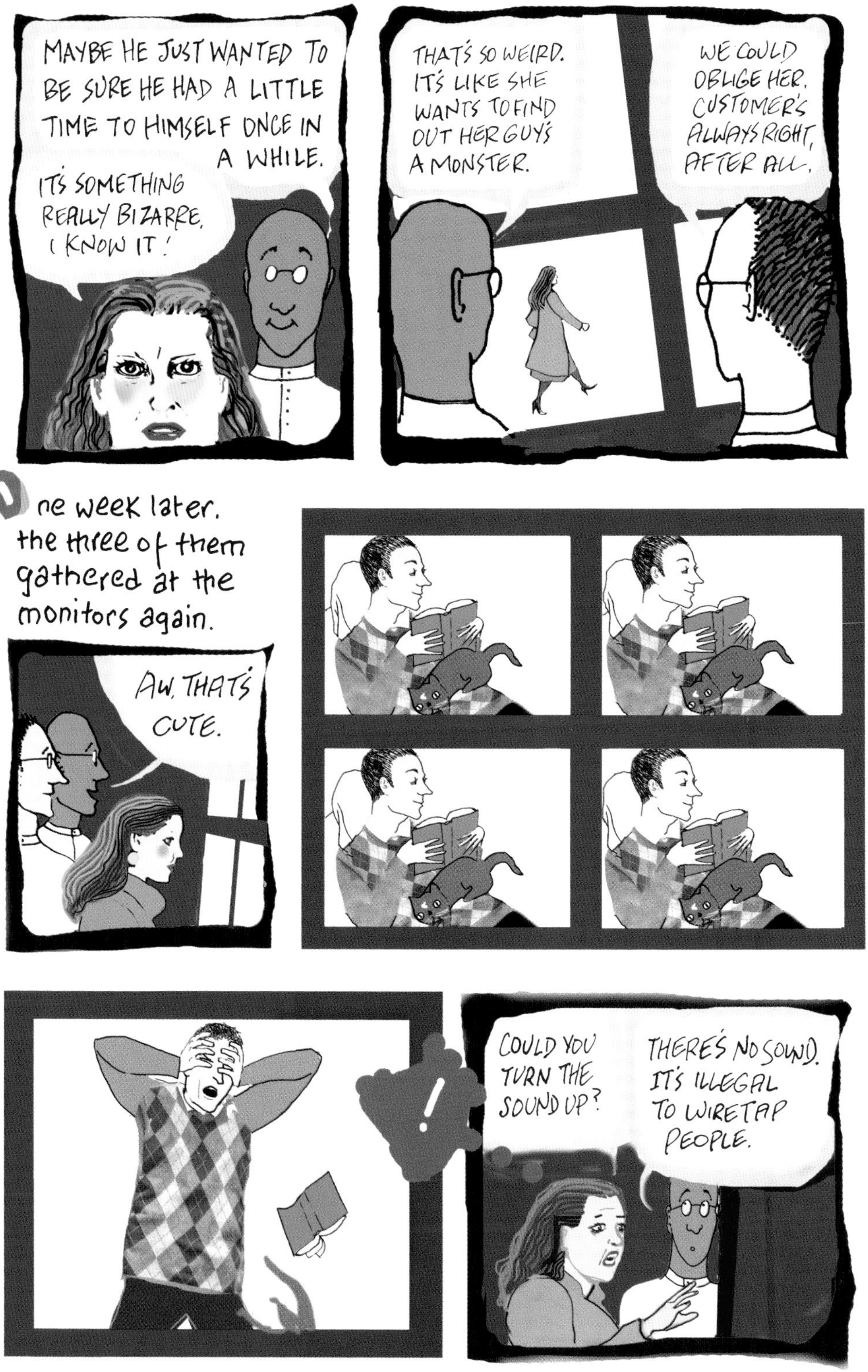
MAYBE HE JUST WANTED TO BE SURE HE HAD A LITTLE TIME TO HIMSELF ONCE IN A WHILE.
IT'S SOMETHING REALLY BIZARRE, I KNOW IT!
THAT'S SO WEIRD. IT'S LIKE SHE WANTS TO FIND OUT HER GUY'S A MONSTER.
WE COULD OBLIGE HER. CUSTOMER'S ALWAYS RIGHT, AFTER ALL.
One week later, the three of them gathered at the monitors again.
AW, THAT'S CUTE.
!
COULD YOU TURN THE SOUND UP?
THERE'S NO SOUND. IT'S ILLEGAL TO WIRETAP PEOPLE.

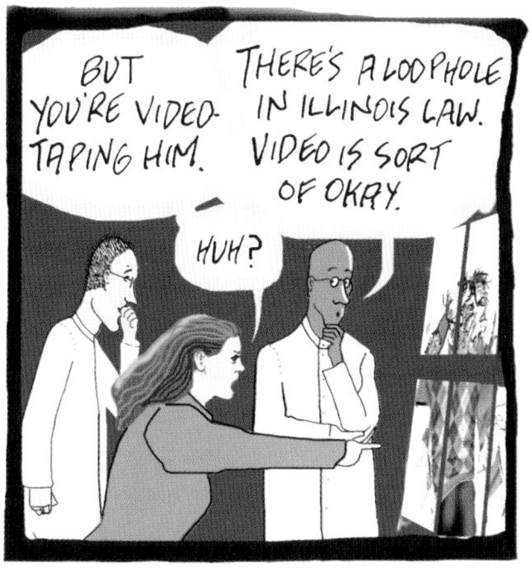
BUT YOU'RE VIDEO-TAPING HIM.
THERE'S A LOOPHOLE IN ILLINOIS LAW. VIDEO IS SORT OF OKAY.
HUH?

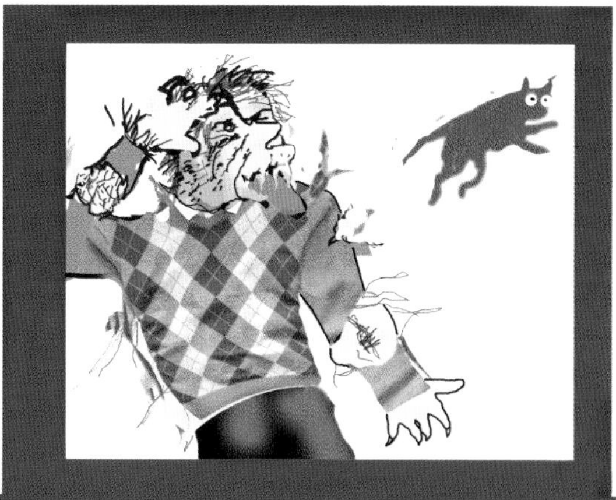

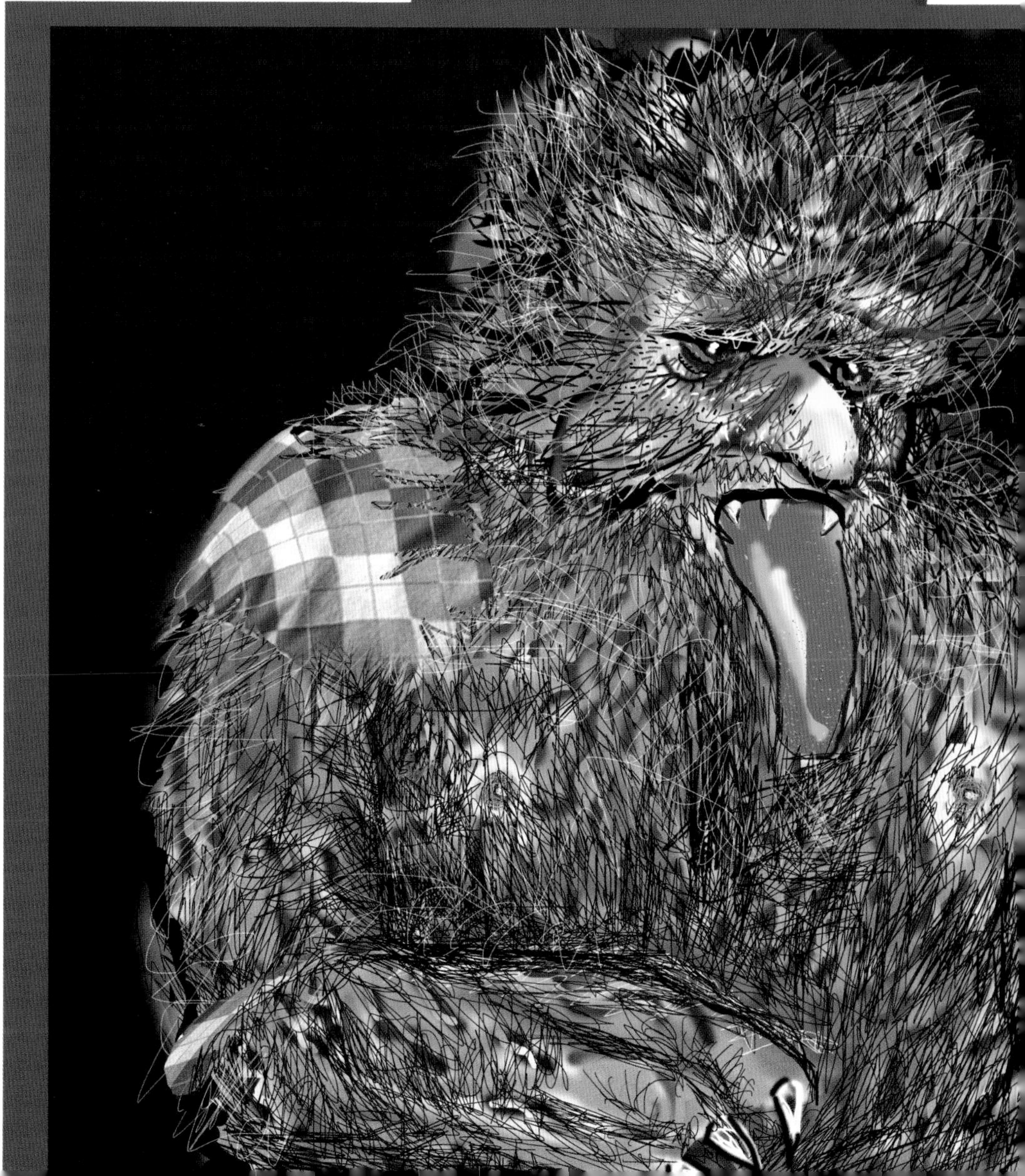

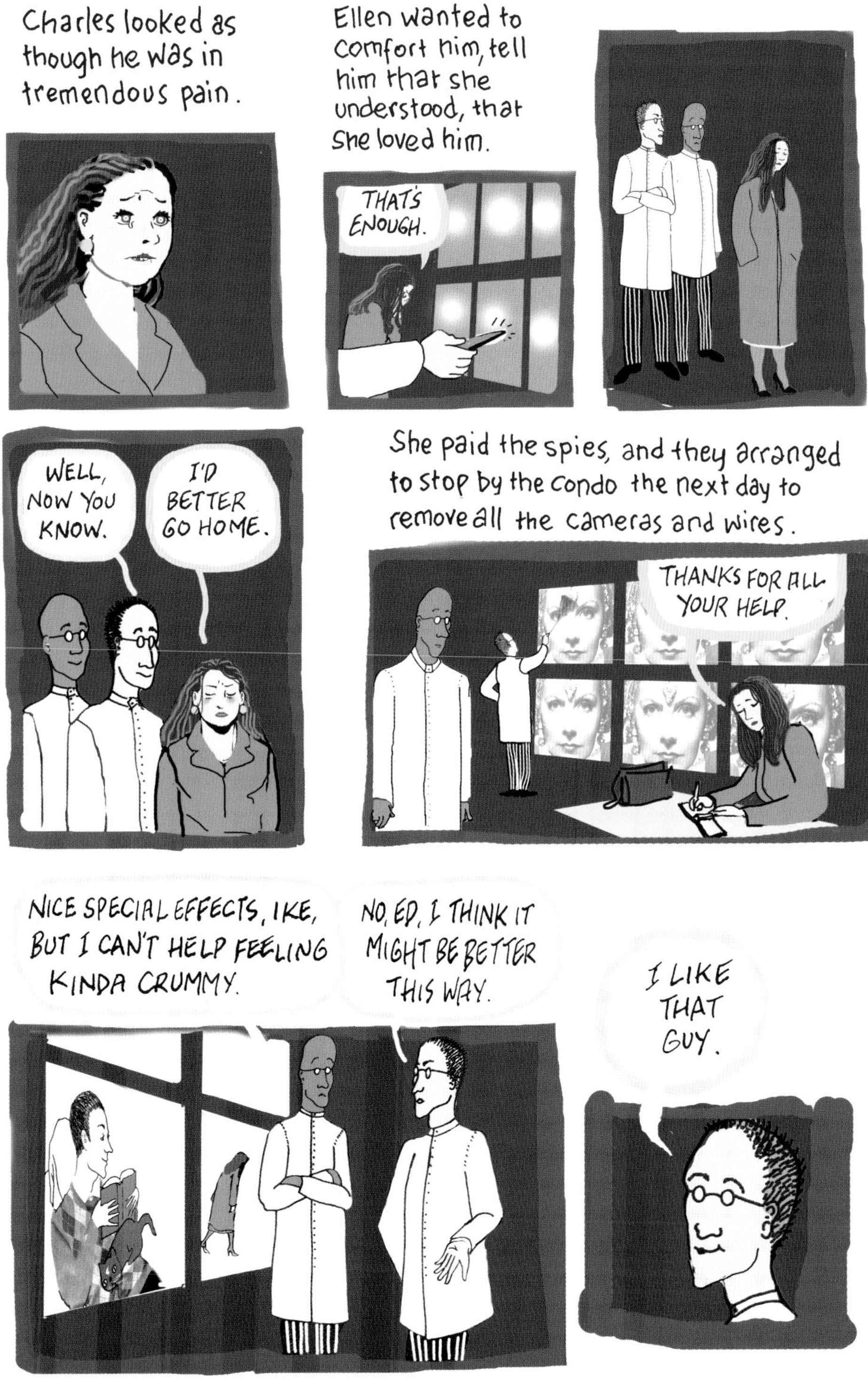

Charles looked as though he was in tremendous pain.
Ellen wanted to comfort him, tell him that she understood, that she loved him.
THAT'S ENOUGH.
WELL, NOW YOU KNOW.
I'D BETTER GO HOME.
She paid the spies, and they arranged to stop by the condo the next day to remove all the cameras and wires.
THANKS FOR ALL YOUR HELP.
NICE SPECIAL EFFECTS, IKE, BUT I CAN'T HELP FEELING KINDA CRUMMY.
NO, ED, I THINK IT MIGHT BE BETTER THIS WAY.
I LIKE THAT GUY.

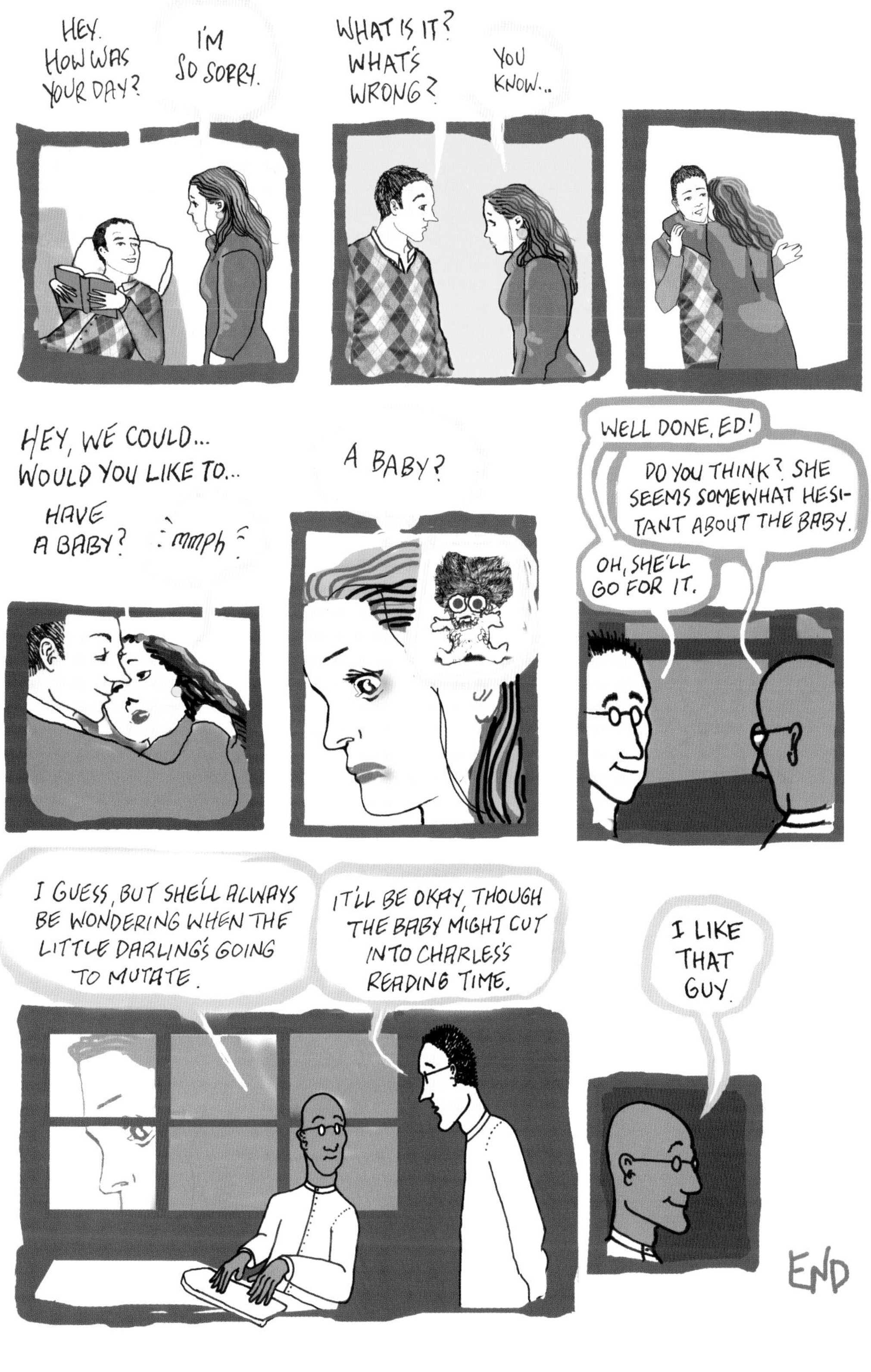
HEY. HOW WAS YOUR DAY?
I'M SO SORRY.
WHAT IS IT? WHAT'S WRONG?
YOU KNOW...
HEY, WE COULD... WOULD YOU LIKE TO...
HAVE A BABY?
:MMPH:
A BABY?
WELL DONE, ED!
DO YOU THINK? SHE SEEMS SOMEWHAT HESI-TANT ABOUT THE BABY.
OH, SHE'LL GO FOR IT.
I GUESS, BUT SHE'LL ALWAYS BE WONDERING WHEN THE LITTLE DARLING'S GOING TO MUTATE.
IT'LL BE OKAY, THOUGH THE BABY MIGHT CUT INTO CHARLES'S READING TIME.
I LIKE THAT GUY.
END

The Composite Boyfriend

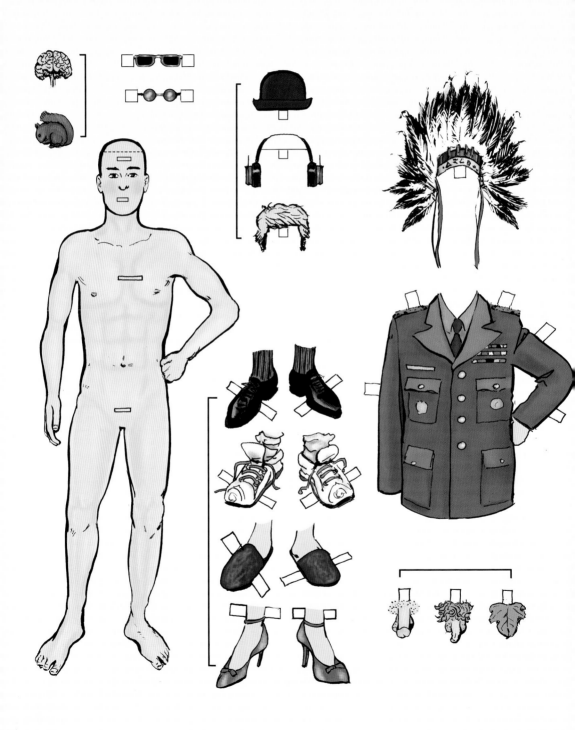

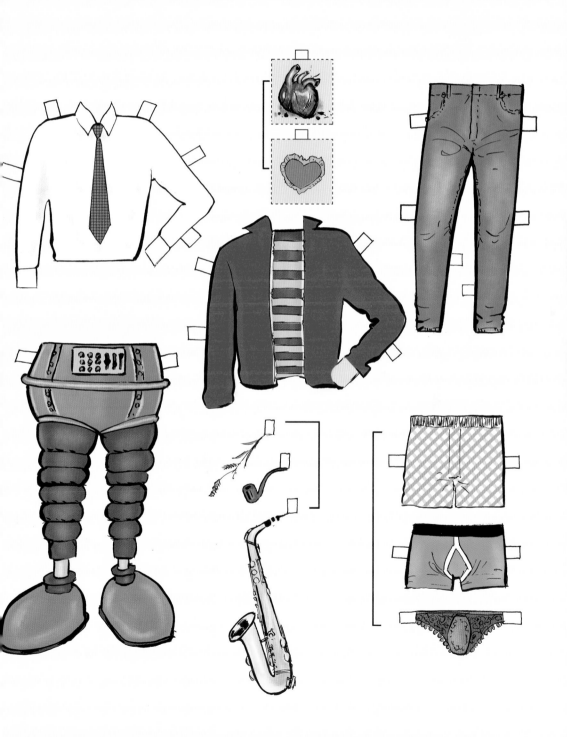

I met him at the Isabella Stewart Gardner Museum in Boston, where he worked as a guard. I met him in a class I was taking. I met him at a school where we both taught. I met him at a party; we smiled at each other across a crowded room. We were introduced to each other by our mutual friend Paula, an Austrian immigrant who had escaped from the Nazis as a young girl.

I asked him a question about a painting; we chatted; we went out to a club that night; afterward, I brought him to meet my best friend, who was ill and in the hospital. I was taking a trip to Amsterdam, he was Dutch, we went out for coffee so he could tell me what to see when I got to Holland. I ended up spending New Year's Eve with him at his mother's house in Arnhem. I gave him my phone number but accidentally transposed two digits because I had just changed it. He managed to call anyway. I saw him standing alone at a party, smiling at me. "Who's that?" I asked Sylvia, because he was handsome. It was her party. She sighed and told me I didn't want to know him, but she wouldn't tell me why not; I ended up driving him home. I don't remember how we began. Somehow we did.

It was 1985. It was 1997. It was 1992. It was 1996. It was 2001. It was spring, winter, summer, autumn, winter.

He was an artist, a neurobiologist, a writer, a legal secretary, a musician. He was writing his dissertation on Wittgenstein. He was tall and didn't drive; he always wore a blue windbreaker and went everywhere on his bicycle. He was shorter than me and had an accent. Until I got used to it I replied to many of his utterances with "What?" He was extremely good-looking, movie-star handsome, but his hands were always quite red, as though he had been boiling them. He smiled a lot and was a good ballroom dancer. He loved the Cubs, barbequed ribs, and high-heeled shoes.

He wasn't patient but he was very well-read. He hardly read at all and went to the movies a lot. When he was a child he was obsessed with *Star Wars*. He was obsessed with *A Clockwork Orange*. His parents were divorced, and each had remarried to people he didn't like. His father had died the year before we met; one day I went over to his apartment and saw a jahrtzeit candle burning for his dad.

I loved listening to him practice the flute. His apartment had almost no furnishings, and the sound filled the rooms and reverberated in my chest. I didn't think he was attractive, except when he was absorbed in drawing or watching TV or concentrating on what someone else was saying. Then his face was transformed—it was wise. I liked driving him places, having aimless conversations, smoking sometimes, despite his asthma. He always drove fast, as though we were late for a movie.

He made beautiful photographs. He was writing a novel about a man with eidetic memory. He had terrific hair. He was going bald. He didn't have any tattoos.

The sex was great, the sex was okay, the sex was a huge problem. The religious scruples, the foot fetish, the antidepressants, the porn addiction, the irrational fear of STDs, the lack of sleep, the boredom of monogamy, inexperience, mismatched expectations.

We talked about getting married. I was standing in a dirty phone booth in Penland, North Carolina, talking to him long-distance in Boston, when he proposed. I waited eagerly for him to ask me to marry him, but he never did. He proposed when it was too late, after I'd left him. I knew it was going nowhere; we had no future. I kept hoping, even when it was obvious that he was going to dump me.

The obsessive-compulsive disorder he hid so brilliantly: He lived like a deranged squirrel, all his possessions wrapped in plastic and stored in Tupperware containers stacked up to the ceiling. He was recently divorced but insisted he was over it. He mentioned his ex a lot. He lived across the country and stopped calling. Three months later he called at two a.m., drunk, asking if he could borrow money. He placed a personal ad while we were still dating. A friend showed it to me; I called the number and left a message. We never spoke again. We were getting into bed one night when he said, "I think we should see other people." He was already dating someone else. He found me sexually boring and stopped touching me. I found him unattractive and refused to sleep with him.

It ended.

We are still friends. We go to the movies sometimes or out for dinner. He called once, years later. We don't speak. He and his wife sat next to me in a café; I ignored them, and they asked for another table. We once considered getting back together but thought better of it.

Next time he will be perfect. Next time.

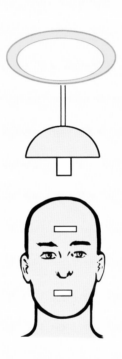

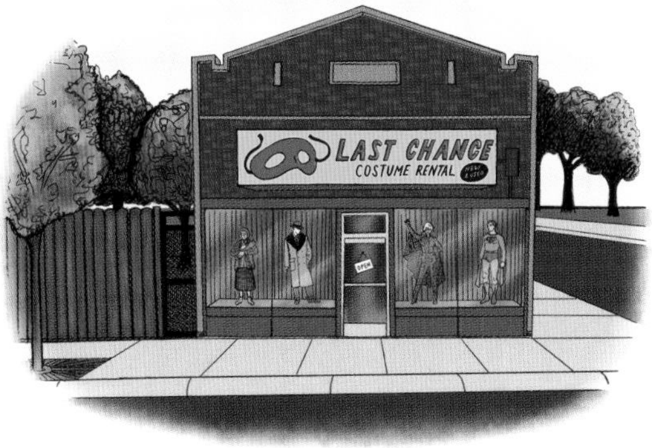
LAST CHANCE
COSTUME RENTAL
NEW & USED
OPEN

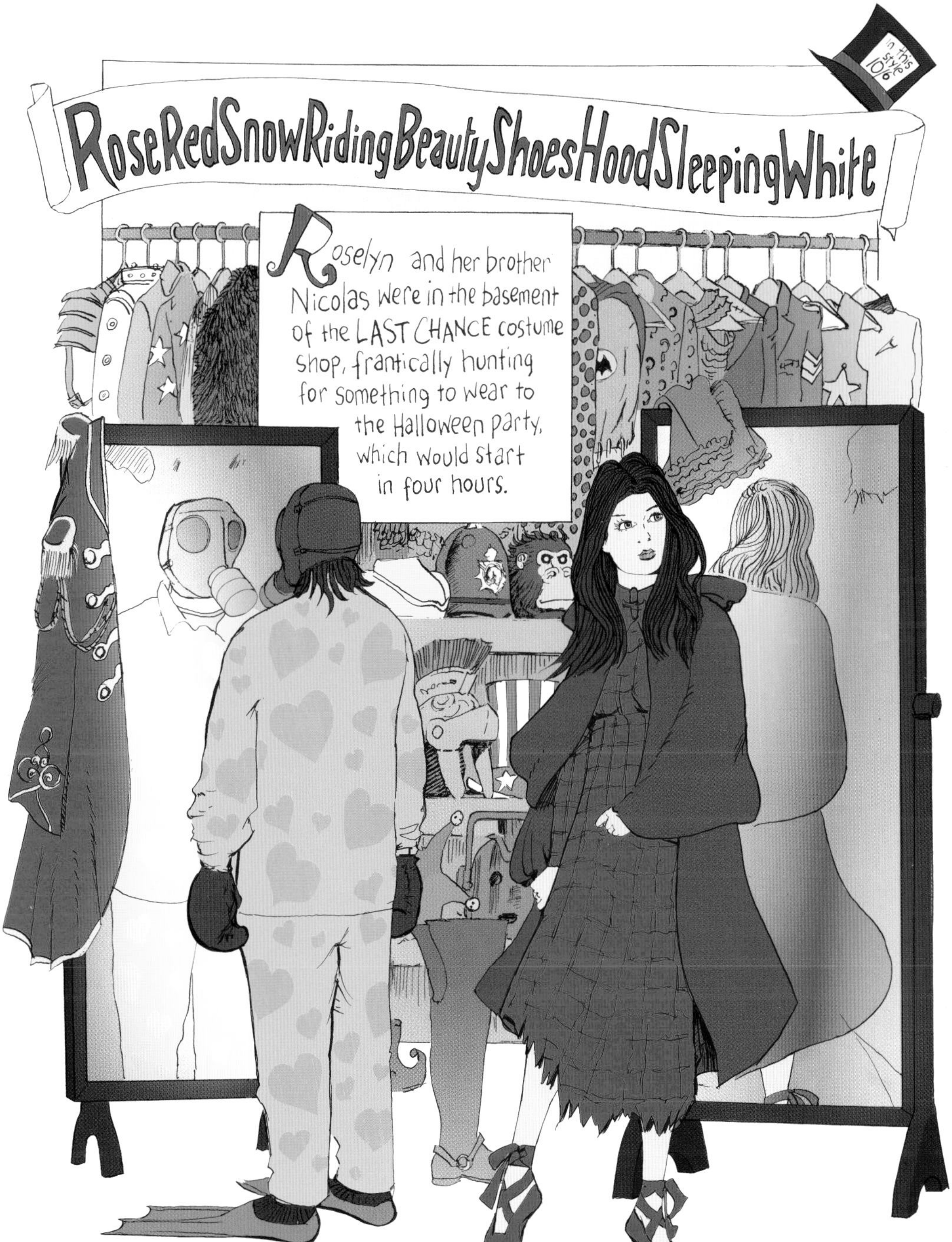

RoseRedSnowRidingBeautyShoesHoodSleepingWhite
in this style 10/6
Roselyn and her brother Nicolas were in the basement of the LAST CHANCE costume shop, frantically hunting for something to wear to the Halloween party, which would start in four hours.

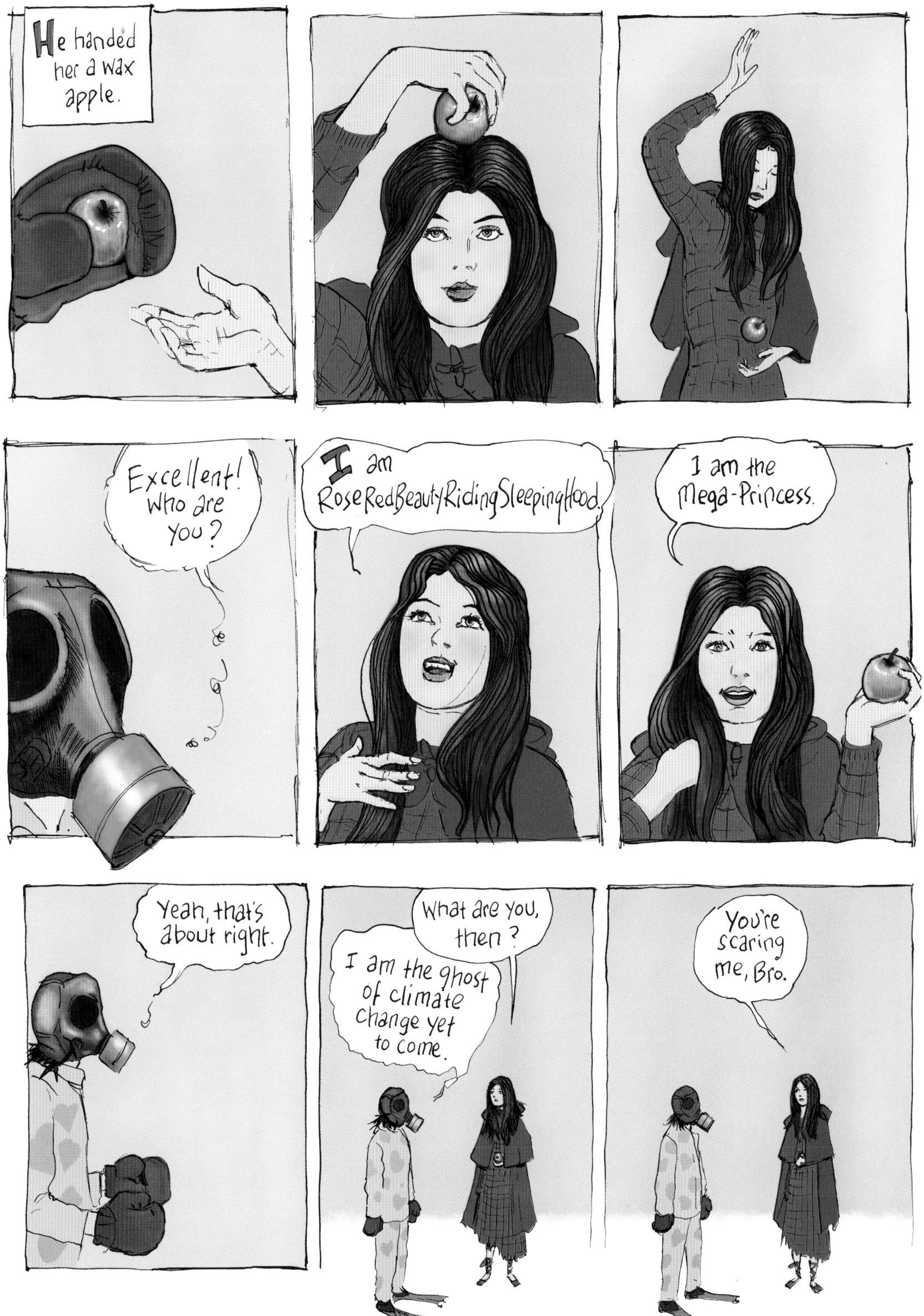
He handed her a wax apple.
Excellent! Who are you?
I am RoseRedBeautyRidingSleepingHood.
I am the Mega-Princess.
Yeah, that's about right.
What are you, then?
I am the ghost of climate change yet to come.
You're scaring me, Bro.

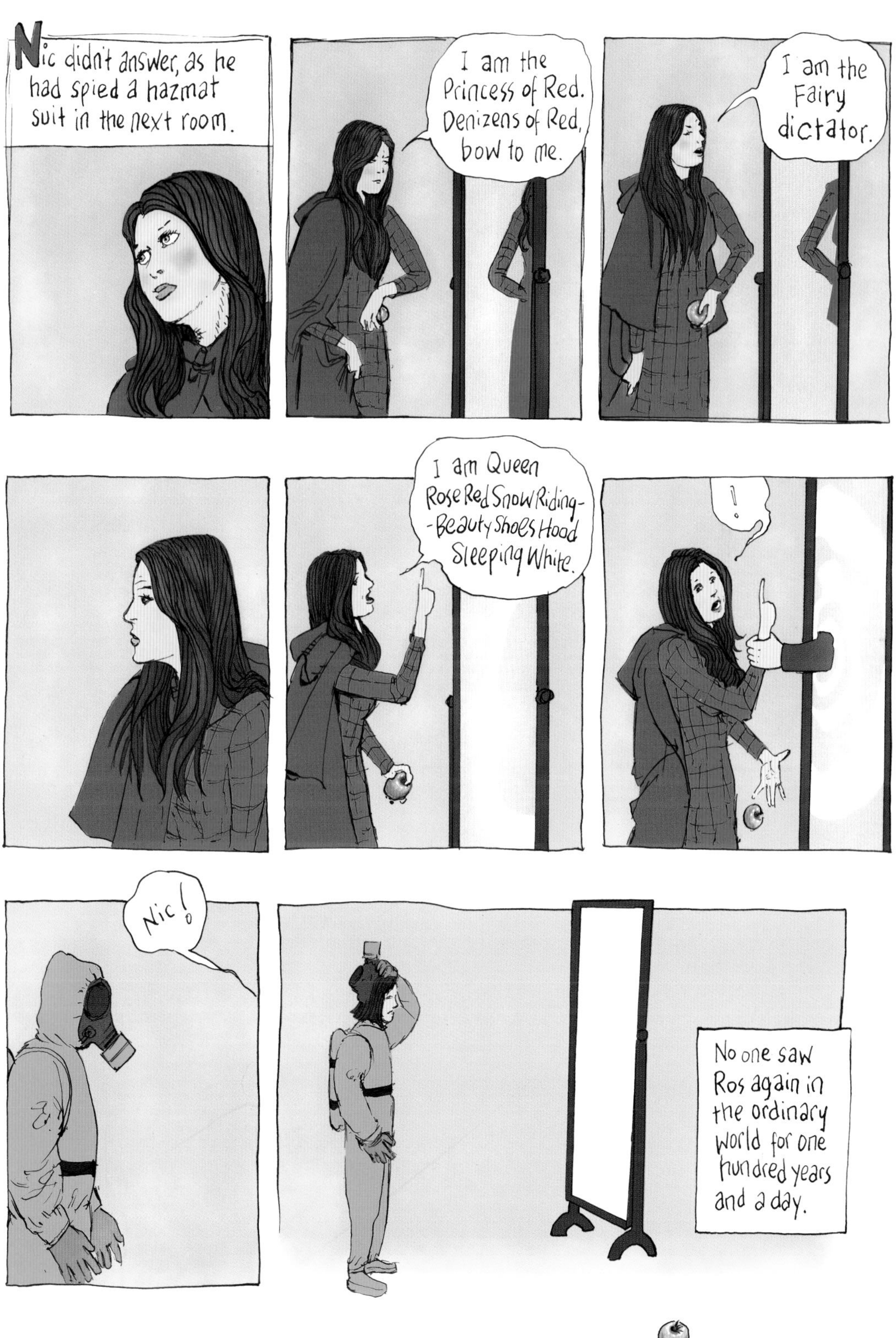
Nic didn't answer, as he had spied a hazmat suit in the next room.
I am the Princess of Red. Denizens of Red, bow to me.
I am the Fairy dictator.
I am Queen Rose Red Snow Riding--Beauty Shoes Hood Sleeping White.
!
Nic!
No one saw Ros again in the ordinary world for one hundred years and a day.

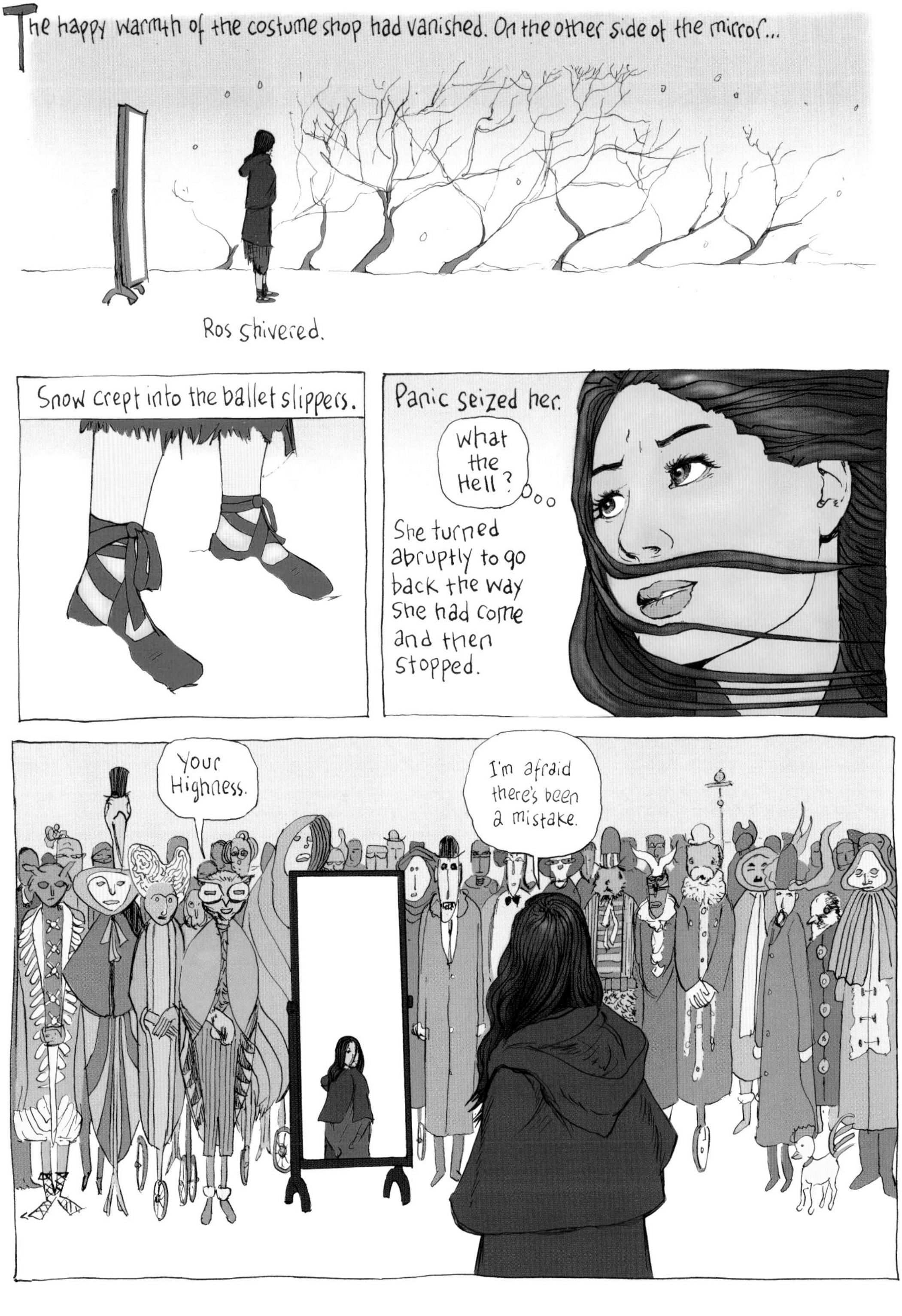
The happy warmth of the costume shop had vanished. On the other side of the mirror...
Ros shivered.
Snow crept into the ballet slippers.
Panic seized her.
What the Hell?
She turned abruptly to go back the way she had come and then stopped.
Your Highness.
I'm afraid there's been a mistake.

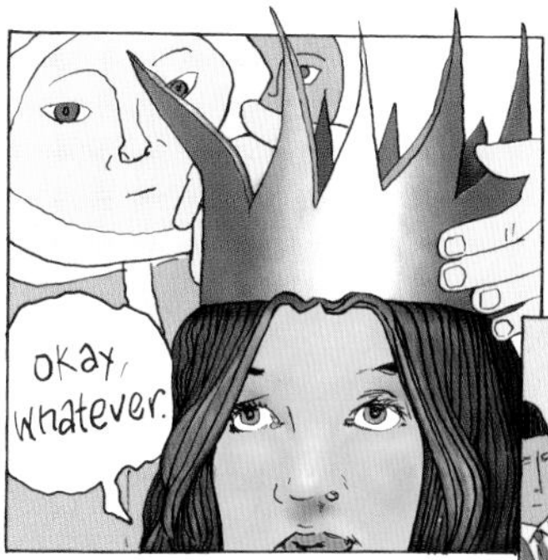
okay, whatever.

Someone brought her a velvet cape and mittens and a flask of whisky.

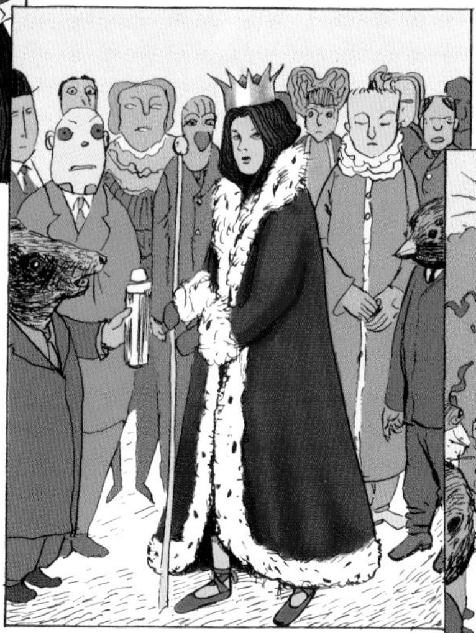

And once Ros had warmed up, she embarked on her glorious reign over the citizens of that land.

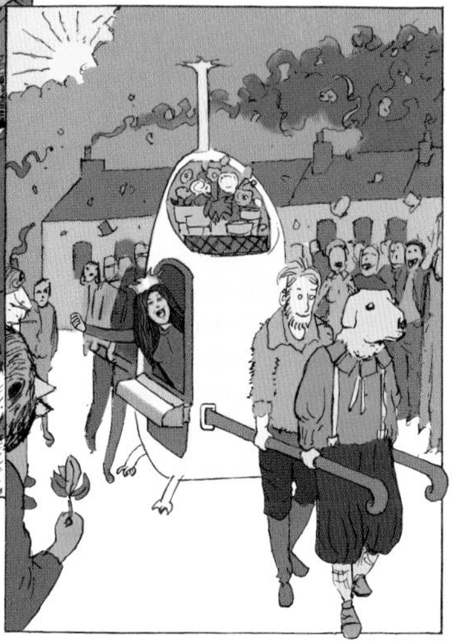

Ros discovered quickly that the Kingdom was rather provincial and behind the times. Sure, they had magic and almost no litter or traffic jams, but there was no art, no science, the food was dreadful, and the buildings tended to be squat, cold, and lumpen, with endless dark rooms and not enough closets.

Ros introduced microwave cooking, oil painting, the steam engine, mint juleps, something like coca-cola (she never quite got the recipe right), rock'n'roll, photography, hand lotion, galoshes, capitalism, and fish fingers.

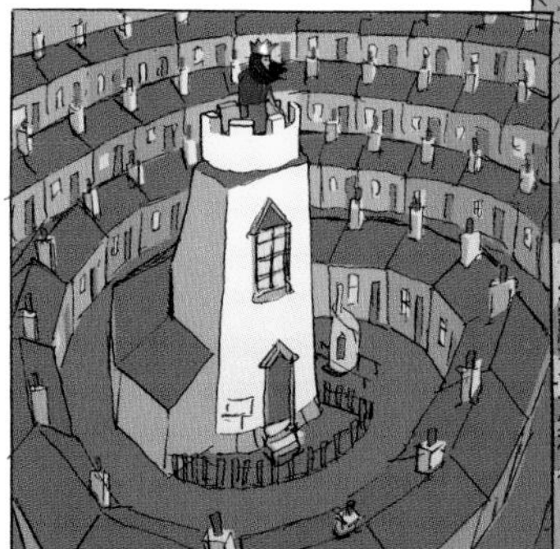

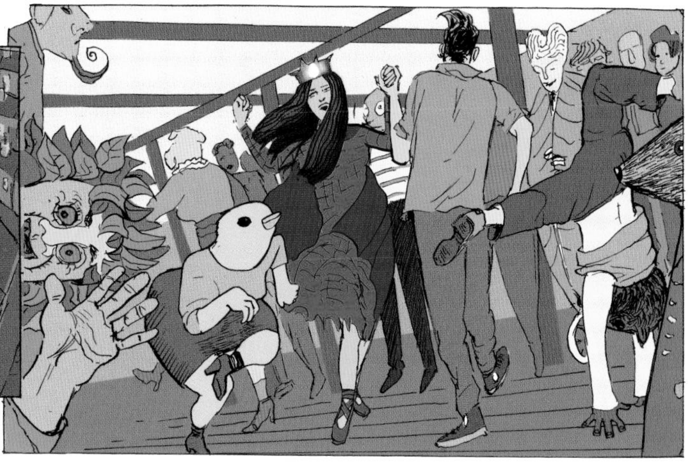

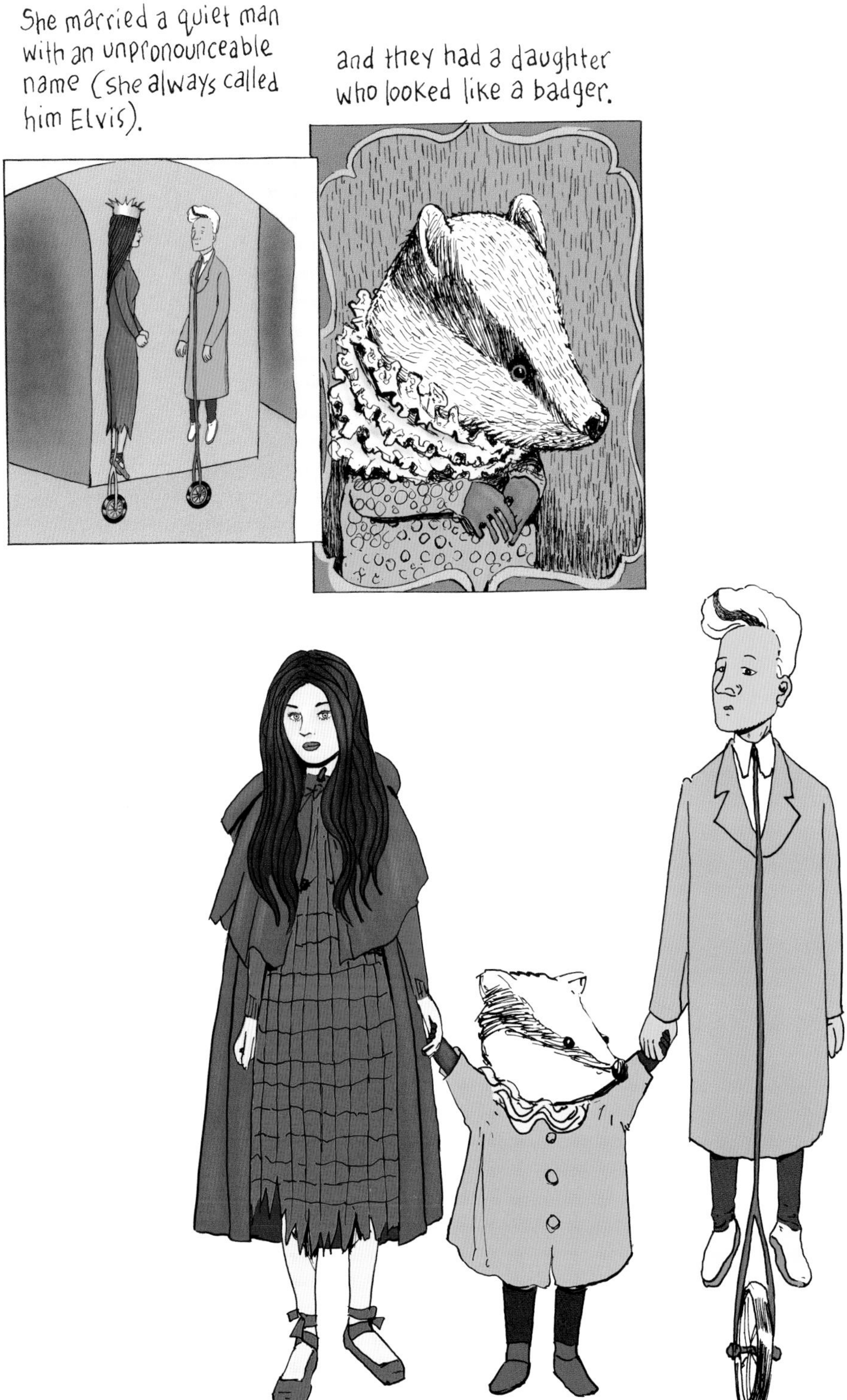
She married a quiet man with an unpronounceable name (she always called him Elvis).
and they had a daughter who looked like a badger.

Ros made her subjects celebrate the Fourth of July (they liked the fireworks)

and Christmas (which mystified them, though they enjoyed setting puddings on fire).

She never initiated any wars. She made sure everyone had enough food and occupations and hobbies.

Occasionally she would redistribute all the money just to keep things interesting. When she thought the time was right, Ros introduced democracy.

But even though she changed her job title from Queen to President, the citizens still elected her repeatedly.

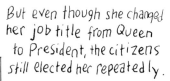

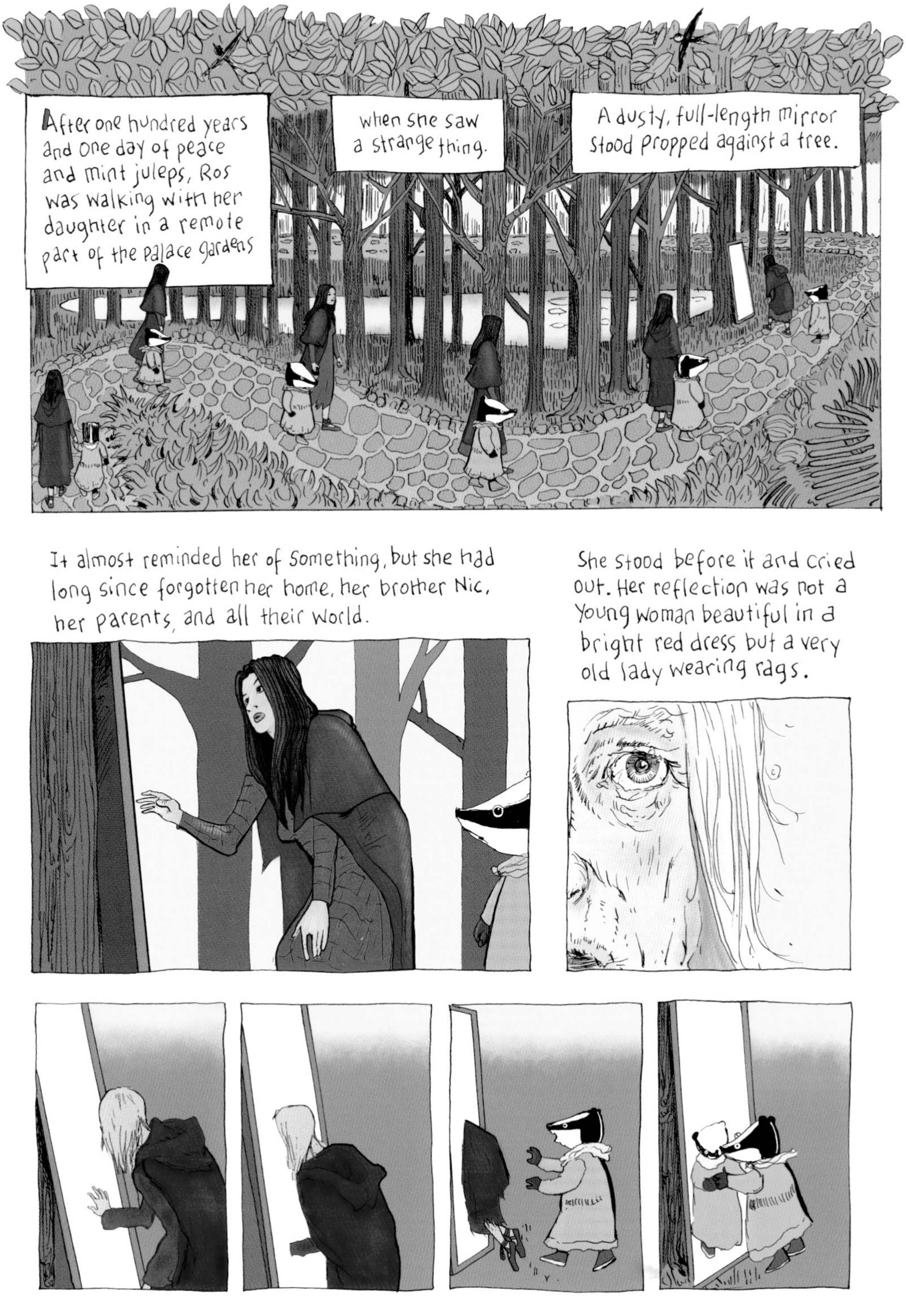
After one hundred years and one day of peace and mint juleps, Ros was walking with her daughter in a remote part of the palace gardens
when she saw a strange thing.
A dusty, full-length mirror stood propped against a tree.
It almost reminded her of something, but she had long since forgotten her home, her brother Nic, her parents, and all their world.
She stood before it and cried out. Her reflection was not a young woman beautiful in a bright red dress but a very old lady wearing rags.

When she came to, she was in an unfamiliar city. She stood up slowly and made her way through the streets. No one noticed her. She had nothing in her pockets.

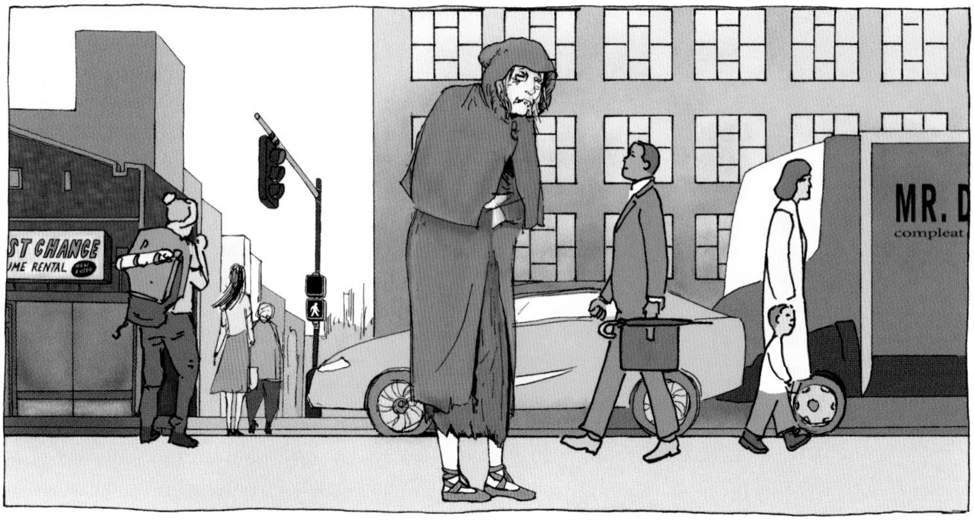
ST CHANGE
UME RENTAL
MR. D
compleat

She wondered what had become of her badger daughter and realized she might never see her again.

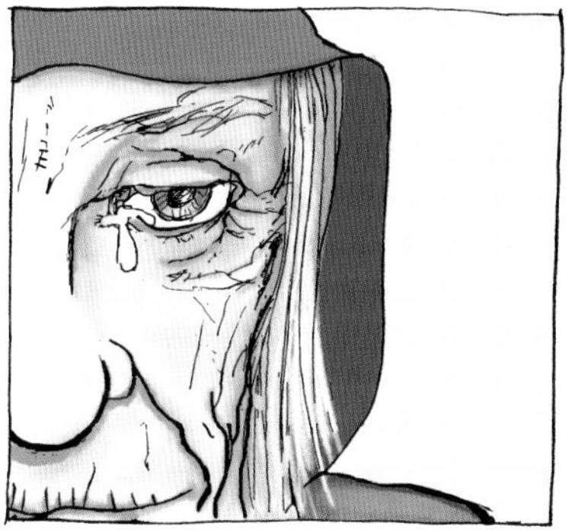

After hours of wandering, she came to a park. It looked green and inviting.

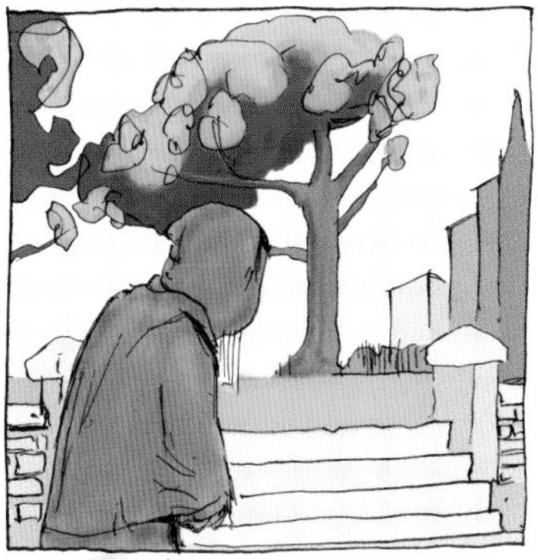

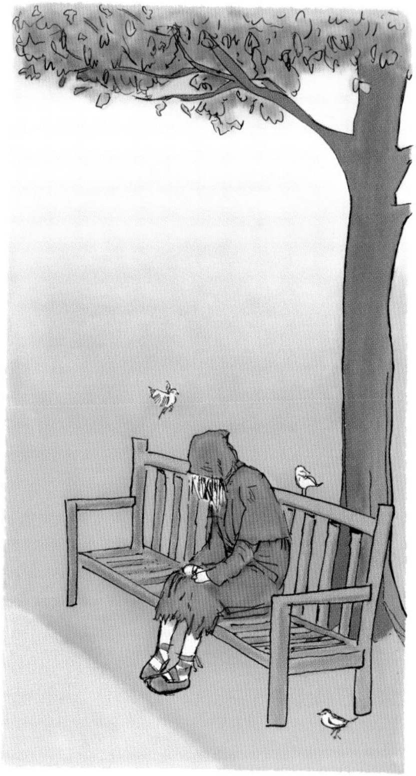

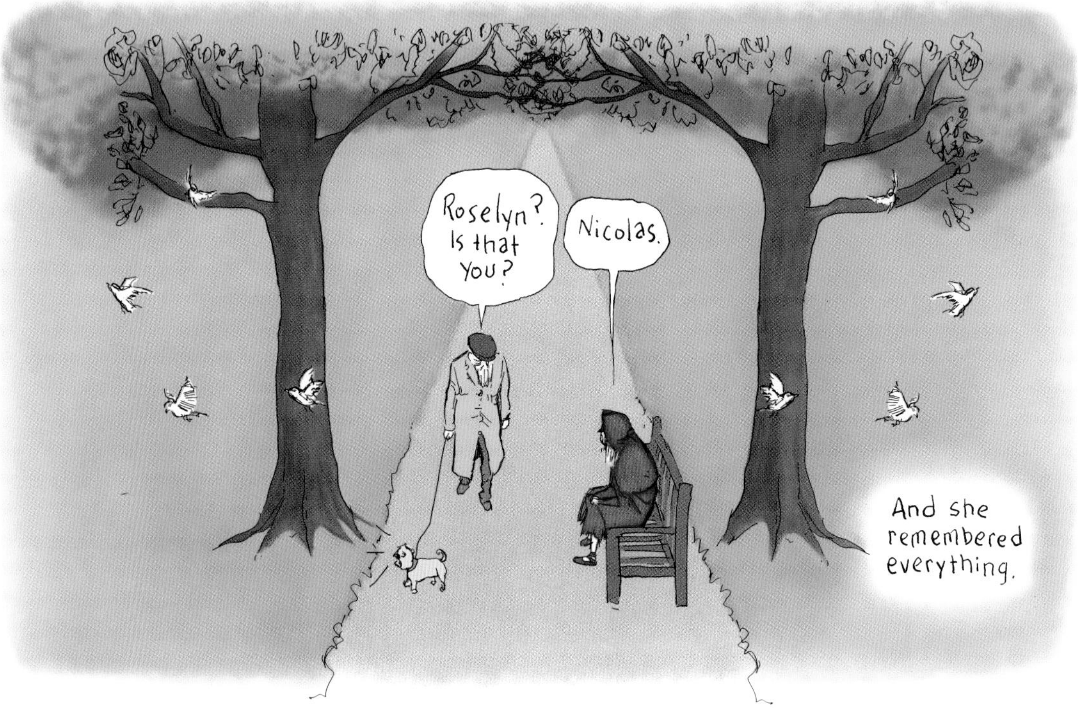
Roselyn? Is that you?
Nicolas.
And she remembered everything.

end

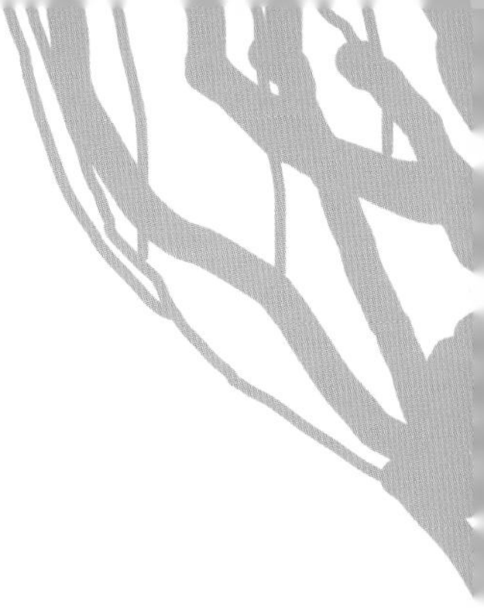

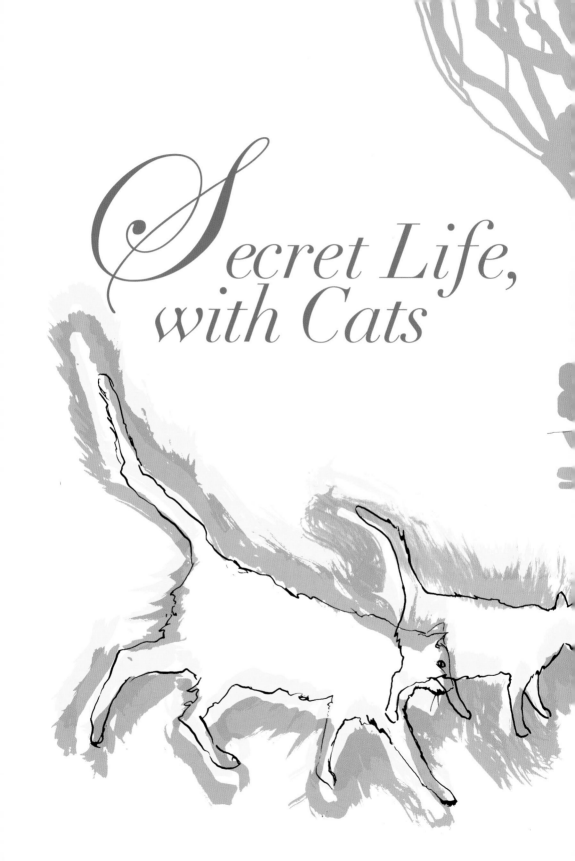

Secret Life, with Cats

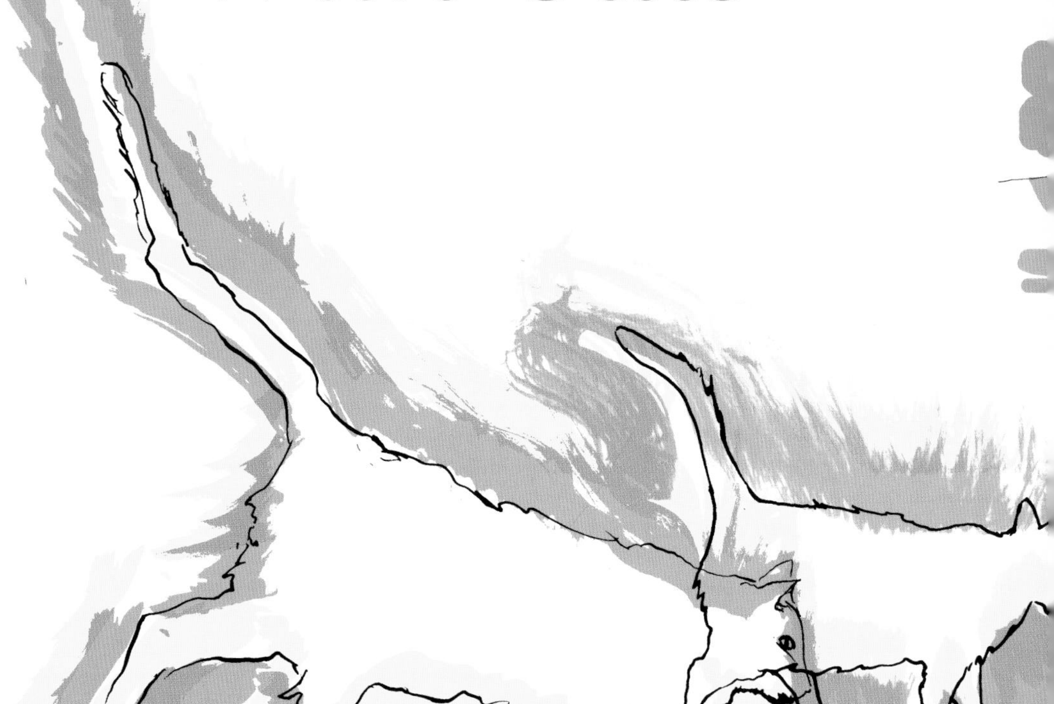

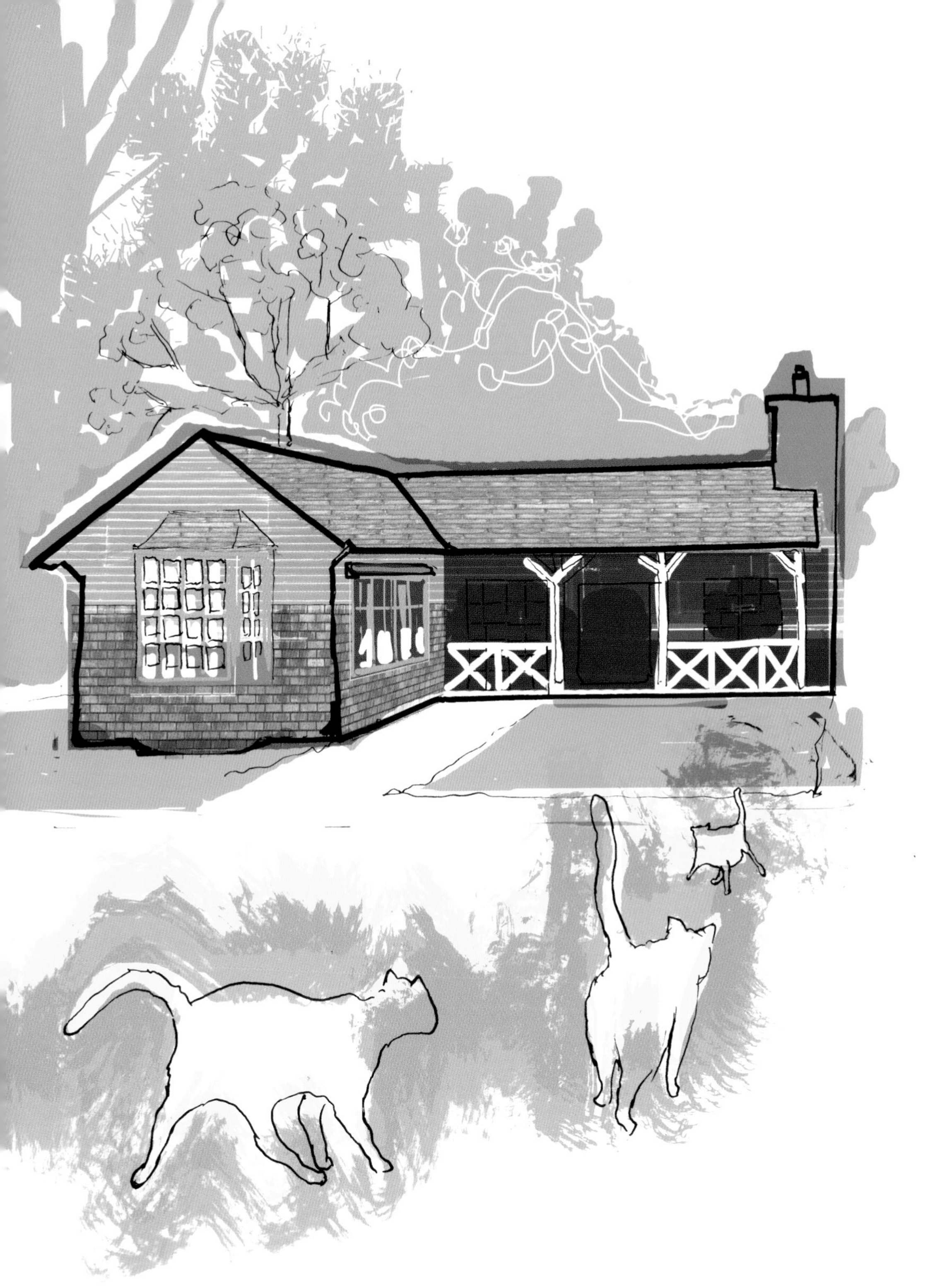

I don't know why Ruth left me her house, with all its attendant complications. Perhaps she sensed that I longed for change, for an adventure. Perhaps she pitied me. Maybe she knew what I would do with such a gift, though I did not know myself.

You might think that I was an unlikely heiress. I was forty-two years old, married, no kids. My husband, Jim, was older than me. He was a real estate agent and spent his days stalking through other people's homes, extolling their bathrooms and evaluating their roofs. Houses meant money to Jim. When I met him, he was a tenure-track professor in the anthropology department at Northwestern University. He was thirty-five, and I was twenty. I sat in the front row of Methodologies of Urban Ethnography, entranced by his easy, confident lectures, his Brooks Brothers suits, his longish brown hair and sensual green eyes. He was studiously pale in those days, and his hands had never held a hammer, much less a pneumatic staple gun. He gave me a B+ for the semester and asked me out on the last day of class.

I am not a terribly practical person. I was not an asset as a faculty wife; I was too shy, pretty, and had a knack for blurting out non sequiturs to full professors. In the third year of our marriage, Jim was denied tenure, and a year later, after our health insurance was gone, I was diagnosed with ovarian cancer. Debt piled up. Jim taught part-time at Chicago City Colleges and began selling real estate.

At first, real estate was a stopgap. I would lie on the couch in our tiny south Evanston apartment, bald from chemo and ravenous from steroids, and Jim would sit with my bloated feet on his lap, wearing his Century 21 vomit-yellow jacket. He'd tell me stories. There was the two-flat with the racing pigeon empire on the roof, the illegal apartment in the basement of a house full of Haitian tenants who followed Jim and his buyer from room to room but never spoke a word. Jim began every story the same way: "Beatrice, you've never seen anything like it." The possessions of the sellers, their bad taste, bad habits, their misconceived notions of what might attract buyers—these fascinated Jim in much the same way that the subjects of his ethnographies once had. He sold his first house, and we gloated over the commission; even though it went directly toward hospital bills, Jim was as hooked as any gambler. He stopped teaching and sold real estate full-time. Every house sold was a triumph.

I got well. We became solvent, and then we became well-off. At the time that Ruth bequeathed me her house, Jim and I had been living in a spacious Victorian on Judson Avenue for ten years. We had relentlessly improved it. We'd remodeled the kitchen and the bathrooms, rewired, re-roofed, added a gazebo and a family room, moved and expanded closets, punched new doorways through old walls. Sometimes when I got up in the night to go to the toilet, I got lost. The house was Jim's baby. It was beautiful and hungry, and he tended to it with the same solicitude he had once lavished on me. The houses he sold fed the house we lived in.

As our house became sleek and lovely, I began to fade away. I have aged as pretty blond girls do: My pink cheeks are too red, my hair is shot with gray, my blue eyes are pale and watery. My skin is chamois-soft, and there are lines in my face from frowning; my hips have spread, and veins have made dark spots on my legs. When Ruth left me her house, all these things were only beginning to happen, and now they are well on their way. Now I don't mind, but at that time I was unhappy, because I knew Jim hardly saw me when he looked at me. I couldn't be the mother of his children, and so I had become the mother of his house.

I was in charge of keeping the house. I washed its windows, vacuumed its floors, waxed it and painted it and helped choose wallpaper for it. Jim made a point of consulting me about the house. Would I like stainless steel appliances? Overstuffed Crate & Barrel leather chairs? Chinese or Persian carpets? Rosewood shoe racks? I didn't really care, and I noticed that Jim tended to wind up doing whatever he wanted anyway. I kept it all clean. Then we hired a cleaning service, and I didn't even do that anymore.

I met Ruth at the Happy Cat Home. I realize that this is ironic. Jim was allergic to cats, and I began to volunteer at this no-kill shelter in Rogers Park just to have something alive to care for.

Ruth had been a volunteer for years. She was the first person I met there. The reception room was cinder-block-ugly and clean. It was full of scratching posts and carpeted cat perches. There was a desk, a folding chair, a bank of filing cabinets, and a chintz couch. There was one cat in the room, asleep on the couch. He was a Siamese named Reginald who lived at the shelter. Ruth sat at the desk and filled out paperwork with me. I drank coffee out of a Styrofoam cup and looked at her while she asked me questions.

"You have cats at home?"

"Actually, no—my husband's allergic. I had a cat when I was a child."

Ruth was small, sharp, and quick. Her face was heart-shaped, and her eyes were dark. She seemed to me like a silent-movie starlet who had become careless with her looks. She must have been in her seventies then, and her clothes often sported safety pins; her shoes were always on the verge of splitting from the soles, and there were usually stains on her sleeves. She always had a cup of coffee in hand. She drank it almost white, more milk than coffee. Ruth had an educated voice. If I closed my eyes while she was talking, I could swear I was listening to NPR.

"What days can you come in?"

"Any day. I'm a housewife."

Did I imagine it, or did Ruth wince when I called myself a housewife?

"Well, you can work as many hours as you want. We're chronically short of volunteers."

"What will I be doing?"

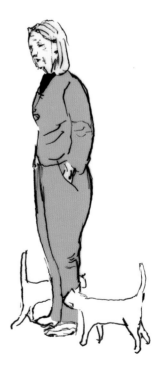

"Feeding, scooping out litter pans, running the cats to the vet if you drive. Show them to people, try to find them homes." Ruth smiled. "And of course there's the socializing, playing with them and petting them—that's the fun part."

I smiled back, and perhaps it was then that we began to be friends.

I never have had many friends, and I didn't have siblings either. I was so quiet as a girl that other children tended to forget I was there. I liked to lie on my bed and read or play odd little games with dolls or watch TV. I had a best friend in high school, but then her family moved to Maryland. In college, my few friends seemed to melt away when I started dating Jim. So I was a little intoxicated by Ruth.

It wasn't what she said so much as how she was. She was confident, but she listened. She was compelling. Oh, I'm afraid I'm not doing such a good job of conjuring her up for you. She was like an older sister to me, a clever sister; it was as though we somehow shared a past that there was no need to speak of, about which too much had already been said, even though we'd never talked about it at all.

Ruth had a preternatural ability to divine the desires of the cats, and to command them. They flocked to her and deferred to her. They loved her, and so did I.

Ruth could feed liquid medicines to cats from a spoon. She would hold it out to a sick old cat and coo, "Drink up, sweetie." The cat would make a face and lap the nasty stuff up, like a child. Once we had an orange tom named Lump who was dying of kidney failure. He hung on and on; finally the staff decided it was time to put him down. I was getting ready to drive him to the vet when Ruth came in. She sat down next to the panting cat and whispered in his ear. Lump dragged himself onto her lap, closed his eyes, and died.

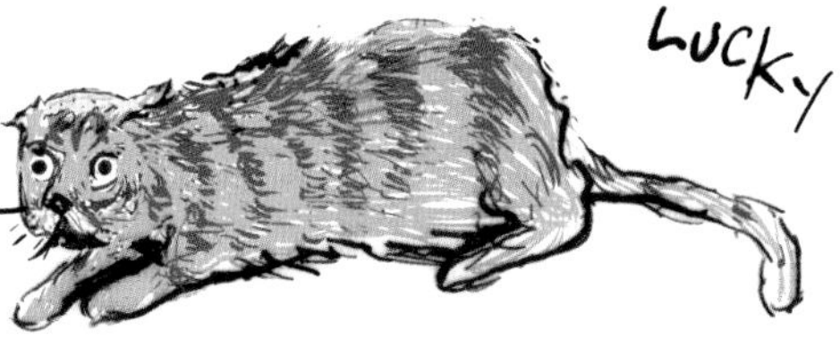
LUCKY

"What did you say to him?" I asked.

Ruth shook her head. "It's private" was all she said.

My own relationship with the cats was more difficult. I was a little frightened of them. I tried not to let Ruth see this, but of course she knew. If a cat hissed at me, I froze. When two cats fought, I could only stand helplessly by; Ruth would snap her fingers, and the combatants would slink apart apologetically. The other volunteers sprayed them with squirt guns.

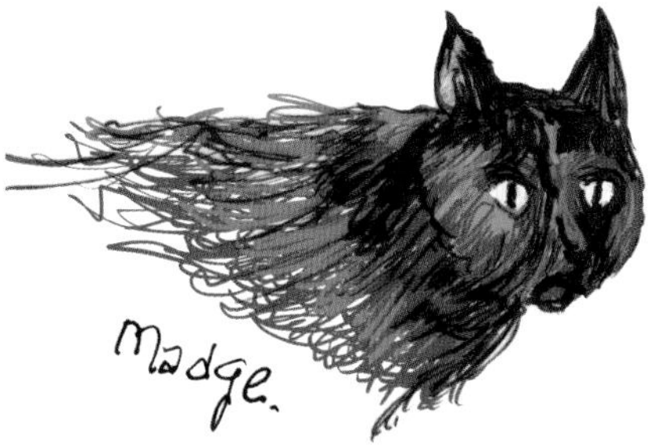
Madge.

I slowly developed a rapport with certain cats. My favorites were Lucky, an earless, balding thing who loved to sit in my lap for hours; Madge, a tortoiseshell who bit everyone but me; and Fabio, a fat blond cat who followed me everywhere and enjoyed chewing on my wristwatch band. I loved the kittens, but everyone loves kittens. They never stayed around long enough to be memorable.

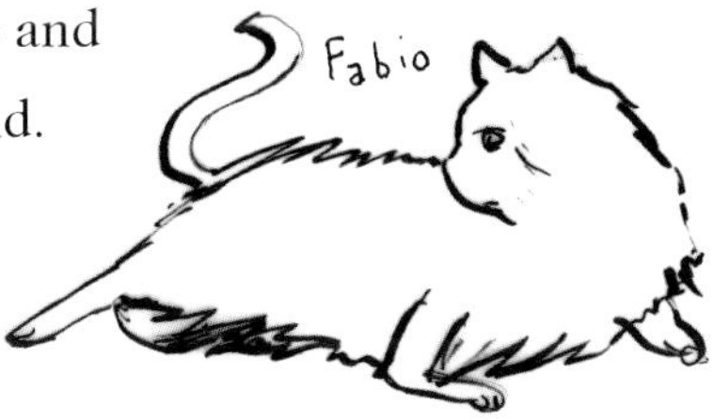
Fabio

Ruth and I would sit in the lunchroom and play cards, each with a cat on our lap and more curled around our ankles. We played simple games like Hearts and Crazy Eights. Ruth never told me anything about her life outside the shelter, and I didn't talk about Jim or real estate or our house. One Monday morning I came to work with a black eye.

"What happened?" Ruth asked.

"I walked into a door." This was the truth; I had gotten up in the middle of the night, thirsty and sleep-fuddled, and had collided with one of the recently relocated doors in my search for the bathroom. I could see that Ruth was drawing her own conclusions.

"No, really. I do that a lot."

Ruth now looked extremely skeptical. "You don't do it here."

"Yes, well, my husband isn't remodeling the Happy Cat Home. He has an insatiable urge to make closets where no closets were before." That was all we said about it. I admit that I felt a little glamorous. Without doing a thing, Jim had incurred Ruth's dislike. No one else at the shelter asked me about the black eye, and I imagined Ruth telling them my closet story, which was not even a story but actually true. That night Jim came home with steaks. I put one on my eye for a while to please him, and then we ate them.

Things went along this way for a few years. Cats came and went; the young, pretty ones tended to go, and the old, broken ones tended to stay. I got more relaxed and skillful with them; I could give the diabetic cats insulin and clip claws without getting scratched. Jim continued to put our house through startling transformations and finally installed a bathroom right off the master bedroom. Ruth and I went to the movies now and then, but mostly we spent our time at the shelter, wrangling cats and playing cards.

Then Ruth died.

I don't know how it happened. One Wednesday in July, she didn't show up for her shift at the shelter. No one answered her phone. Jim and I were on vacation in Nova Scotia, so I heard about it the following Monday from Ellie, the director of the shelter. They had gotten worried; after all, Ruth was old, though she didn't complain about her health. They'd called the emergency number on her volunteer application, but it was disconnected. It had been hot all week, in the upper nineties. They went to Ruth's house and rang the bell. No answer. I had never been to Ruth's house. Ellie said it was a small brick ranch-style place. She went around and looked in all the windows, which were open. No sign of Ruth. The police couldn't find her either. "Maybe she went on vacation and just forgot to tell you, ma'am," the officer suggested.

Ruth never came back. There was no body, no funeral, no grave.

I worried and felt spurned. I couldn't imagine Ruth leaving without saying good-bye. Something terrible must have happened to her. But no one knew anything. Jim suggested that she might have amnesia, but he liked to listen to *Radio Mystery Theater*, and I knew that sort of thing only happened in melodramas.

At the end of the summer, I received a registered letter at the shelter. I remember holding it in my hand, the weight of it, the pause before opening it, my puzzlement as to who might send me a letter at work. It was from a downtown law firm, and it informed me that Ruth had died and left me her house and its contents.

I'm ashamed to say that my first response was relief: Ruth hadn't abandoned me; she had only died.

That evening Jim came into the kitchen as I was making dinner
and said, "How was your day?" I opened my mouth to tell him about
Ruth, about her house . . . and I said, "Just a day. How about you?"

Ruth's house was on Pratt, near Ridge Avenue; it was a ten-
minute walk from the Happy Cat Home. Jim would have
called it a teardown. The house was small and sat far back
on a double lot. It was a single-story brick house, neat and plain,
built in the sixties. Elm trees that had somehow eluded Dutch elm
disease loomed over it. A sprinkler sat unused in the middle of a
beige lawn.

I let myself in the front door.

The house itself was silent; a shimmer of cicada singing came in
the open windows along with a warm breeze. I stood in the entryway
and felt like an intruder. This was Ruth's house. Ruth was a very
private person. Standing there looking at her couch, her dining table
and chairs, her desk, I felt reluctant. *But she gave it to you. She
wanted you to be here.* The thought came into my head as though

someone was urging me to accept hospitality. *Come in, come in.* I set my purse on an armchair and began to wander slowly through the rooms.

Ruth must have furnished her house in the nineteen seventies. All the furniture was teak or covered in nubby off-white fabric. There were batik throw pillows and a beanbag chair. Her dishes were heavy stoneware; the carpeting was brown shag. Everything was somewhat worn.

I opened one of the desk drawers. It was empty. There were circles on the windowsills where plants had been. There was nothing in the kitchen cabinets but curling shelf paper, nothing in the bathroom except an extra roll of toilet paper. In the bedroom closet I found two dresses that had belonged to Ruth. I leaned in and smelled them. They smelled like the Happy Cat Home.

But what about Ruth's cats? There was no cat hair anywhere. No furniture had been clawed; there was no evidence of a litter box. And yet I remembered Ruth sharing stories of her cats' antics. Perhaps whoever had taken the plants and the rest of it had taken the cats, too. What were their names? I couldn't remember.

I sat down on Ruth's bed. The curtains moved in the breeze. I felt watched. "Thank you," I said to Ruth, in case she could hear me. Then I felt silly. I got my purse, locked up the house, and left.

I didn't go back for a week. There was no reason to go. I worked my shifts at the shelter, but without Ruth it seemed dull and sad. I sat down one day to eat by myself in the shelter's squalid lunchroom, and suddenly it occurred to me that I could eat at Ruth's house; it was so close. I gathered my food and left.

A bus was letting children off on the corner as I walked toward the house. They stared at me and whispered to each other as I let myself in.

The house was exactly the same. I sat at the dining room table and ate my yogurt and my tuna fish sandwich. When I was done, I folded up the brown paper bag and put it in my purse. It seemed wrong to leave any trash behind, even in the garbage can.

I stood in the kitchen looking out at the backyard. There was a small patio with a few old lawn chairs randomly placed, a planter full of dirt. Then I sat on Ruth's bed. I took off my shoes and lay down on top of the bedspread, experimentally. The bed was very soft.

I didn't mean to sleep. Even as I was falling asleep I thought, *No, I must get back to work,* but I knew I was sleeping already. It was the kind of sleep that is like dropping into a hole. Then I was half-awake and had a curious sensation: There was a weight on the bed, leaning against me, and as I moved in my waking, the weight went to the edge of the bed and fell off. It landed with a thud on the floor.

I sat up and looked at the floor, but there was nothing there. I looked at my watch. Only a half hour had gone by. I put on my shoes and went back to the shelter.

I came back the next day. I decided to turn on the sprinkler and watched it fling water in a circle as I ate lunch. When I walked into the bedroom, there was a dead sparrow on the bed, neatly centered on the pillow I had used the day before. And somehow I understood.

That evening Jim and I were eating dinner out on our deck. Jim had recently purchased an elaborate gas grill, so we were eating ribs and grilled vegetables. I knew that I would be the one who got to scrub the burnt barbeque sauce off the new grill when dinner was over.

"Jim?"

"Mmm?" He had his mouth full.

"I'm going to Boise tomorrow." Boise was where my mother lived. "I'll be back in a week or so."

"Hmm. Everything okay?"

"Sure, but it's been a while."

"Well, give her my love."

"Okay."

That was the last conversation we had. After twenty-one years of marriage, there's not a lot to say.

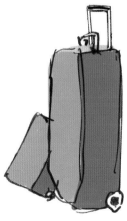

I left the next morning. I didn't bring many things: a suitcase full of clothing, a few books. I had a checking account Jim didn't know about. I'd been saving my clothing allowance for a long time, not for any particular reason, just to have some money of my own. I took all the evidence of that with me.

I bought some groceries. I bought bath towels and dish soap and a small radio. I drove to Ruth's house, now my house, and put the car in the garage. Now I was invisible. No one knew where I was.

The first few days were uneventful. I often had the feeling that something was moving at the edge of my vision—a slight blur, a dark shape. I read my books and ate chocolate. I listened to *All Things Considered* and took long baths.

On the third night, I woke up suddenly. A large cat was sitting on the bed, looking at me. Its eyes reflected pale green. I offered my hand to it. It considered this for a moment, then flicked its tail and jumped off the bed. There was a slight thump as it landed, then silence. I looked all over the room but didn't find it.

The next day I put a dish of cat food on the kitchen floor. I watched it for a while; nothing happened. A few hours later I checked again, and the food was gone.

The days began to blur together. Purring sounds in my ear. Aluminum foil balls rolling of their own volition across the floor. Invisible cat feet making soft dents in the bedspread. I woke up close to dawn and saw cats swarming around the bedroom, colorless in the half-light, an uncountable number of them. I was afraid then.

A few days later I was vacuuming the living room when I noticed something dark on the white wall. I got down on my knees to look at it. It was writing, small and cramped. It said: *You could probably levitate if you wanted to.* The thing that frightened me and thrilled me was that the words were so low to the ground—just above the baseboard.

I stood up. The house seemed expectant. I didn't know if I wanted to levitate. I had never thought about it. I went outside and stood on the patio. After a while I went back inside. Curtains were moving slightly in the breeze; otherwise the house was still. There was a feeling of disappointment, but I did not know if it was mine or someone else's.

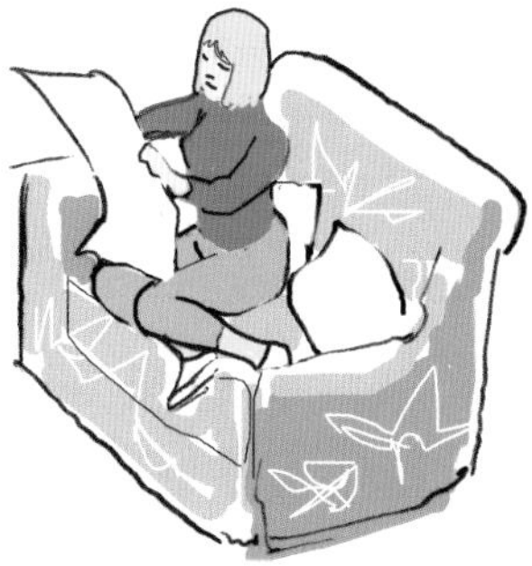

I had been living in the house for two weeks. It was early evening. I was curled up on the couch, reading the newspaper. It was October, and chilly. I had closed all the windows and turned on the heat. I was content.

I had begun to distinguish between aloneness and loneliness. In Ruth's house I was alone; the phantom cats and NPR were company enough. But I wasn't lonely, and I realized this only by how lonely I had been before.

Now I had the familiar sense of being watched. I put down the newspaper. There was a white cat sitting in the armchair. It was very thin, with green eyes and a rather haughty manner. We stared at each other. It seemed to be considering me, judging me.

"Well, come on, then," it said. It rose, stretched, jumped to the floor, and stood looking at me expectantly. When I didn't get up instantly, it turned its back and marched off toward the bedroom. I hesitated, then followed it.

The closet stood open. I had hung a few dresses and skirts next to Ruth's; these had been pushed aside, and the back of the closet was now another doorway. I couldn't think how I had failed to notice this door. The white cat stalked through it, and I followed.

There were stairs, which led down. The house was built on a concrete slab; these stairs had no business being there. There was hardly any light, and I felt my way with my hands touching the walls and with my feet seeking each step before advancing. The walls and the steps seemed to be made of earth. Sound was deadened. I had no idea if the white cat was still with me. I went down and down . . . finally there were no more stairs. I was in a hallway that led to a door. The white cat sat in front of the door with its tail twitching.

"There you are. You're very slow." It nudged open the door and disappeared through it. I followed.

The room was big and low-ceilinged. It smelled of earth and unbathed flesh, meat, baby powder, damp wood, old sweaters. The room was full of things, in no order at all, and cats were everywhere. The cats were playing, napping, eating, yawning, fighting, and they were doing all this in the midst of shoes, hats, dresses, books, dead plants, papers, a typewriter, a few small lamps with chewed cords, underwear, knickknacks, a footstool, a child's rocking chair, suitcases, combs, a toothbrush . . . all the things that had been missing from Ruth's house were here. Some of the cats wore pieces of costume jewelry I remembered seeing on Ruth.

They all ignored me, or pretended to ignore me. The white cat was nowhere to be seen, and I wondered why I'd been brought down here. The disorder was oppressive. I felt large; at first I thought I was the only thing in the room over two feet tall.

"Hello, Beatrice." Her voice came from a dark corner. I took a step forward and stopped. Where was she?

Ruth was sitting in a metal folding chair, the kind people take to parades. She was wrapped in a blanket. All I could see of her was her face. Ruth looked tired but otherwise not too different from when I'd seen her last.

"Ruth! I was so worried about you! What are you doing down here? Are you okay?" I was so relieved to see her, and so confused. I edged a little closer.

Ruth chuckled. It was such a familiar sound—it evoked all those games of Crazy Eights in the Happy Cat House lunchroom. "Well, darling, I don't think I would exactly describe myself as 'okay'; I'm dead, after all, so 'okay' is a little beside the point, don't you think?"

"But—?" I remembered that I had no idea how she'd died.

"It wasn't that big of a deal. I slipped and cracked my head in the bathtub. It was very tidy." Ruth's voice was kind, but I could tell she thought I was focusing on the wrong thing. *Barking up the wrong tree* would have been her way of putting it.

"Yes, but Ruth—no one could find you. We checked, we looked for you, but you had just . . . vanished." I knew I sounded a little petulant. I couldn't help it.

Ruth smiled, as though she was proud of how she'd mystified us all. "That's right. They couldn't find me, because the cats ate me."

"*Ate you?*"

"Yep. Every little bit of me. It's such a cliché, isn't it? But they didn't do it for the usual reasons. They weren't hungry; they weren't locked in the house. They did it to bring me down here, with them. So we could be together."

The longer I stood here listening to Ruth in this dark, smelly, chaotic room, the more revolted and sad I felt. The cats had gradually stopped milling around. Now they sat silently, listening. Ruth waited for me to respond. Finally I said, "Won't you come upstairs? We could be together—with the cats, too, of course." There was a deep stillness among the cats now, as they waited to hear what Ruth would say.

"Oh, Bea. I wish I could, I really do. Remember how much fun we had?" Ruth smiled, and I thought, *She is the only person I have ever truly loved.* "But you see," she continued, still smiling, "I can't do that. I belong here now, with my sweeties." There was an audible hum in the room, all the cats purring. "Plus, I'm afraid I'm not exactly ambulatory."

"Why not?" I asked without thinking.

"Well . . . they are cats, after all. They aren't doctors or mechanics. I'm afraid they did a rather poor job of reassembling me." Ruth nodded at her own blanket-wrapped form. The cats looked at her, anxious, loving.

"We tried, Ruth," said the white cat, who had reappeared and was sitting at her feet.

"I know you did, Thaddeus," said Ruth in her most gentle voice. The cats began to surge around her, rubbing against her blanket with sorrowful expressions on their faces.

I stood there watching, at a loss. Tears ran down my face. "Oh, God, Ruth . . . what can I do?"

She looked back at me calmly. "I don't think there's much you can do, darling. But how are you? How do you like the house? You're living here now, aren't you?"

I had a sudden vision of myself, living in Ruth's house, calmly going about my life upstairs while she was down here, with the cats . . .

I cried out, turned, and stumbled toward the door. Ruth called out, "Beatrice, wait!" but I ran up the stairs without answering her. I could hear the cats hissing. I reached the closet and slammed the door behind me. Within minutes I was in my car, driving blindly down Pratt, away from Ruth and her house, away from those cats.

I sold the house to a developer. It was on the market for two days. A few weeks later Ruth's house was a pile of rubble, and I was driving to New Mexico. I bought a condo in Albuquerque, filed for a divorce, and got a German shepherd puppy named Millie.

I think about Ruth a lot. But it's too late to change anything. And though I've tried to levitate, I can't do it. It's probably just as well.

THE RUIN OF GRANT LOWERY

Grant Lowery was sitting at the bar of the Village Tap
on Racine drinking a beer and thinking about nothing much
when a lady tapped him on the shoulder.

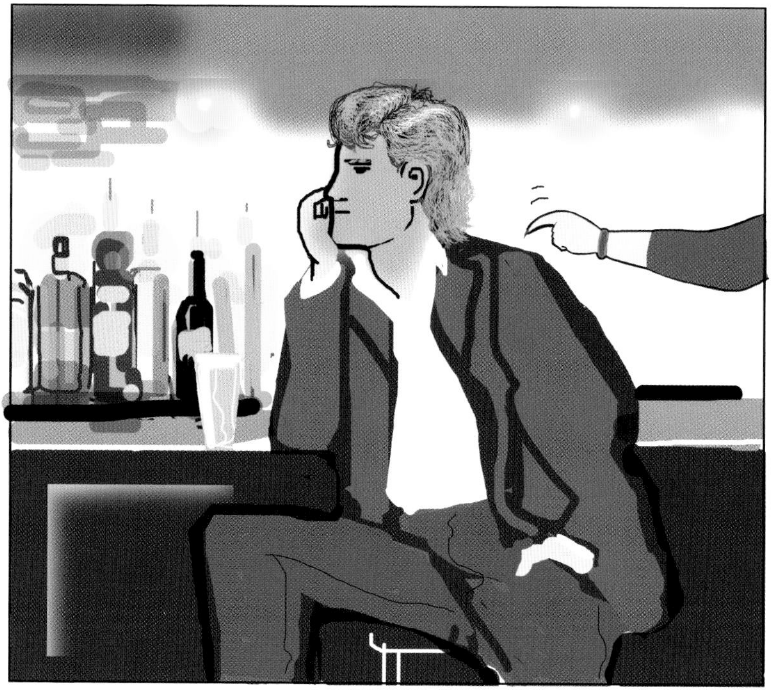

He thought of her as a lady, not a girl or a woman, because there was something imperious and retro about her; the gaze she fixed him with could have belonged to Cleopatra or Margaret Thatcher.

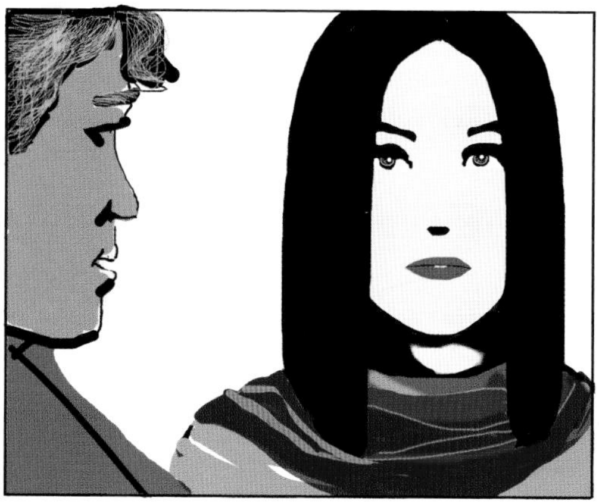

She smiled. It was not an honest, open sort of smile, but the smile of a conspirator, a smile that implied the game was afoot.
Mischief.

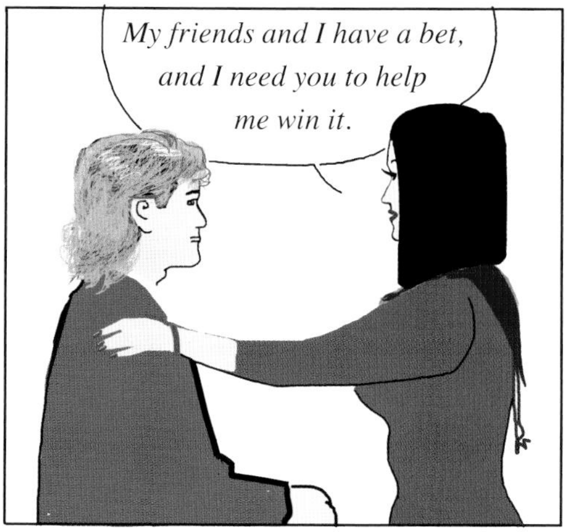
My friends and I have a bet, and I need you to help me win it.

Grant rose from his barstool and allowed the lady to propel him to her table, where two other ladies sat. He shook their hands, and they were introduced to him.

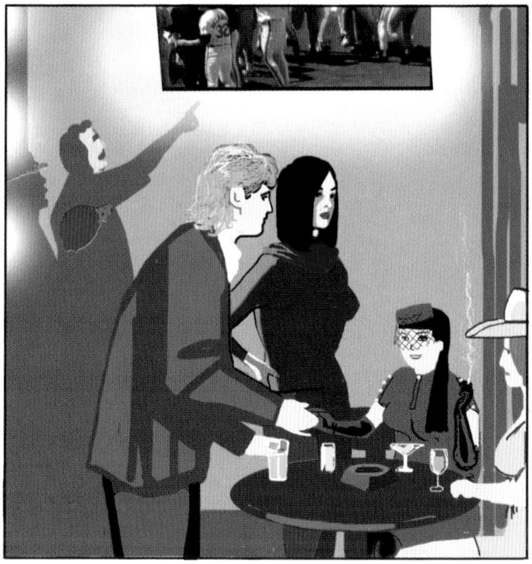

Migly. When she smiled, her expression seemed extremely asymmetrical, and Grant wondered if she had been in some kind of accident.

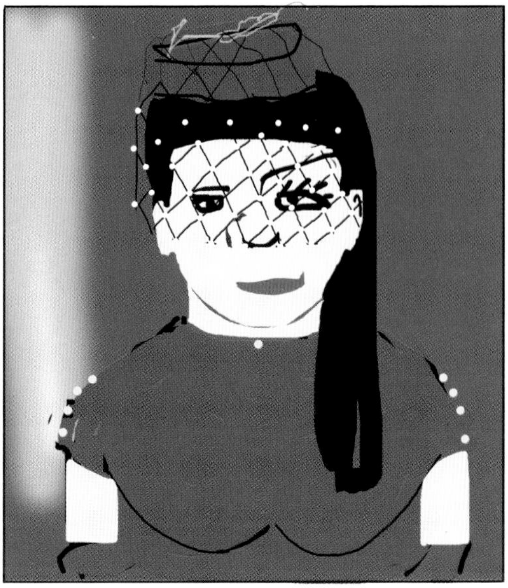

Leticia. Her eyes were dark and her hands were pawlike, with short fingers that she put under the table when she noticed him staring.

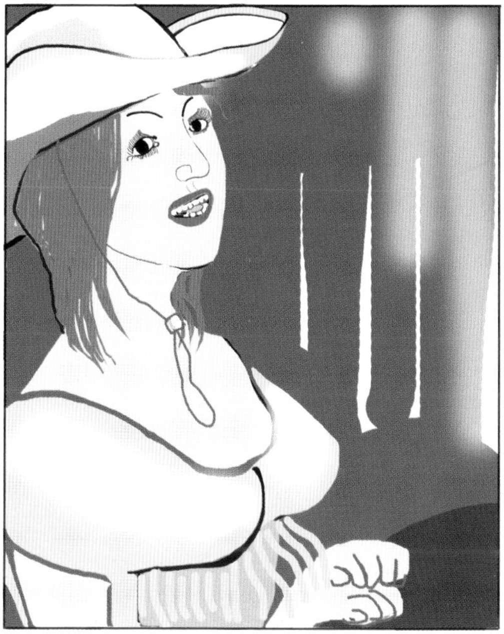

The lady, who had not yet told Grant her name, drew out a chair for him and seated herself. All of the women were drinking peculiar variations on Martinis. Grant smelled chocolate. He was a beer man, himself.

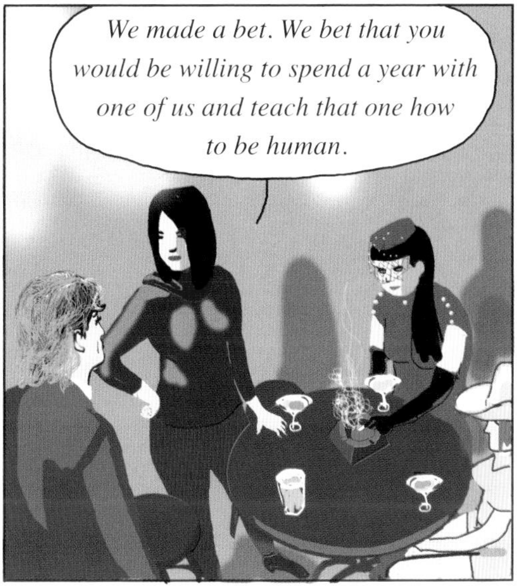
We made a bet. We bet that you would be willing to spend a year with one of us and teach that one how to be human.

Grant thought that he had heard wrong, since the music was loud and there was a TV just above them tuned to the Cubs game, which most of the bar was roaring at.

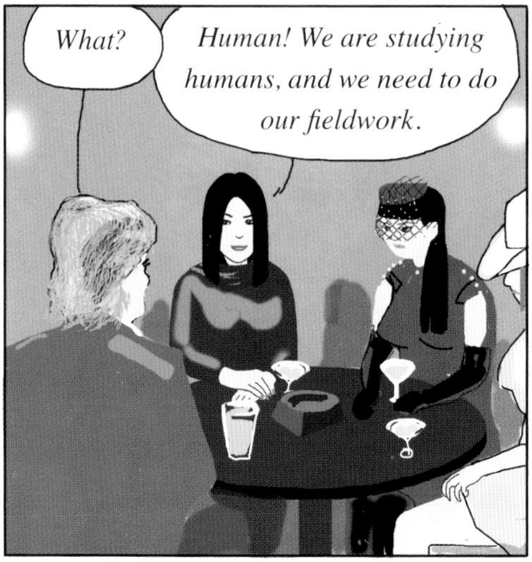
What?
Human! We are studying humans, and we need to do our fieldwork.

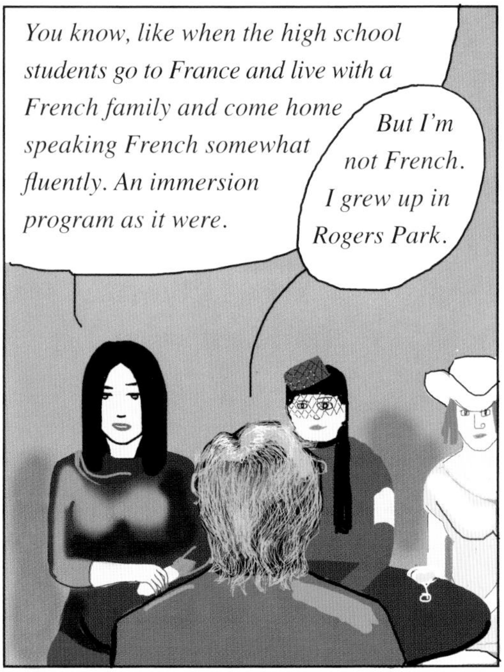
You know, like when the high school students go to France and live with a French family and come home speaking French somewhat fluently. An immersion program as it were.
But I'm not French. I grew up in Rogers Park.

Grant was not actually as dense as he seemed; he'd had a few beers before the lady showed up. This may explain why he didn't resist her, or it may not.

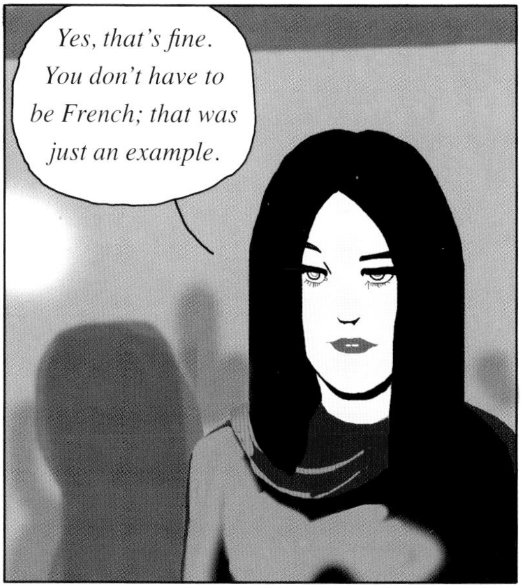
Yes, that's fine. You don't have to be French; that was just an example.

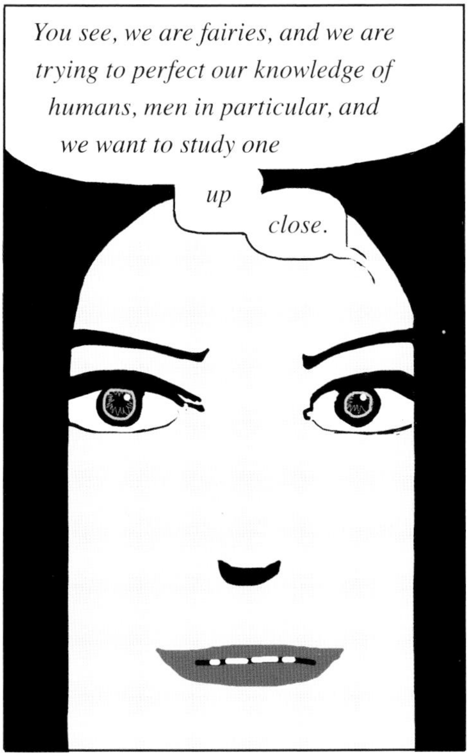
You see, we are fairies, and we are trying to perfect our knowledge of humans, men in particular, and we want to study one
up
close.

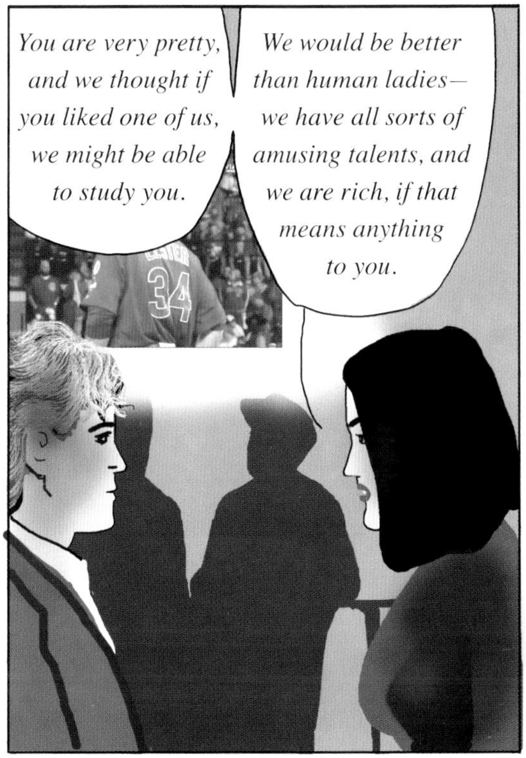
You are very pretty, and we thought if you liked one of us, we might be able to study you.
We would be better than human ladies—we have all sorts of amusing talents, and we are rich, if that means anything to you.
34

Grant, of course, had misunderstood what the lady meant by "fairies," since no one expects to meet actual fairies in a bar in Chicago, only homosexual men who call themselves fairies.

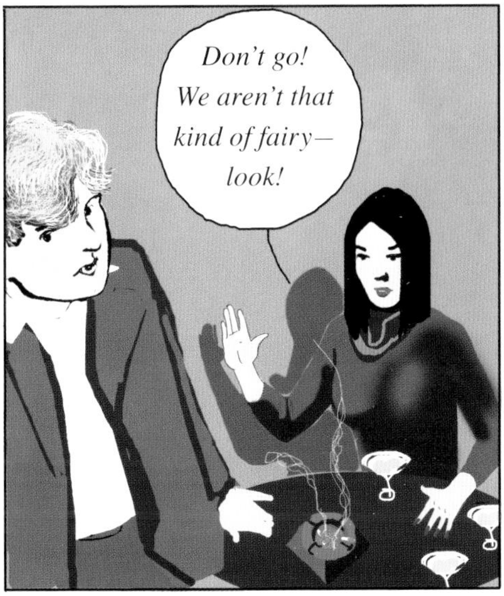
Don't go! We aren't that kind of fairy—look!

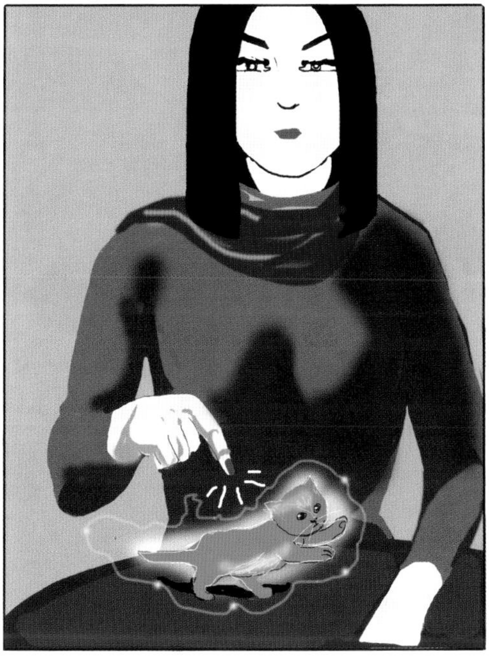

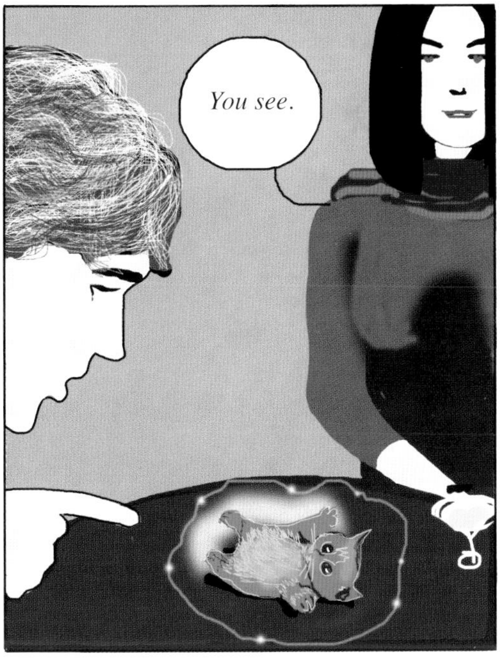
You see.

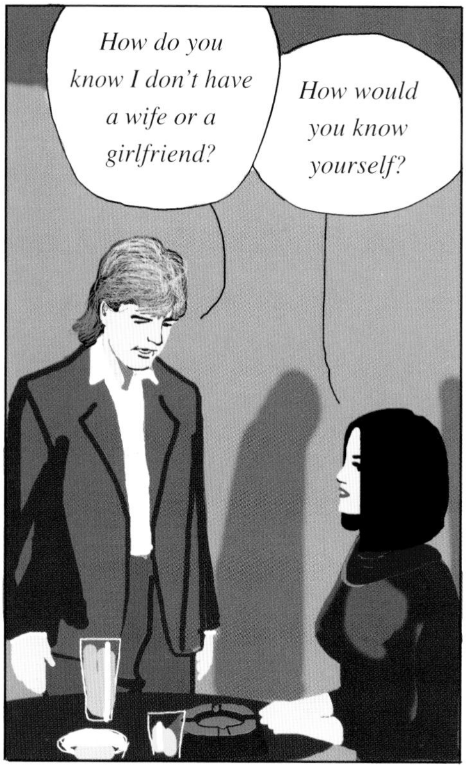
How do you know I don't have a wife or a girlfriend?
How would you know yourself?

Grant had a glimpse, just for a moment, of an entire life that might or might not be his: a girl with blond hair who stood in a sunlit kitchen, stirring something in a pot on the stove.

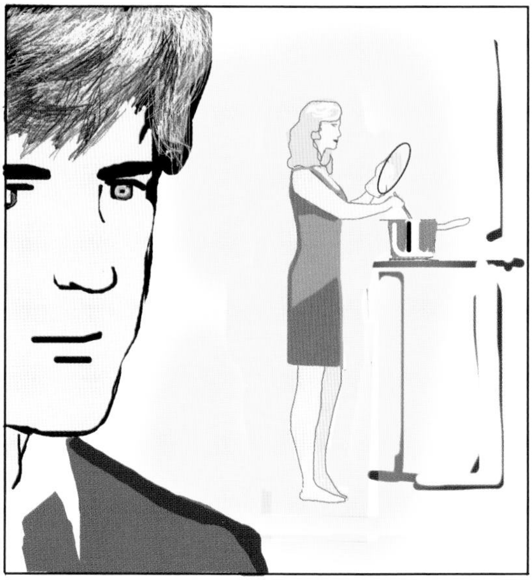

Grant smelled chili. The girl turned toward him with an inviting smile, and was gone.

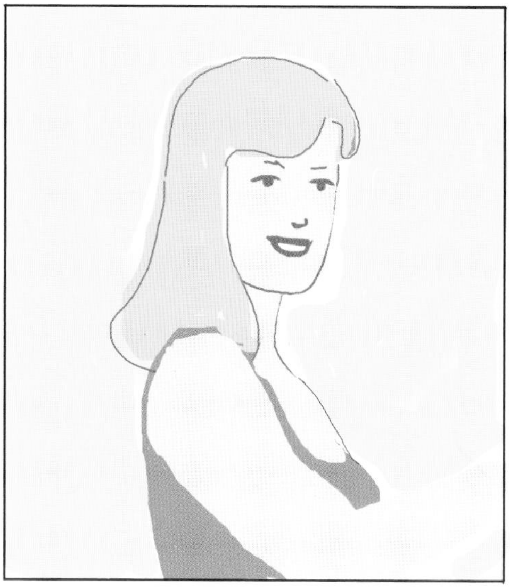

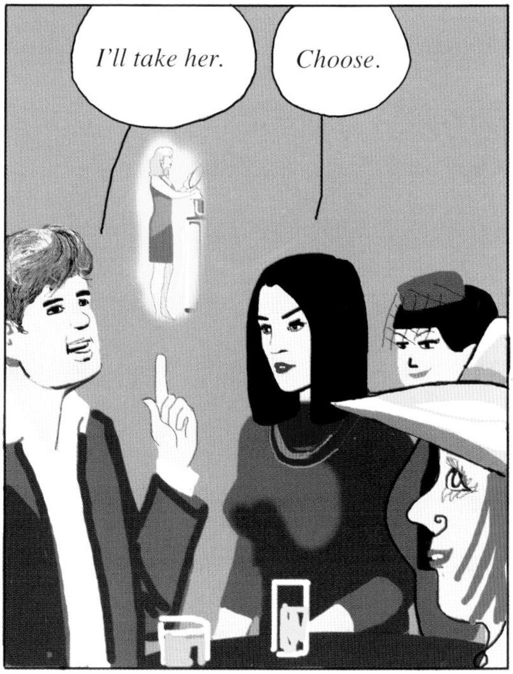
I'll take her.
Choose.

Grant looked at Migly, and she smiled. He thought that she might be the kindest of the three, and maybe he should choose her. Perhaps she would not abuse him or turn him into an ashtray. But Migly, as he looked at her, seemed to become subtly more asymmetrical, until she was almost cubist.

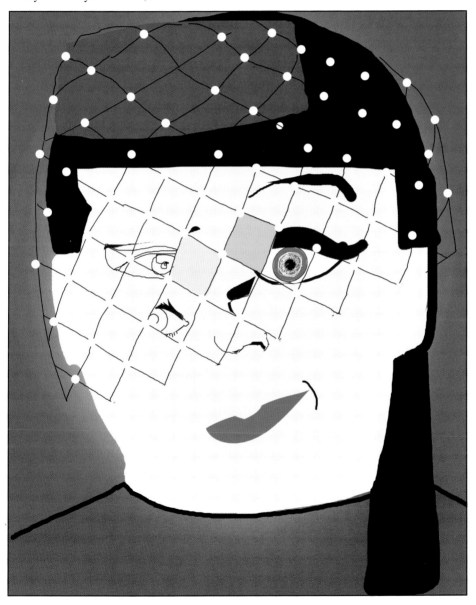

Leticia sharpened and gleamed at him. He was repelled by her feral appearance. She grew whiskers, then retracted them.

Meanwhile, the lady sat, unperturbed, at his side. He studied her, but she continued to smile, confident and lovely. She reminded him of a TV actress he'd had a crush on when he was thirteen. He was a little unnerved by how normal she seemed. Grant thought it was a little unfair of her to pretend to be that TV actress. He couldn't remember the actress's name.

He woke the next morning with a sense of something forgotten, an appointment missed; what day of the week was it, anyway? Someone brewed coffee. Grant felt slightly hungover. He struggled to remember the previous evening but failed.

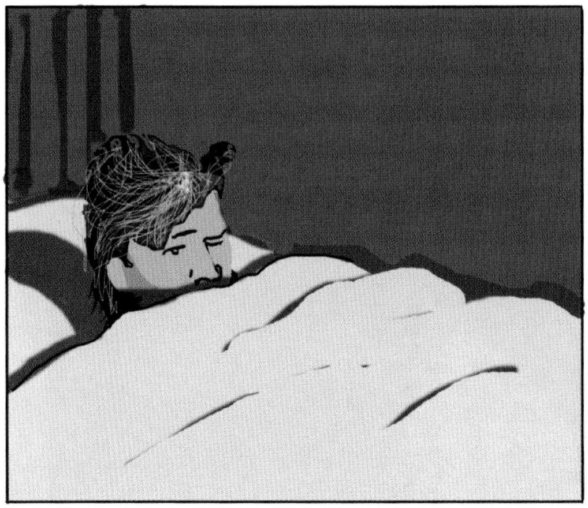

Grant got out of the bed and staggered into the next room tugging at his boxers. The fairy sat in a wingback chair. Two small ocelots sat at her feet. They vanished as she turned her attention to Grant.

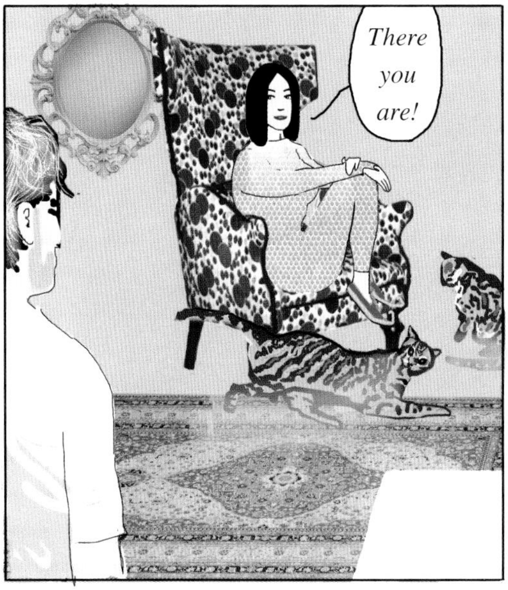
There you are!

At first he thought that he must have gone home with a girl; the apartment was much larger than his, decorated in velvet, Persian rugs, sinuous antique furniture. Maybe this was her parents' place.

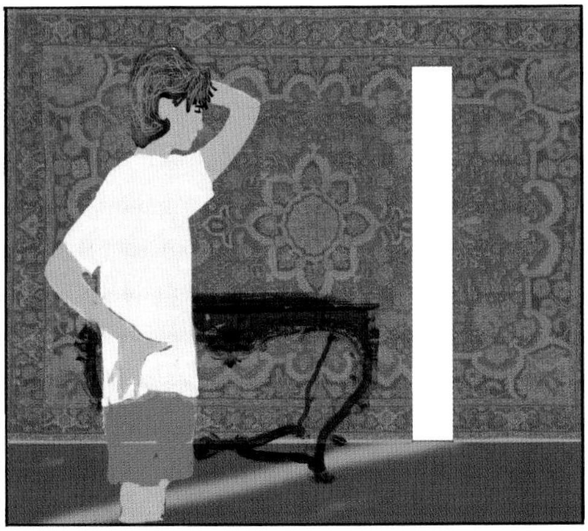

She waved her hand at a large table, which filled up with waffles, strawberries, whipped cream, and syrup, all in staggering quantities. Somewhere in the mess was a pot of coffee.

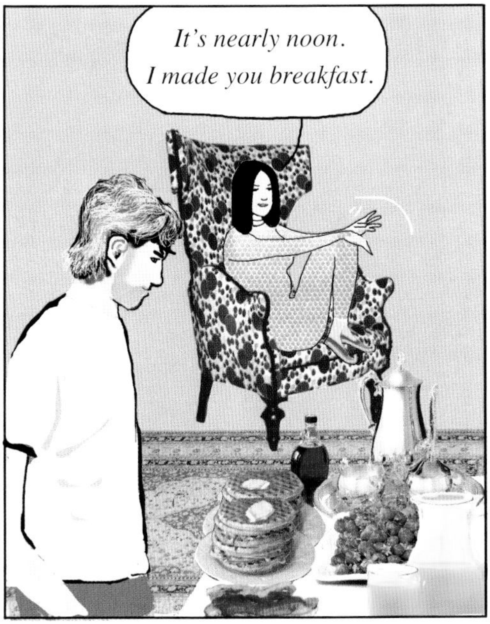
It's nearly noon. I made you breakfast.

Grant went into the kitchen and found a mug. There was something about the mug that seemed familiar.

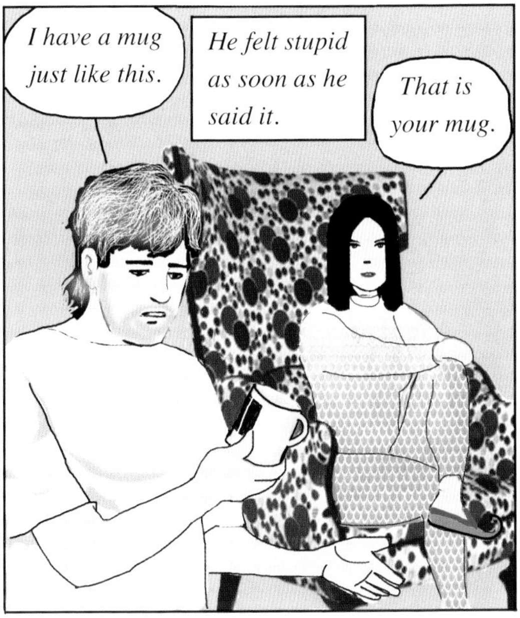
I have a mug just like this.
He felt stupid as soon as he said it.
That is your mug.

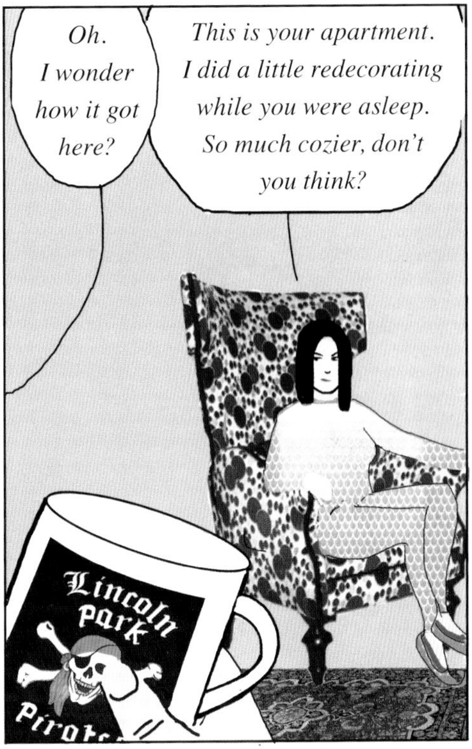
Oh. I wonder how it got here?
This is your apartment. I did a little redecorating while you were asleep. So much cozier, don't you think?
Lincoln Park

Grant thought wistfully of his battered Ikea furniture, his DVD collection, all the PEZ dispensers he had amassed along the baseboards like a little candy army.

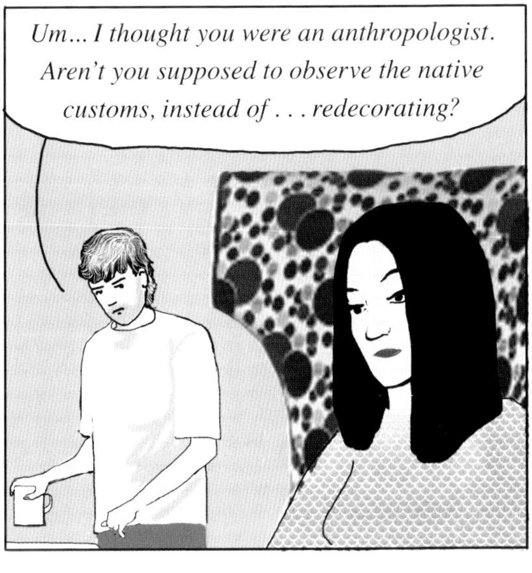
Um... I thought you were an anthropologist. Aren't you supposed to observe the native customs, instead of . . . redecorating?

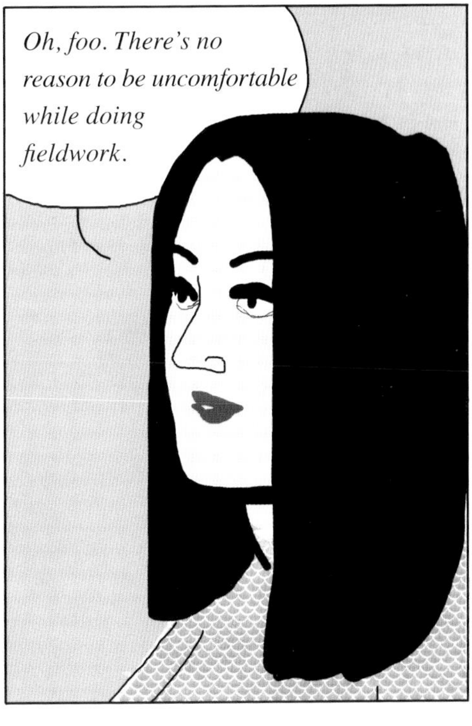
Oh, foo. There's no reason to be uncomfortable while doing fieldwork.

The lady glanced at the table.

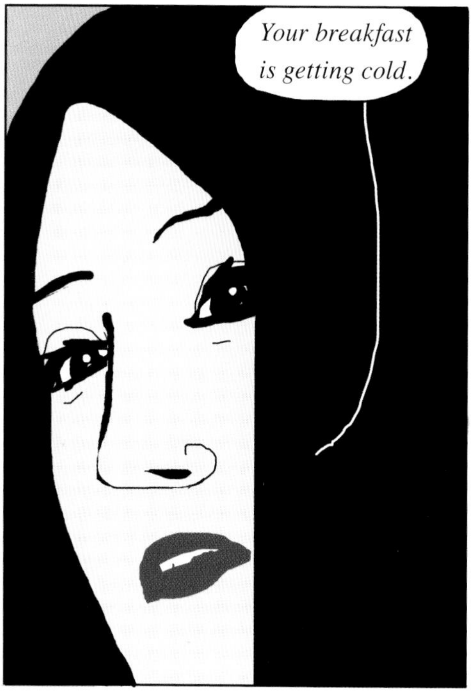
Your breakfast is getting cold.

Grant dutifully picked up a waffle and took a bite. The lady smiled. Grant had no clue that eating fairy food obligated him to serve the lady forever. He ate the rest of it to be polite; it was kind of chalky.

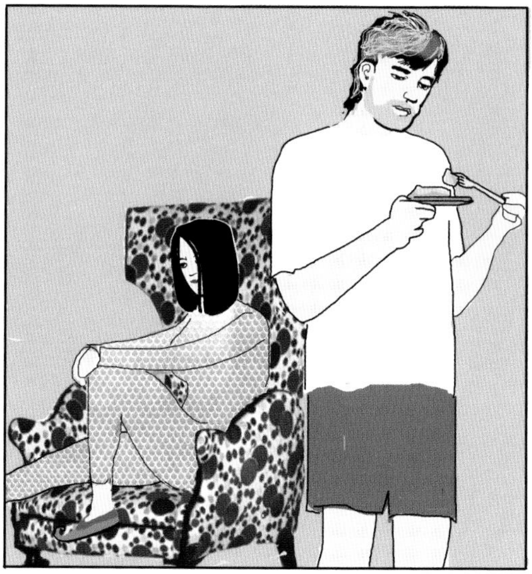

Grant asked the lady her name. He thought he had asked before but couldn't remember what she had told him.

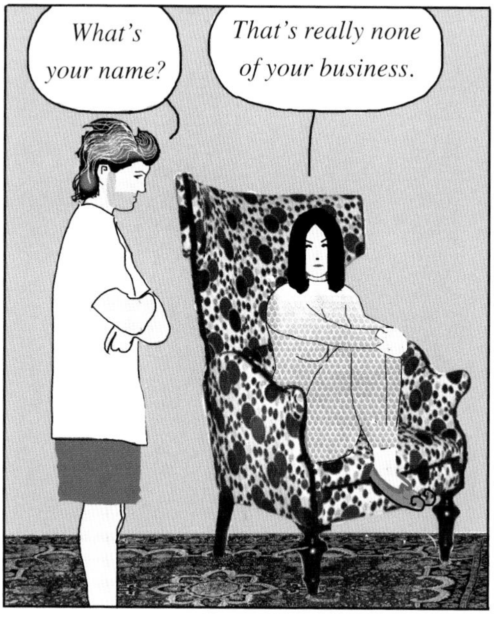
What's your name?
That's really none of your business.

She swept off into another room, leaving Grant to wonder anxiously how on earth he would ever get rid of her.

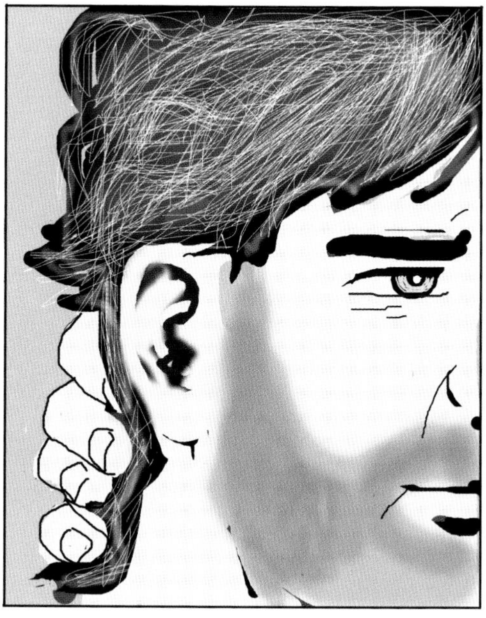

Living with the fairy lady was frightening, dull, mystifying, and aggravating for Grant in equal measures. He didn't seem to have a job anymore.

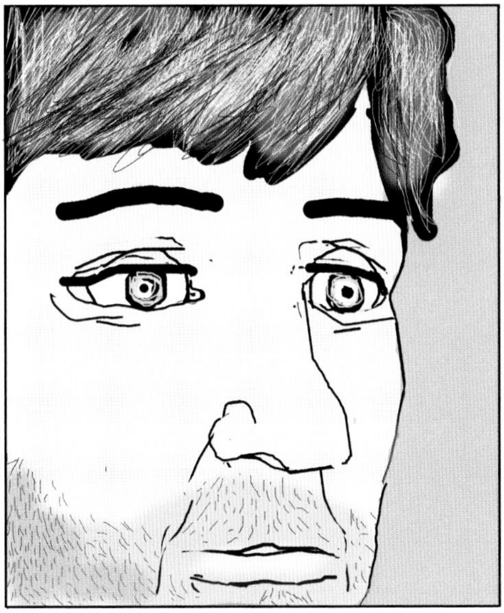

Whenever the lady wanted him to do something for her, he did it. Otherwise he hung around the apartment, fretting. He became rather haggard looking and took a lot of naps. He felt like a pet.

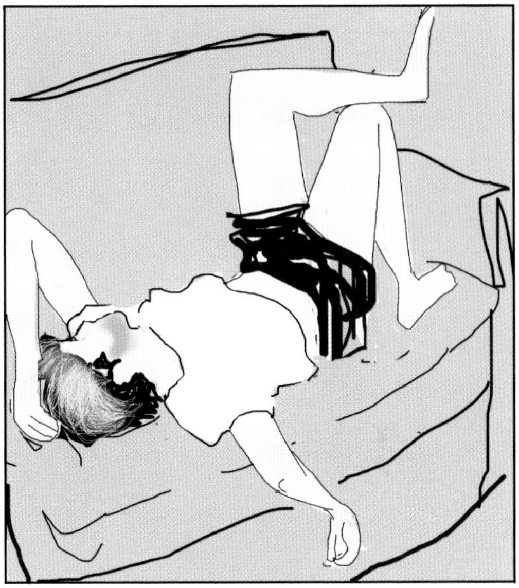

He began having odd dreams. Many of them featured the lady, and Grant resented having to think about her even while he slept. But occasionally he dreamt of the blond girl in the kitchen, the one he had seen in the vision at the Village Tap.

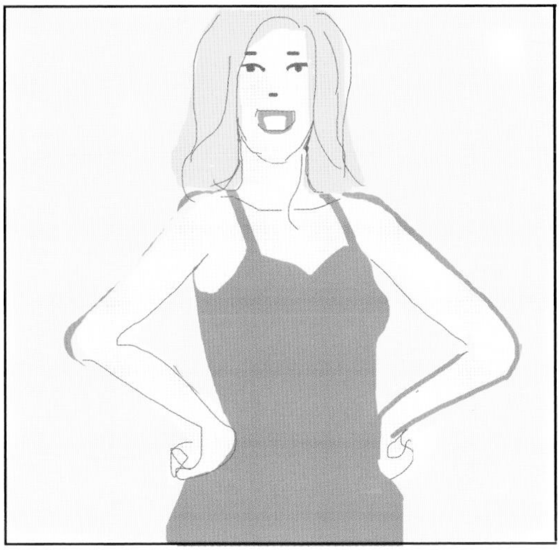

She always smiled at him, then looked alarmed and left the kitchen hurriedly. Grant would call to her, but she never reappeared until the next dream.

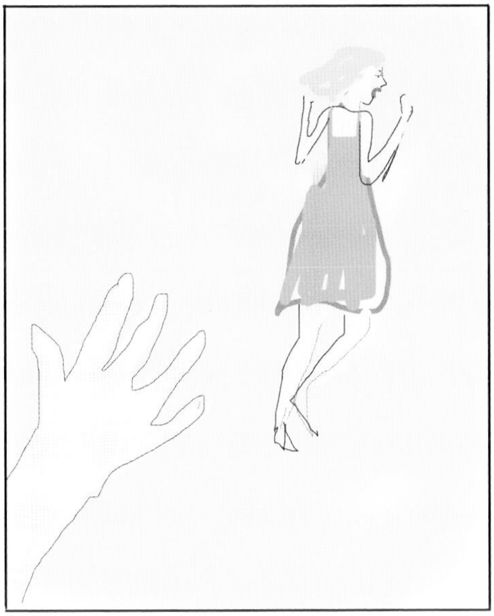

One night he went to bed early with a headache. The lady was playing with her ocelots, a game that involved tossing little animals into the air and letting the ocelots catch them and do terrible things to them.

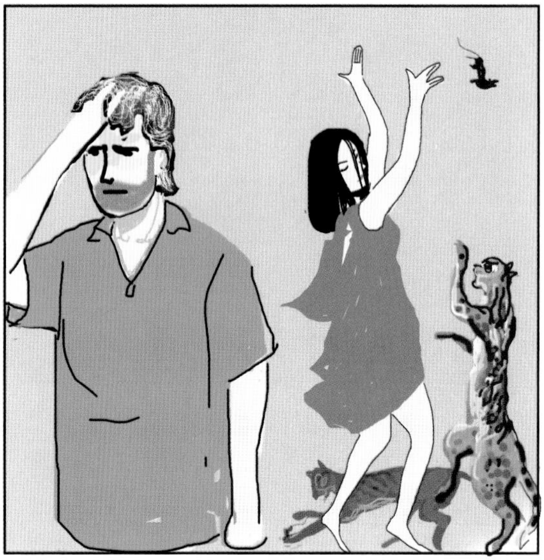

Once he was asleep, Grant immediately found himself in the girl's kitchen. The girl wasn't there, and he turned and saw a tiny door next to the fridge.

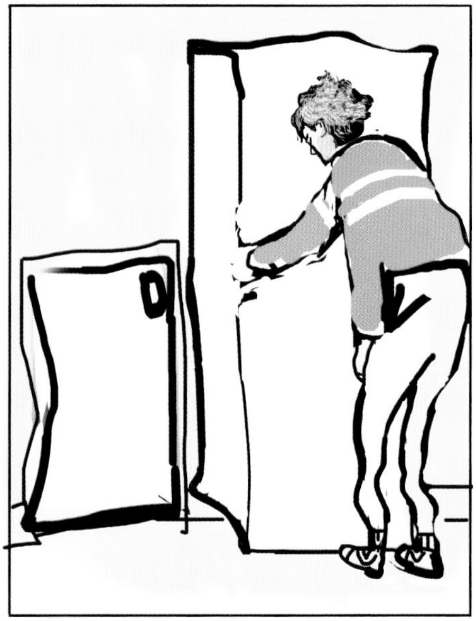

He got on his knees and squeezed himself through the opening. He found himself in his own apartment, with his beloved, decrepit stuff.

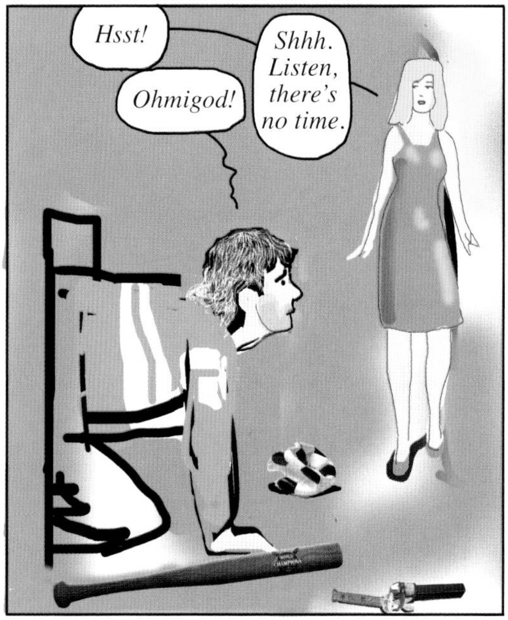
Hsst!
Ohmigod!
Shhh. Listen, there's no time.

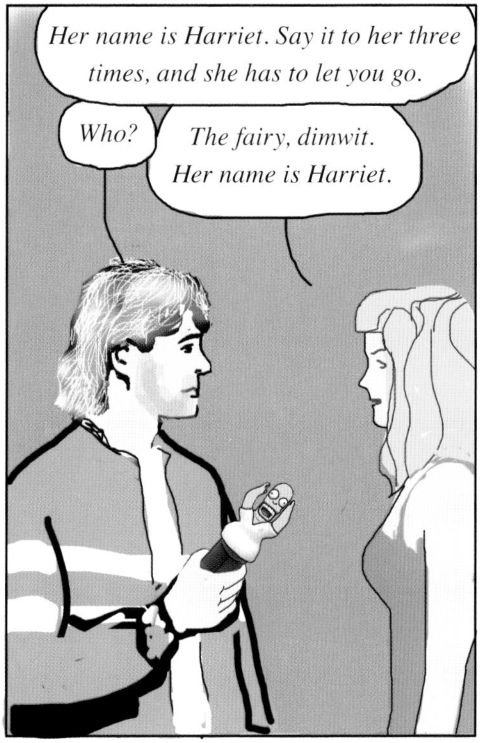
Her name is Harriet. Say it to her three times, and she has to let you go.
Who?
The fairy, dimwit. Her name is Harriet.

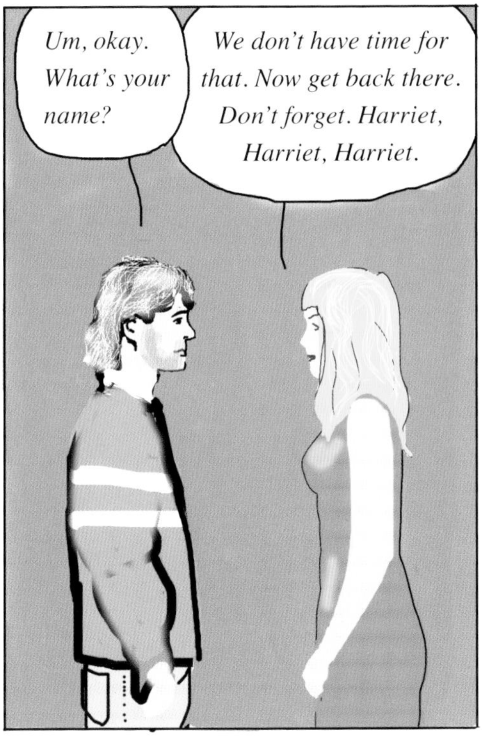
Um, okay. What's your name?
We don't have time for that. Now get back there. Don't forget. Harriet, Harriet, Harriet.

She was pushing him toward the little door when he woke.

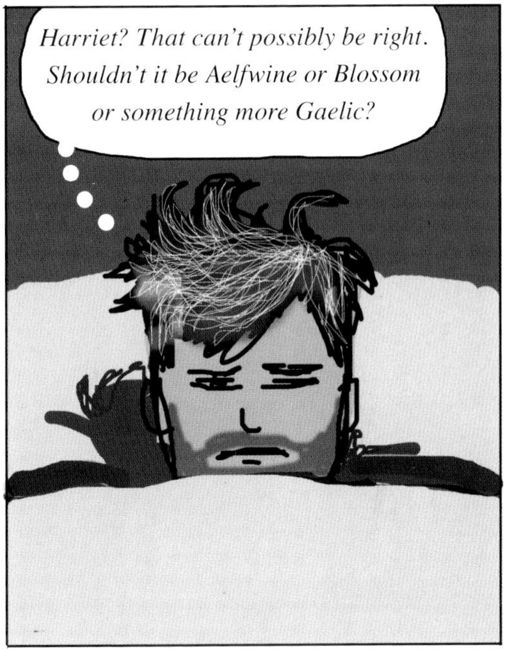
Harriet? That can't possibly be right. Shouldn't it be Aelfwine or Blossom or something more Gaelic?

But Grant was desperate enough to give it a go. He got out of bed and walked into the living room. The lady was levitating the ocelots. They were spinning in midair and didn't seem too pleased about it.

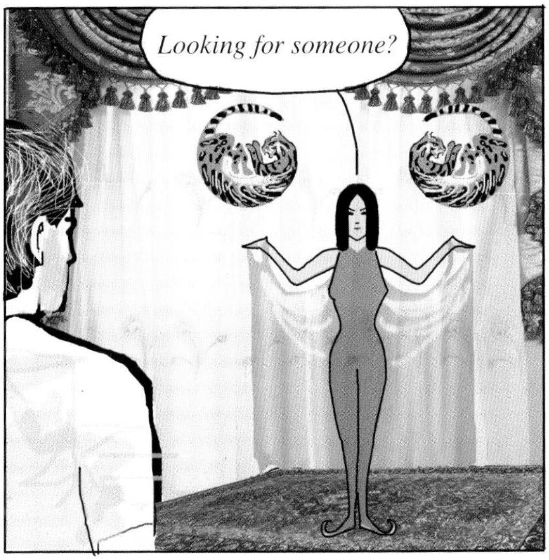
Looking for someone?

Grant expected the lady to say something withering and send him back to bed. Instead she looked furious and vanished.

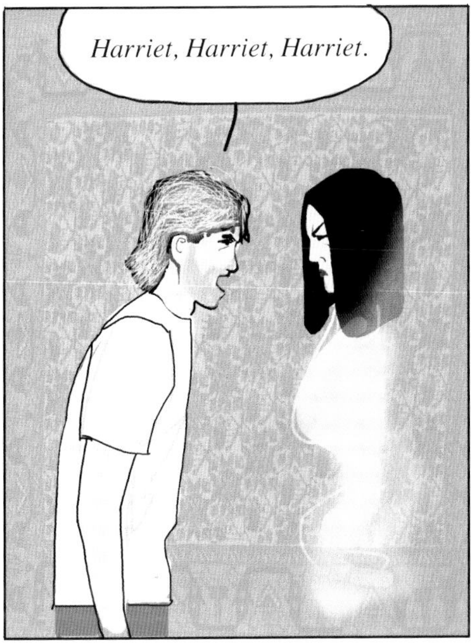
Harriet, Harriet, Harriet.

Grant found himself standing in his own living room; it was uncanny how all the lady's redecorating had utterly disappeared.

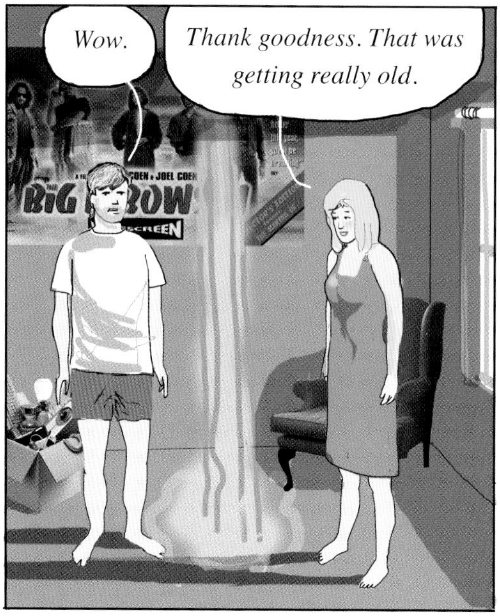
Wow.
Thank goodness. That was getting really old.

Grant turned and saw her in his kitchen doorway. He was about to say, Who are you? but instead blurted,

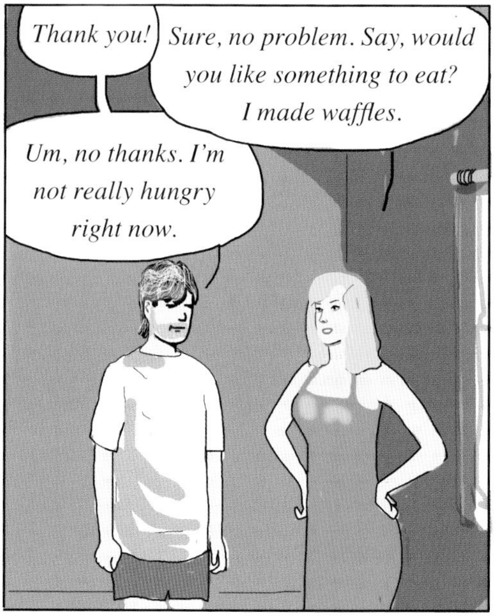
Thank you!
Sure, no problem. Say, would you like something to eat? I made waffles.
Um, no thanks. I'm not really hungry right now.

Grant had a sudden qualm: waffles? The girl looked as though she might cry; her lip trembled, and she seemed very fragile and human standing there, overcome with disappointment.

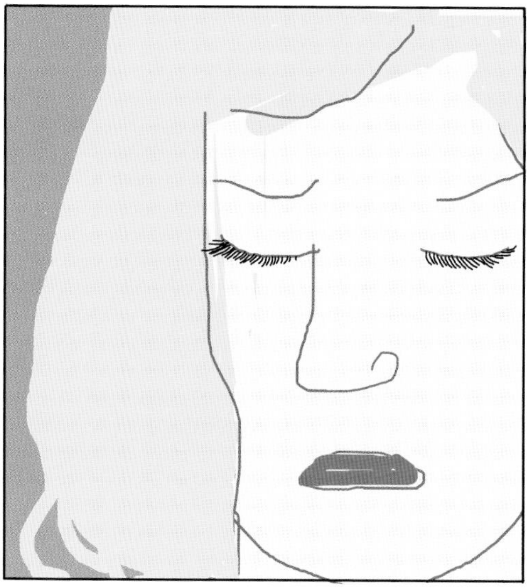

Grant felt terrible. After all, she had saved him from the fairy lady; surely he could eat a waffle if it meant that much to her.

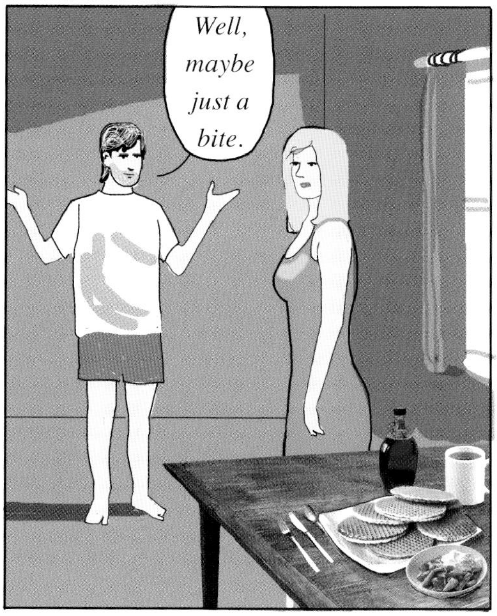
Well, maybe just a bite.

She fetched a dainty plate with one small waffle and set a place for him at his own table. Grant carefully cut off a piece of the waffle, put it in his mouth, chewed, and swallowed.

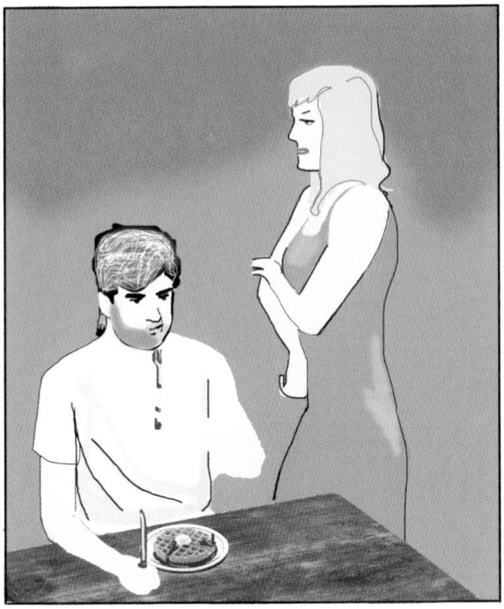

He looked up just in time to see the triumphant expression on the girl's face.

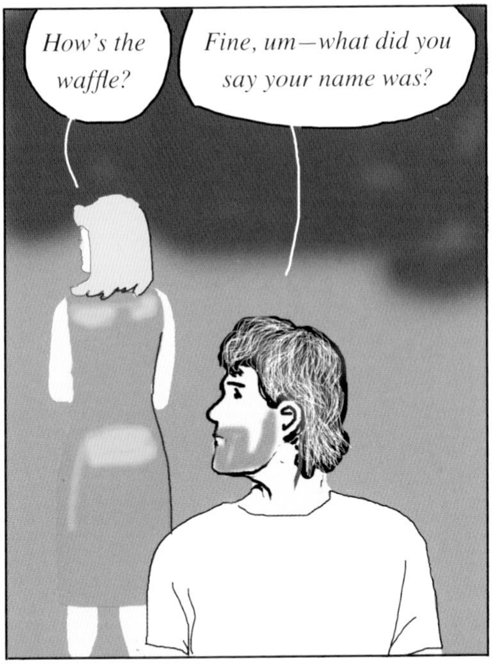
How's the waffle?
Fine, um—what did you say your name was?

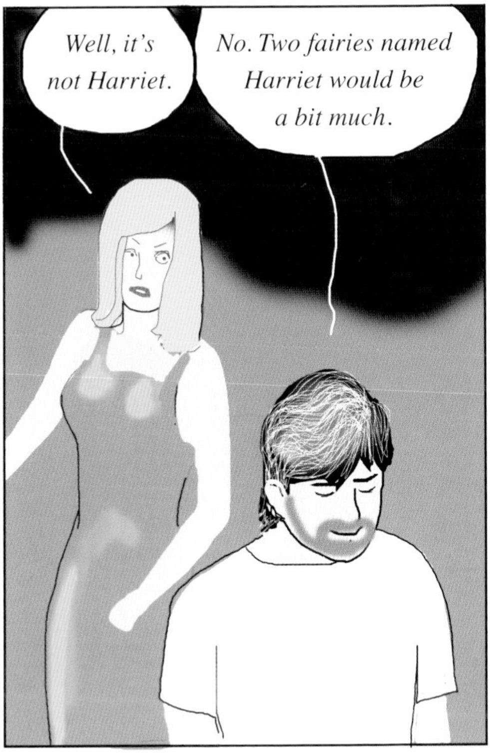
Well, it's not Harriet.
No. Two fairies named Harriet would be a bit much.

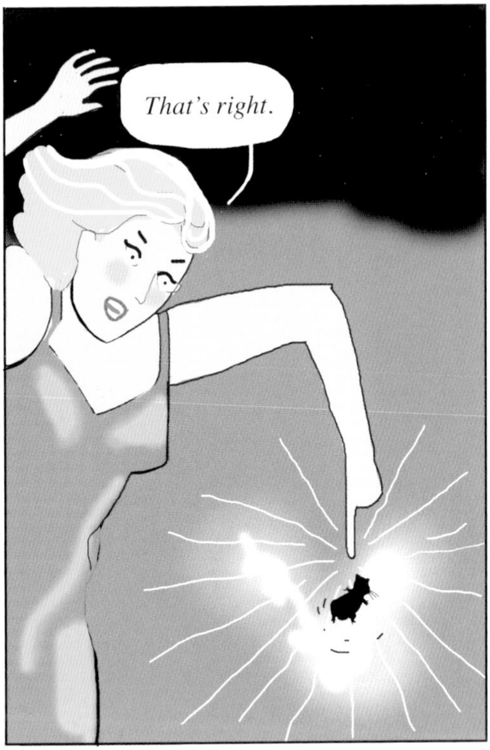
That's right.

And she turned him into a hamster.

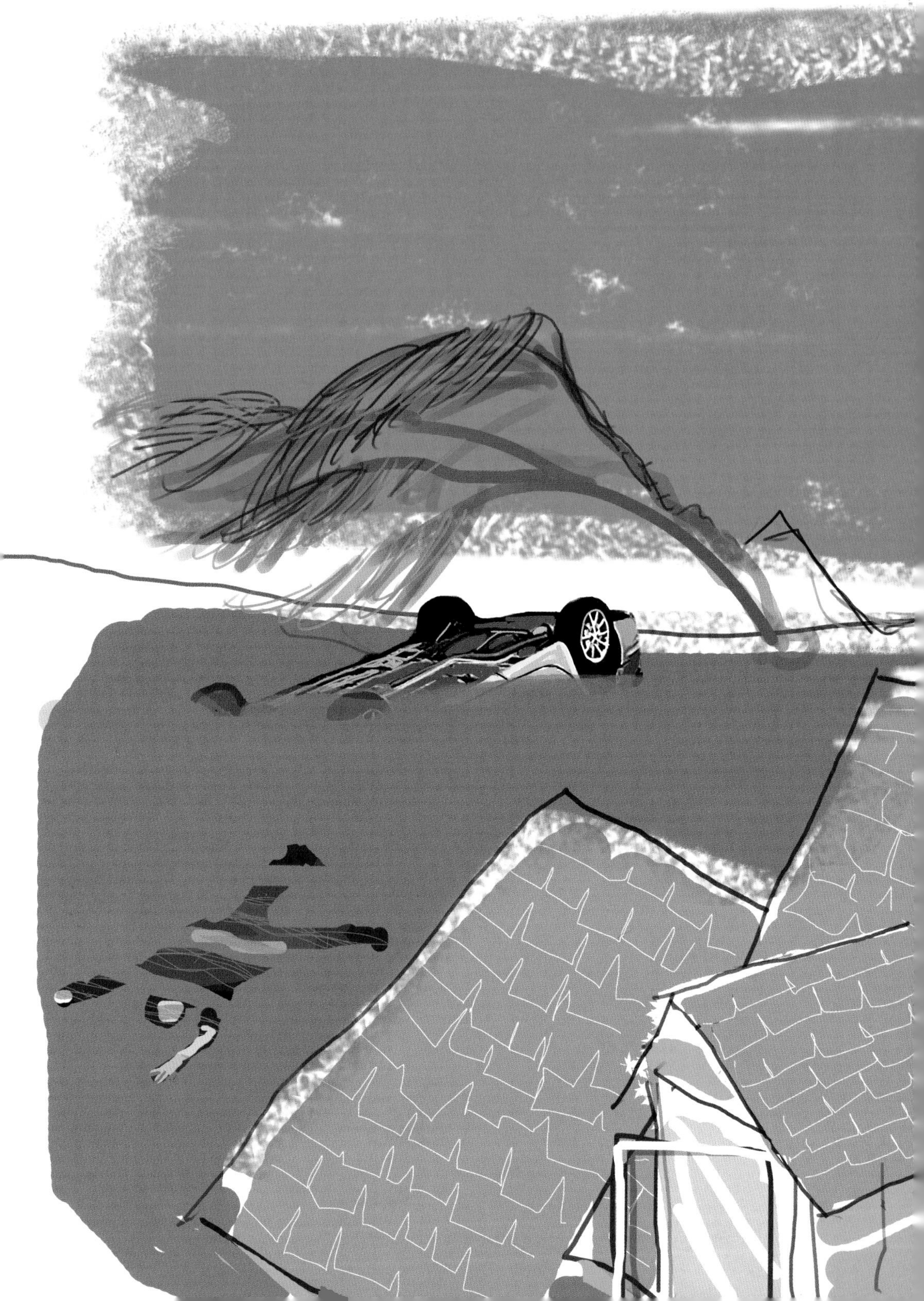

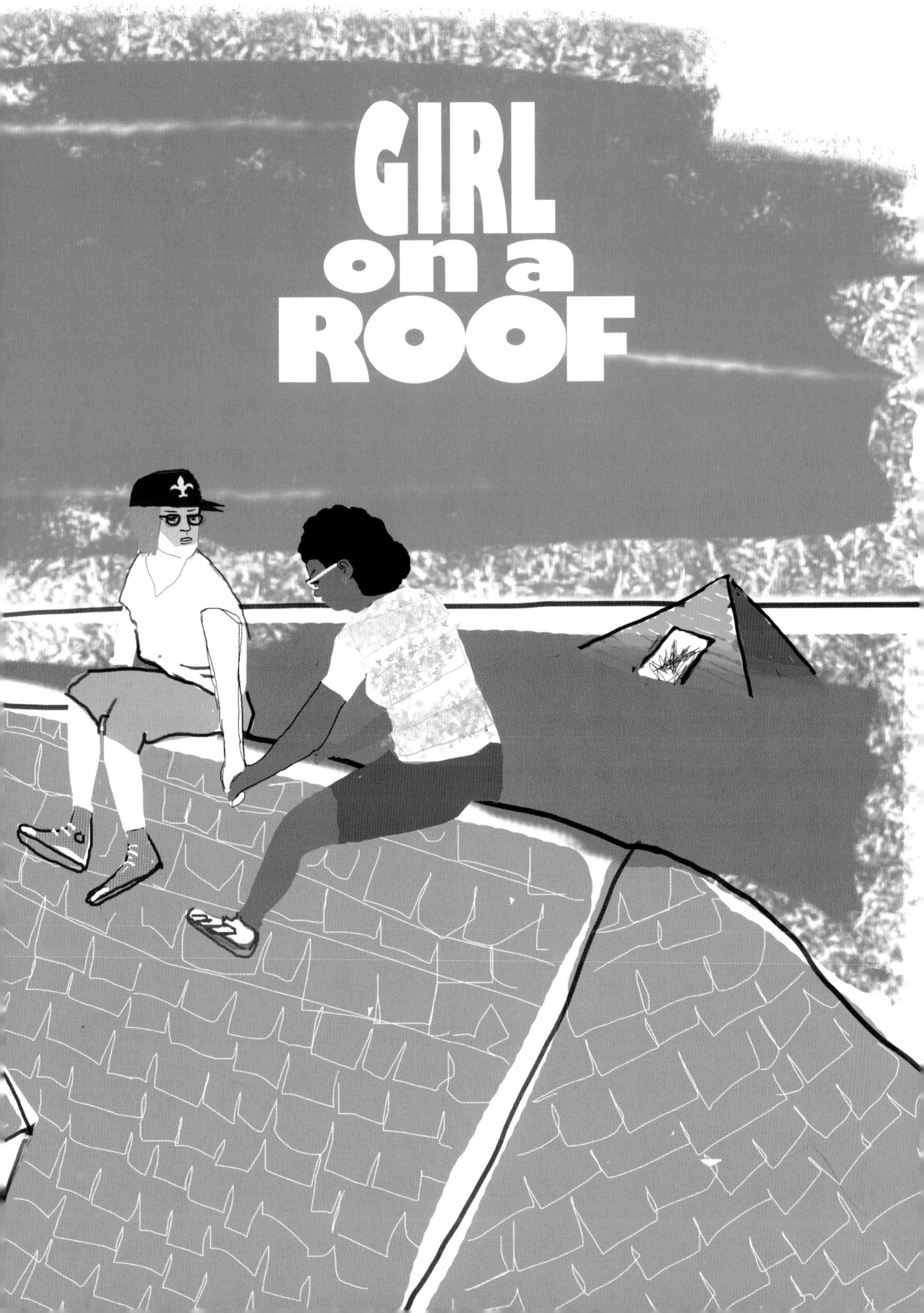
GIRL
on a
ROOF

September 1, 2005

Dear Sylvie,

I'm writing you this letter because I don't know what else to do. Your cell phone is dead. All I get when I call you is a computer voice telling me to call back later. You haven't answered my emails. I've been watching the news for hours, days. Water everywhere, bodies floating down the streets, collapsed highways, abandoned pets. Where are you, Sylvie? I want to go to you, but I'm afraid that if I leave the apartment, you'll show up and I won't be here. I know that you won't read this. There's nowhere to send it anymore.

Last night I dreamt that we were together in your parents' house when the flood came. In my dream we crept up the stairs quietly, as though the water could hear us, as though it would find us—we were its prey, and we went upstairs so silently, holding hands like little kids. And the water rose just as silently. We were afraid to touch the water or to let it touch us. It was formidable, evil. If it touched us, we would die. You kept putting things into my hands, things you wanted to save. We went into the attic. It was full of your mother's clothes, and I knew you were sad that the flood would ruin her extravagant dresses. The water kept rising, and we climbed out the dormer window and onto the roof. We sat side by side on the roof, and the water washed everything away. We saw cars, trees, bodies in the water. All the birds were gone; there was no noise except the sound of the water lapping and swirling; now and then a dog would bark, but there were no other people there. It was an empty world. The water had taken everything. We sat on the roof and looked out at nothing. We made love up there because we had no food or water to drink. The roof was our island. Then I saw the rough green asphalt shingles of the roof through your hands. Your body gradually became transparent, and I was alone on the roof, watching the water invade, watching the city disappear. I looked at the things you had given me to save. I was holding your glasses and a tennis ball.

Sylvie, I hope you aren't in the city. I hope you evacuated. (Though how could you have left the city with no car? Did you ever find your mom? And why haven't you called?) The TV is showing horrible things. There are reports of killings, rapes, looting, old people dying in nursing homes because the staff left them behind. Why haven't you called? I don't know what to do, Sylvie.

Before you left last week I said, *Please don't go.* And you said, *She just wants me home for a few weeks, Nan. I'll be back in Chicago when classes start.* I sit in front of the television looking past the reporters, trying to see your house in the wrecked scenes behind their freaked-out faces. I remember the garden in your mother's backyard, the yellow gladioli and the bright red canna lilies, the honeysuckle that engulfed the garage . . . I remember the scent of the garden at night, how it came in through your bedroom window, so strong I felt almost nauseated. You kissed me in the backyard; I worried that your neighbors might see. You laughed and printed your lipsticked mouth on my white blouse just over my left nipple . . . And in the afternoons, I remember how everyone sat on their porches in the heat, and they all waved at us when we walked to Jimmy's to buy cigarettes and beer. All underwater now. Whole blocks, whole neighborhoods. I stood on our front stoop this morning with the newspaper in my hand, looking at Hyde Park Boulevard, imagining it all underwater.

Do you know how to swim, Sylvie? I never asked you. It's amazing to me how much I don't know. After two years you'd think we'd know everything there is to know about each other. But I guess you never can tell what will be important. Why would it matter if you could swim? We only talk about what we're reading. We eat and sleep and take baths and put on clothes and take them off again and fuck each other delirious and go to classes, and all around us the air fills up with words about books. If New Orleans was flooded with words, I would not be afraid for you, Sylvie. I know you can swim in words. But water . . . can you swim in water, Sylvie?

The apartment seems vacant without you, even though it's crammed with your stuff. Since you won't read this, I'll admit that I've been crying over the stupidest things. Tonight I opened the junk drawer in the kitchen and found your old key ring with the little plastic Pink Panther, and that set me off. I can't explain why. It was just pathetic, I guess. Your possessions seem like they're expecting you; they don't have the slightest doubt that you'll come home. I feel superstitious. If I close my eyes while the phone rings, it will be you. If I take a shower, then the phone will ring, and it will be you. But when the phone rings, it's always other people asking if I've heard from you yet. *No,* I say. *Not yet.* There's not much to say after that. We're all embarrassed by our own politeness. *Call me if there's anything I can do,* they say. *Sure, yeah, of course,* I say. I want to scream at them. I want to howl, like a baby, until you come to me. Oh, Sylvie. You have to be safe, because I am wrecked without you. My levees are breached, and you have flooded me, and I am a city underwater now.

Ugh—I'm getting all metaphorical. Come home and make fun of my bad prose.

It's almost five a.m., Sylvie. I'm sitting at the kitchen table, looking toward the lake. It's funny how we think of the lake being there, a presence even though we can't see it because of all the tallish, ugly buildings. The sky is getting lighter. I remember when I first met you, and you thought it was weird that I always knew what direction the lake was, no matter where we were, as though I had an internal compass that pointed east. How strange it would be if the lake rose up one day and came into the city. It would be like a fairy tale, as though an enchantment had caused the city and the lake to merge, silently, like a painting of a city in a lake. But that's not what I see on TV, Sylvie. On TV there are dead people slumped in folding chairs in the baking sun, and people spray painting Xs on the houses, and everything is either in motion when it should be still or stranded, stopped.

It flooded here once, Sylvie. Someone knocked a hole in the bottom of the Chicago River, and it drained into all the basements in the skyscrapers, the deep basements below the basements. I'm not

making this up. It was a flood no one could see, a sort of conceptual flood, except to the people who had to deal with it; for them it was probably pretty real.

The sun's up, Sylvie. I'm going to bed. Maybe when I wake up, you'll call. Maybe you're on your way here. At least maybe I'll dream about you.

Nan

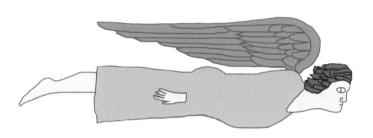

Jakob Wywialowski and the Angels

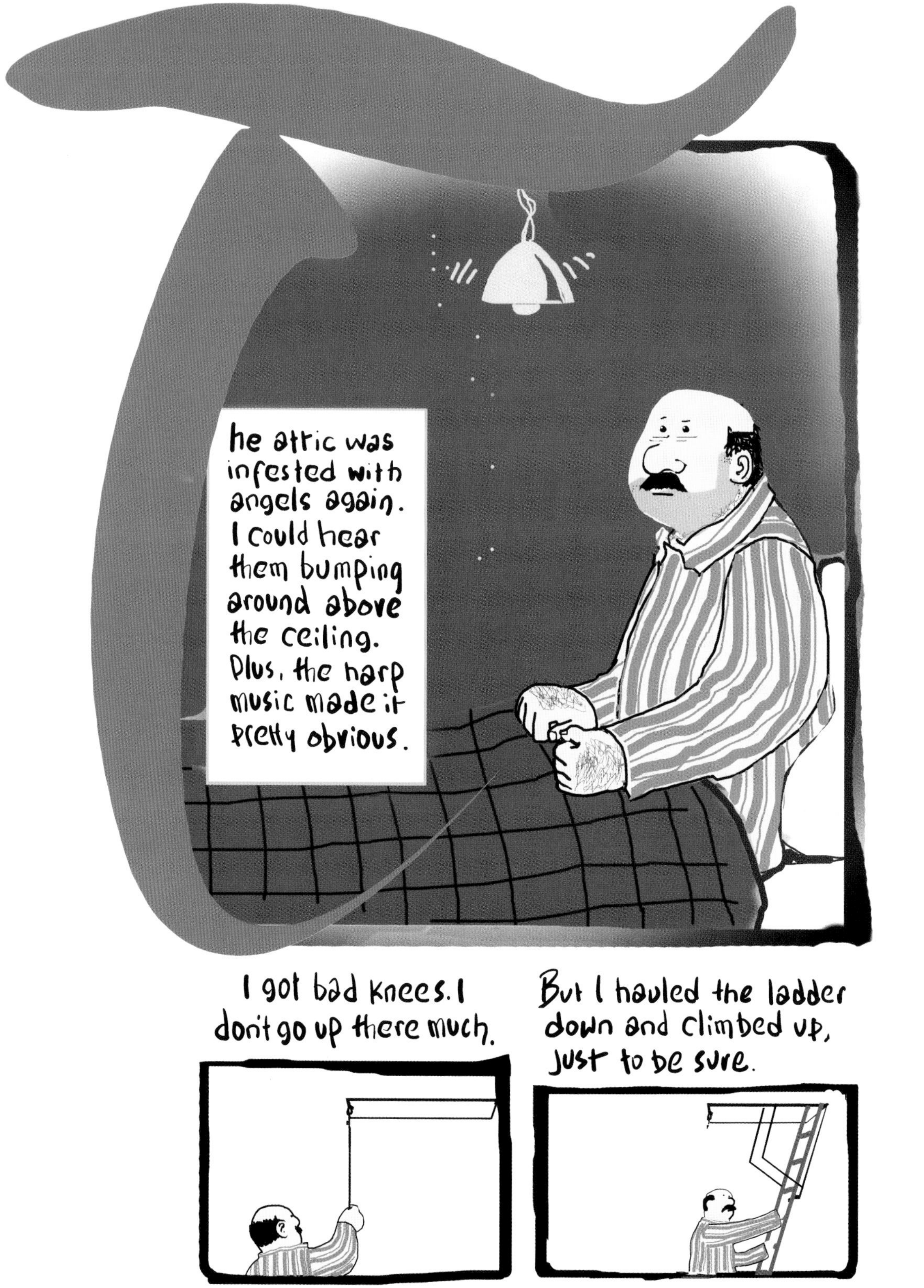
he attic was infested with angels again. I could hear them bumping around above the ceiling. Plus, the harp music made it pretty obvious.
I got bad knees. I don't go up there much.
But I hauled the ladder down and climbed up, just to be sure.

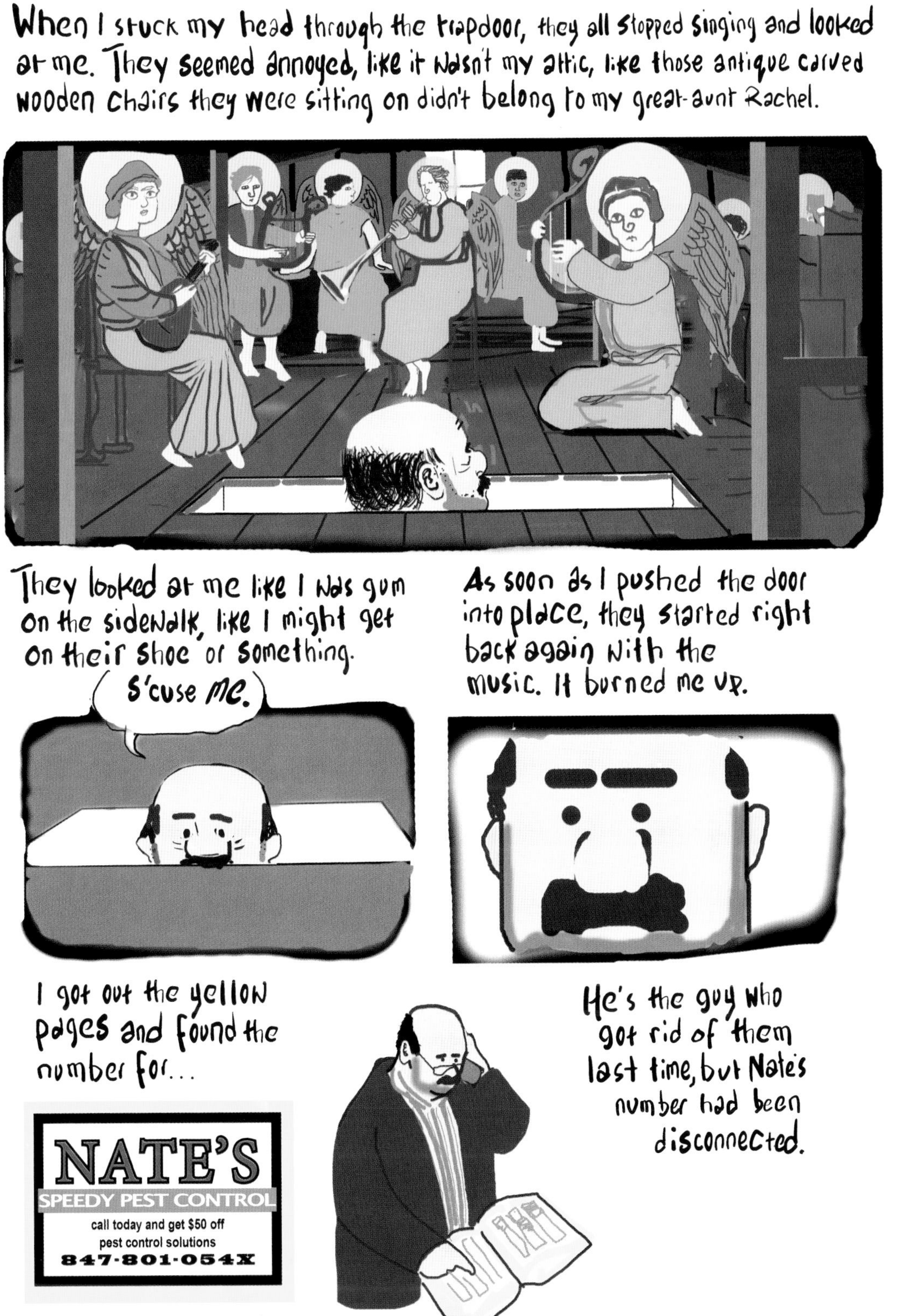
When I stuck my head through the trapdoor, they all stopped singing and looked at me. They seemed annoyed, like it wasn't my attic, like those antique carved wooden chairs they were sitting on didn't belong to my great-aunt Rachel.
They looked at me like I was gum on the sidewalk, like I might get on their shoe or something.
S'cuse *me.*
As soon as I pushed the door into place, they started right back again with the music. It burned me up.
I got out the yellow pages and found the number for...
NATE'S
SPEEDY PEST CONTROL
call today and get $50 off
pest control solutions
847-801-054X
He's the guy who got rid of them last time, but Nate's number had been disconnected.

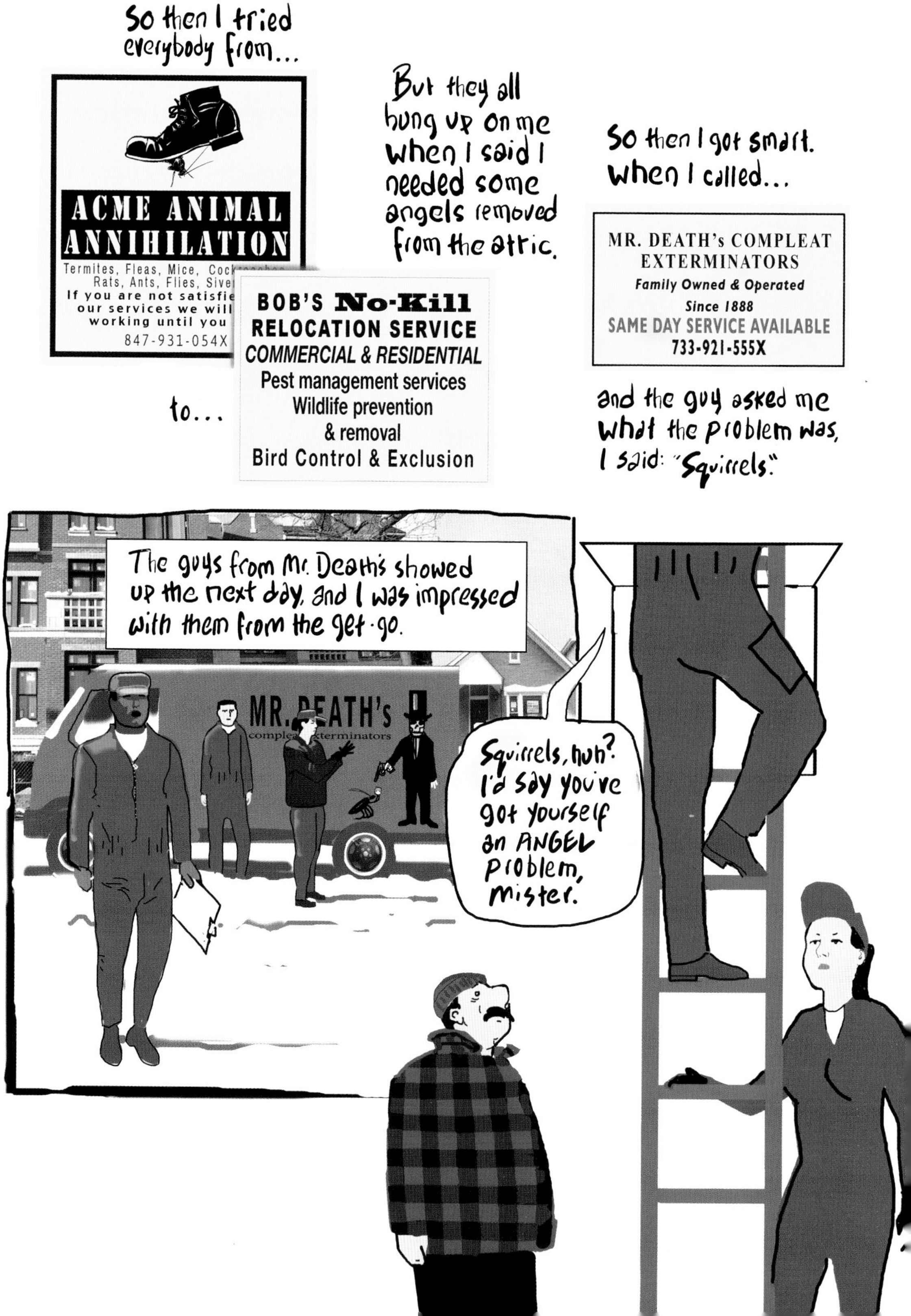

So then I tried everybody from...
ACME ANIMAL ANNIHILATION
Termites, Fleas, Mice,
Rats, Ants, Flies,
If you are not satisfie
our services we will
working until you
847-931-054X
to...
BOB'S No-Kill RELOCATION SERVICE
COMMERCIAL & RESIDENTIAL
Pest management services
Wildlife prevention & removal
Bird Control & Exclusion
But they all hung up on me when I said I needed some angels removed from the attic.
So then I got smart. When I called...
MR. DEATH's COMPLEAT EXTERMINATORS
Family Owned & Operated
Since 1888
SAME DAY SERVICE AVAILABLE
733-921-555X
and the guy asked me what the problem was, I said: "Squirrels."
The guys from Mr. Death's showed up the next day, and I was impressed with them from the get-go.
MR. DEATH's
Squirrels, huh? I'd say you've got yourself an ANGEL problem, mister.

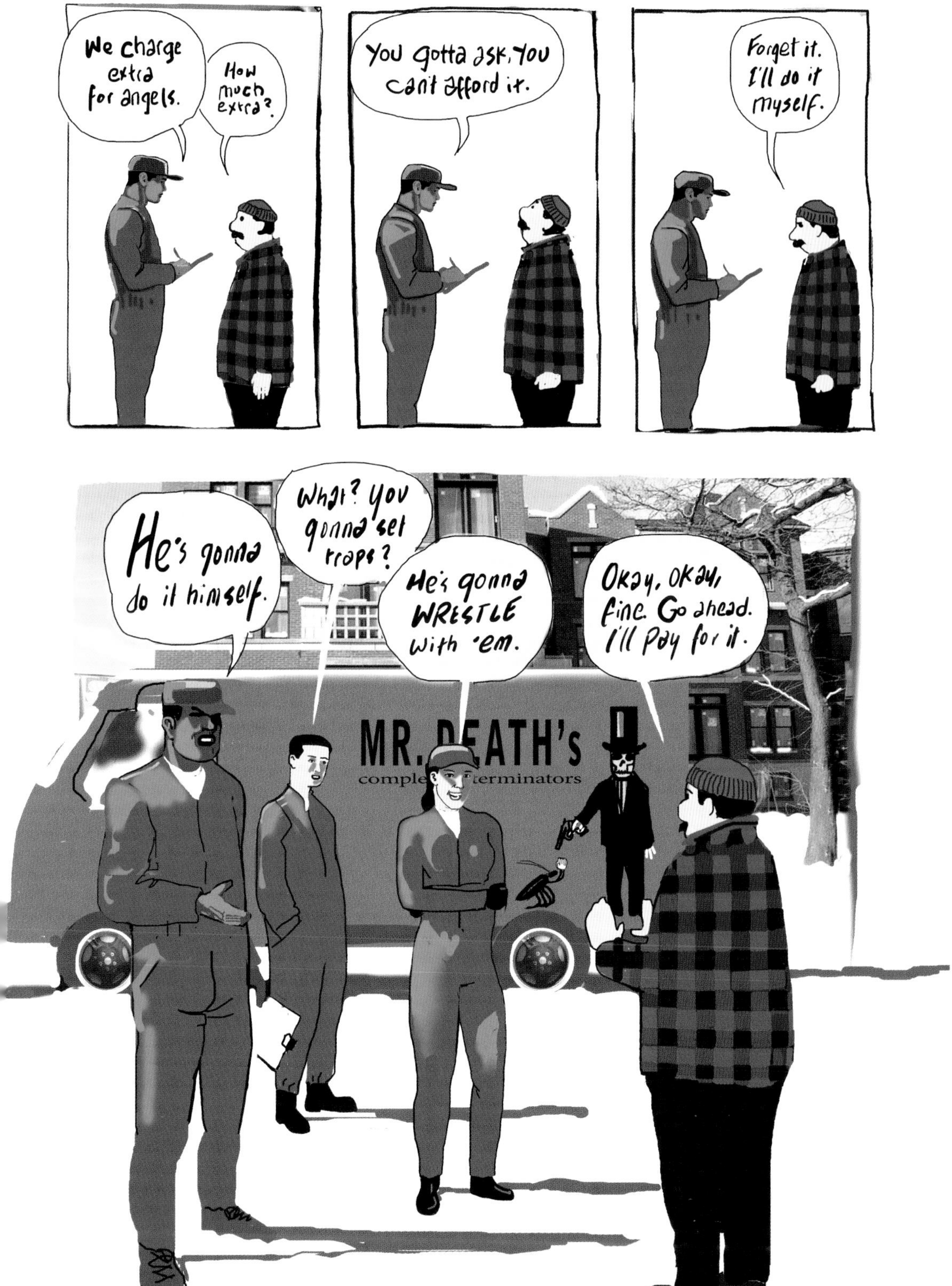

We charge extra for angels.
How much extra?
You gotta ask, you can't afford it.
Forget it. I'll do it myself.
He's gonna do it himself.
What? You gonna set traps?
He's gonna WRESTLE with 'em.
Okay, okay, fine. Go ahead. I'll pay for it.
MR. DEATH's
terminators

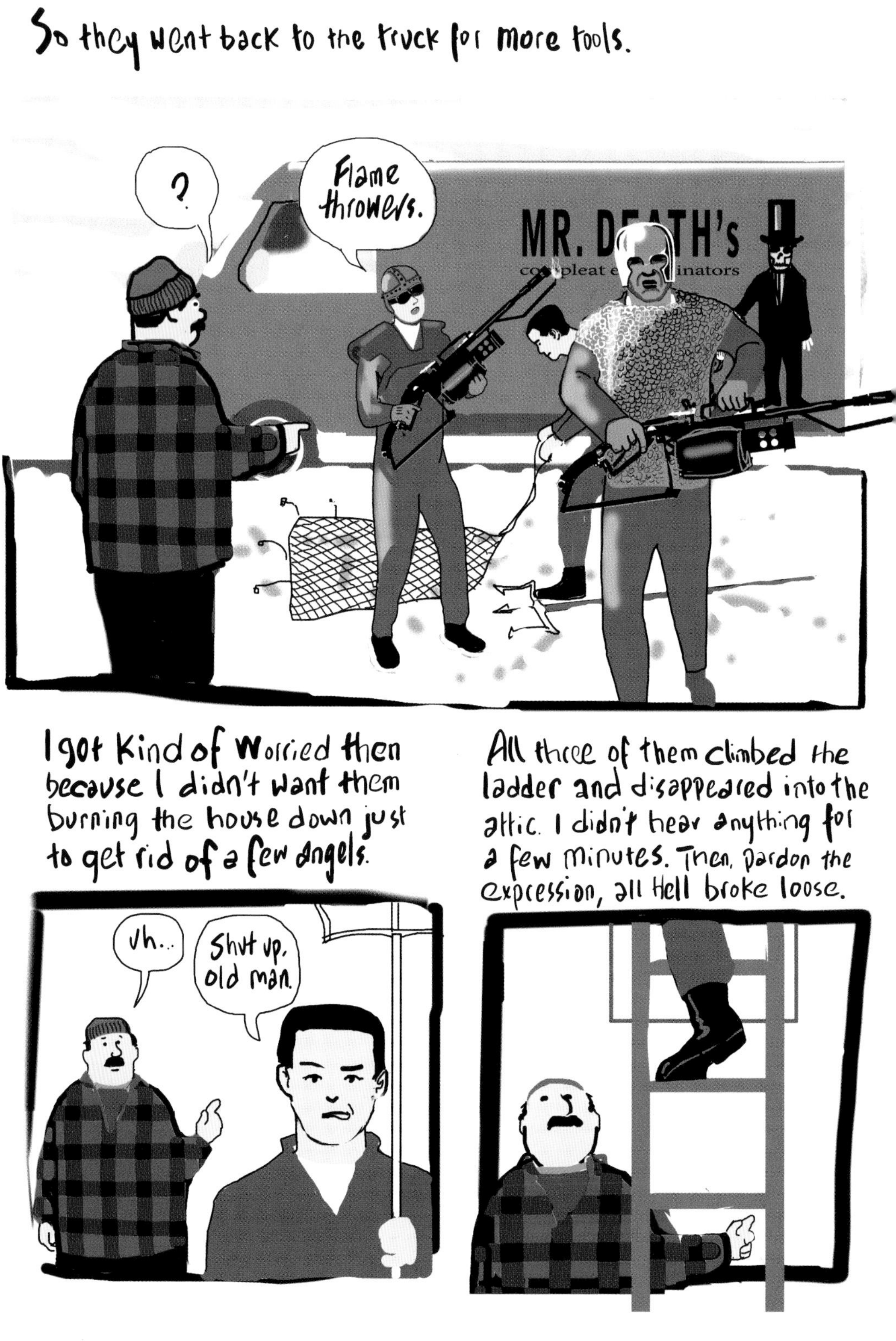
So they went back to the truck for more tools.
?
Flame throwers.
MR. DEATH's
I got kind of worried then because I didn't want them burning the house down just to get rid of a few angels.
uh...
Shut up, old man.
All three of them climbed the ladder and disappeared into the attic. I didn't hear anything for a few minutes. Then, pardon the expression, all Hell broke loose.

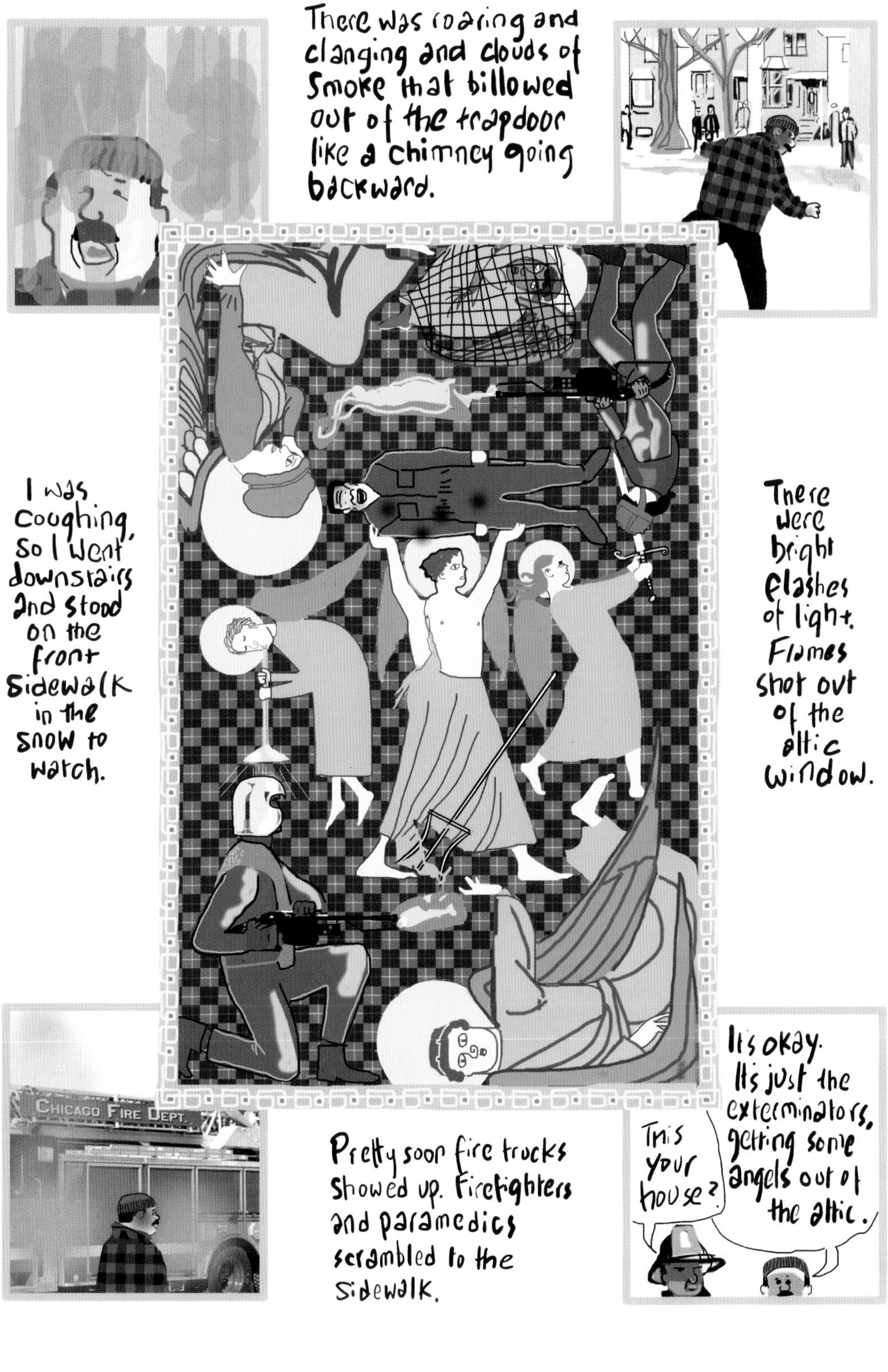
There was roaring and clanging and clouds of Smoke that billowed out of the trapdoor like a chimney going backward.
I was coughing, so I went downstairs and stood on the front sidewalk in the snow to watch.
There were bright flashes of light. Flames shot out of the attic window.
CHICAGO FIRE DEPT.
Pretty soon fire trucks showed up. Firefighters and paramedics scrambled to the sidewalk.
This your house?
It's okay. It's just the exterminators, getting some angels out of the attic.

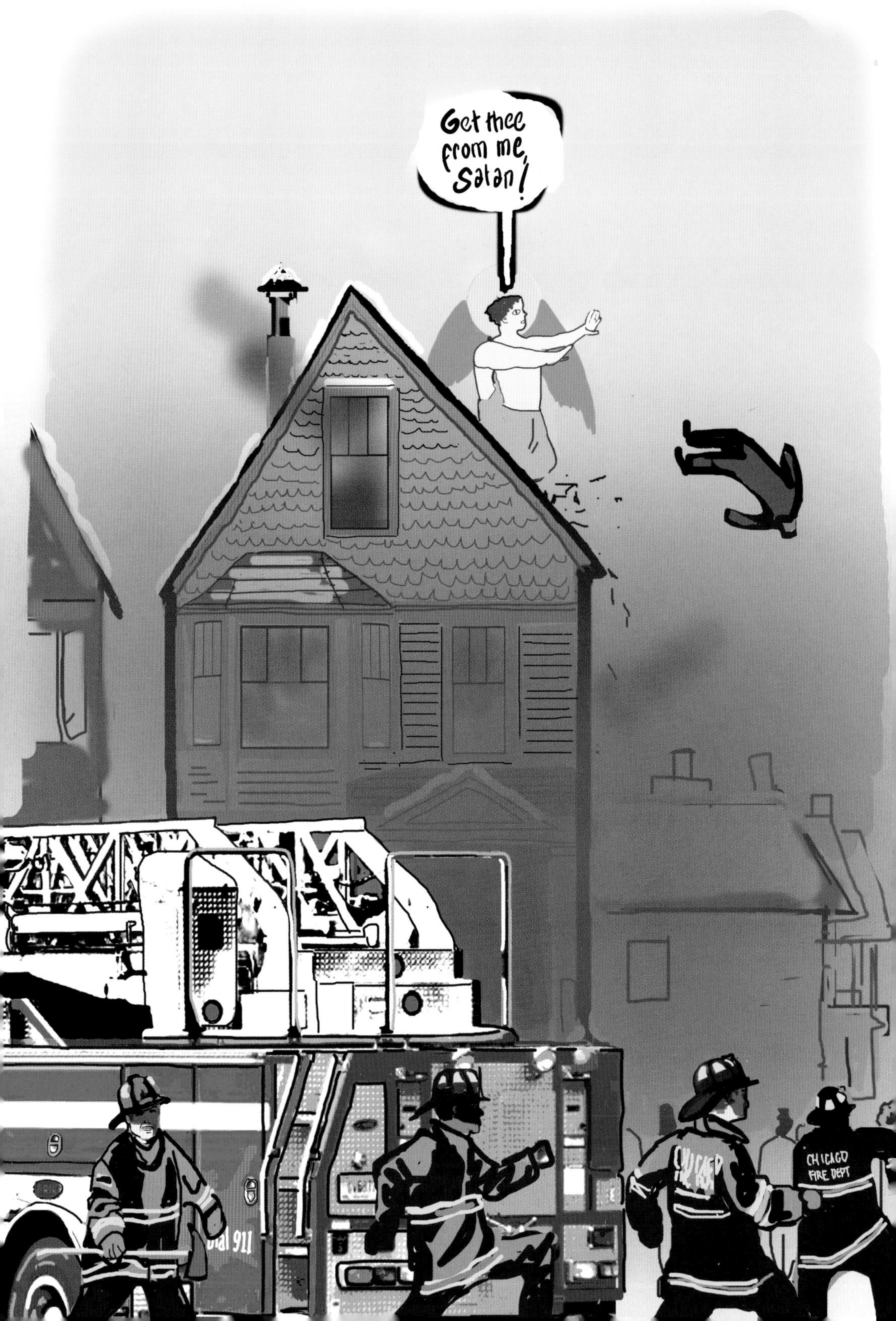
Get thee from me, Satan!
Dial 911
CHICAGO FIRE DEPT

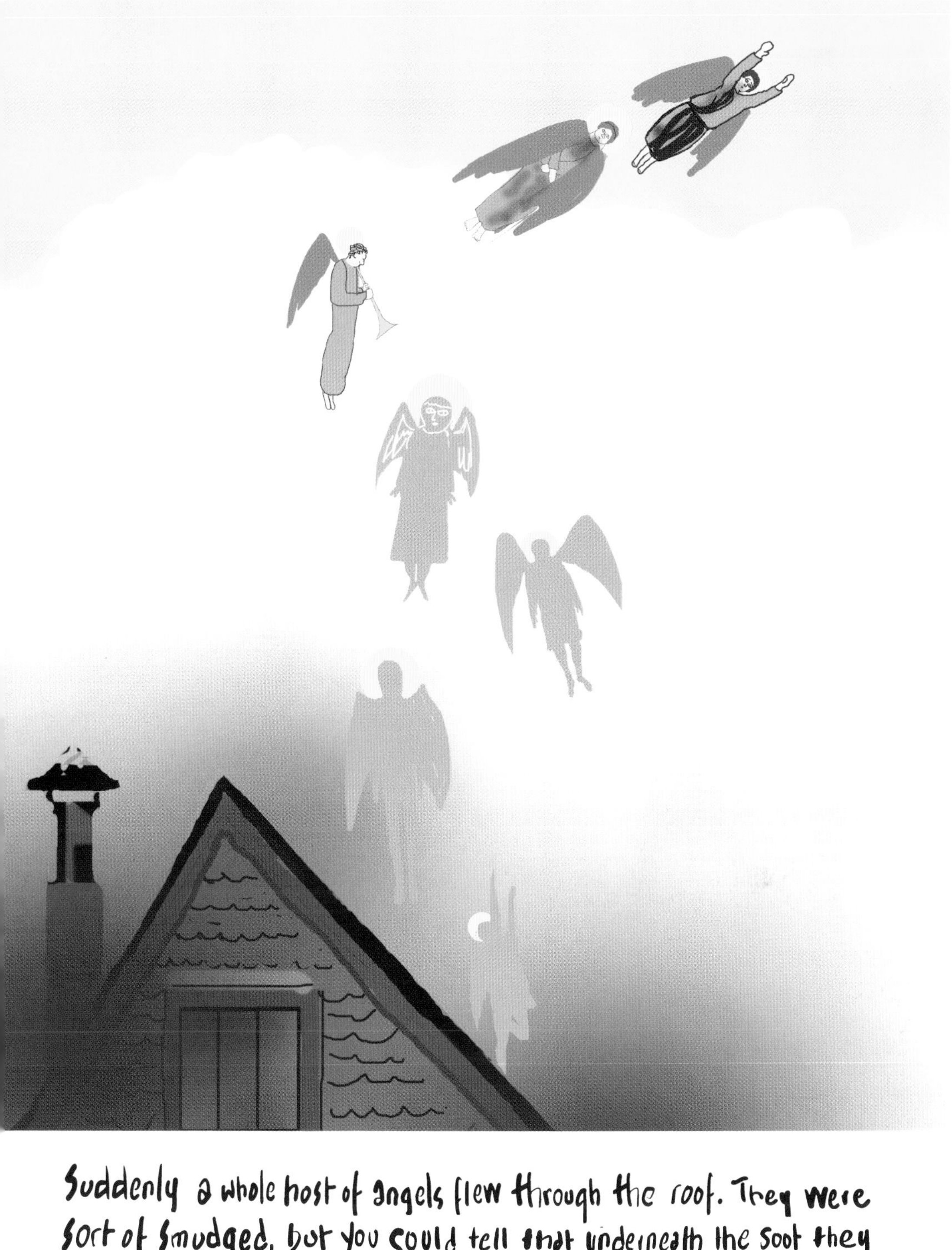

Suddenly a whole host of angels flew through the roof. They were sort of smudged, but you could tell that underneath the soot they were real pretty. I felt bad about throwing them out of the attic, but what was I supposed to do? One thing leads to another, and before you know it, you've got seraphim.

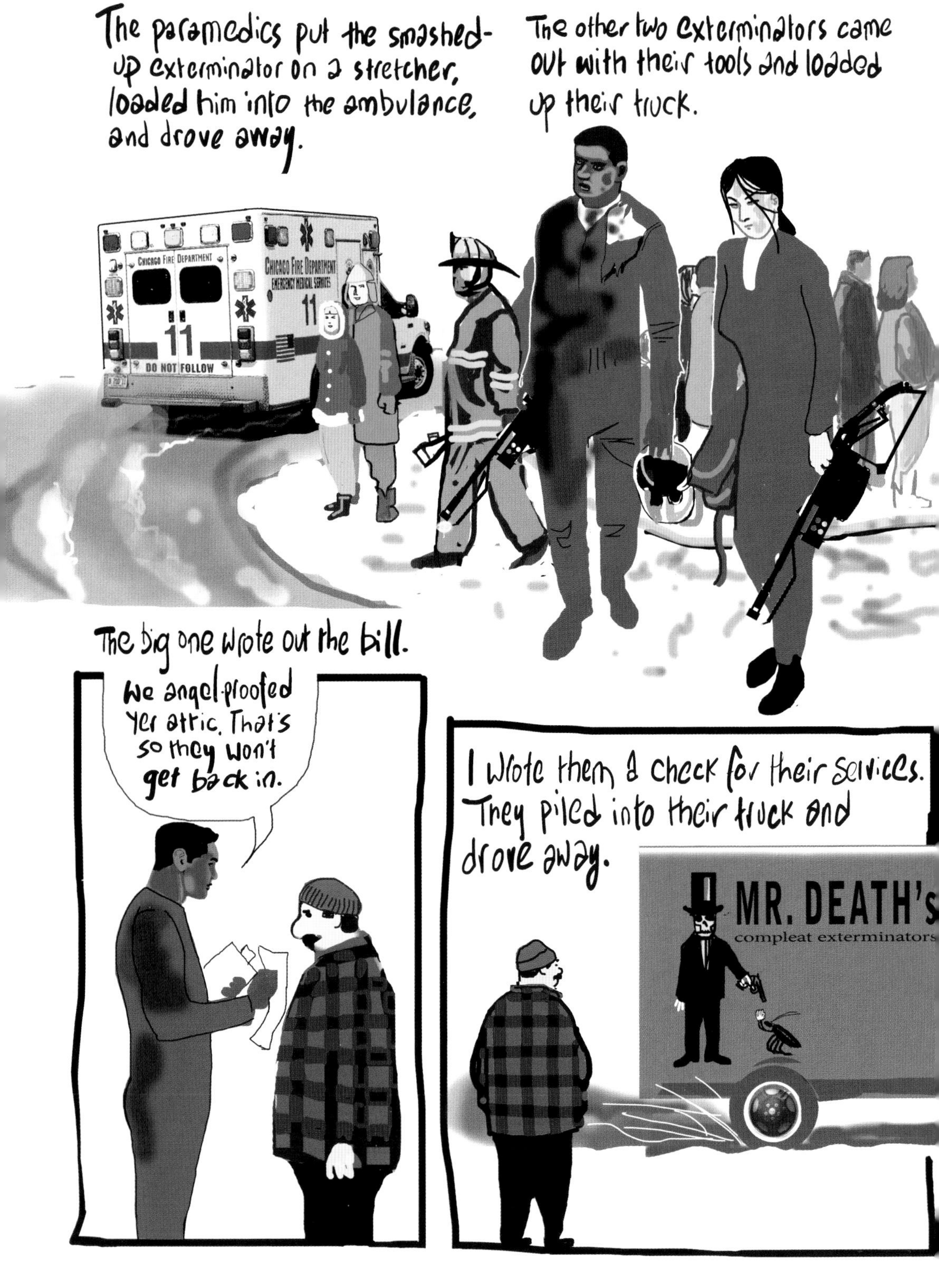
The paramedics put the smashed-up exterminator on a stretcher, loaded him into the ambulance, and drove away.
The other two exterminators came out with their tools and loaded up their truck.
CHICAGO FIRE DEPARTMENT
CHICAGO FIRE DEPARTMENT EMERGENCY MEDICAL SERVICES
11
11
DO NOT FOLLOW
The big one wrote out the bill.
We angel-proofed yer attic. That's so they won't get back in.
I wrote them a check for their services. They piled into their truck and drove away.
MR. DEATH's
compleat exterminators

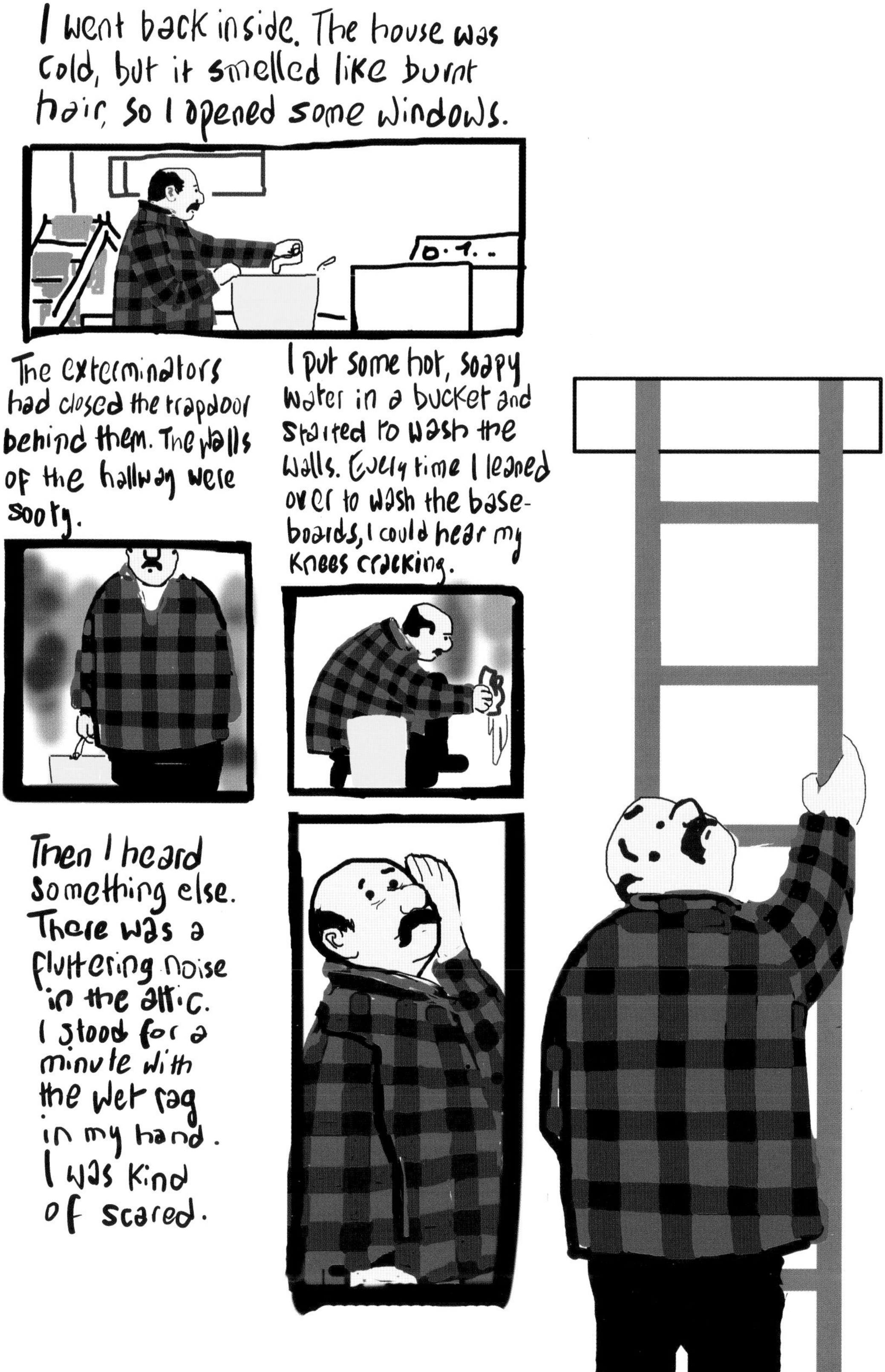
I went back inside. The house was cold, but it smelled like burnt hair, so I opened some windows.
0.1..
The exterminators had closed the trapdoor behind them. The walls of the hallway were sooty.
I put some hot, soapy water in a bucket and started to wash the walls. Every time I leaned over to wash the baseboards, I could hear my knees cracking.
Then I heard something else. There was a fluttering noise in the attic. I stood for a minute with the wet rag in my hand. I was kind of scared.

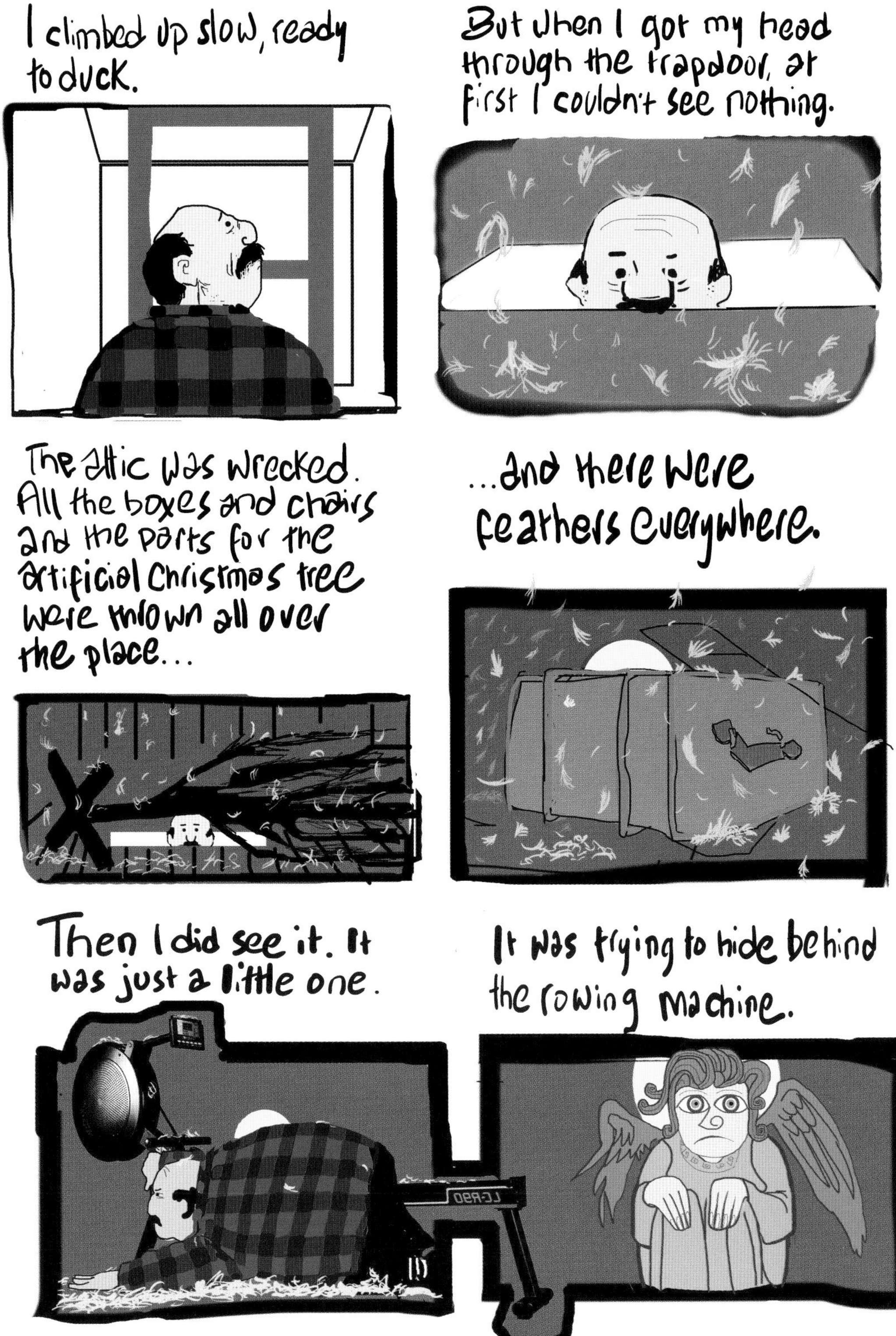
I climbed up slow, ready to duck.
But when I got my head through the trapdoor, at first I couldn't see nothing.
The attic was wrecked. All the boxes and chairs and the parts for the artificial Christmas tree were thrown all over the place...
...and there were feathers everywhere.
Then I did see it. It was just a little one.
It was trying to hide behind the rowing machine.

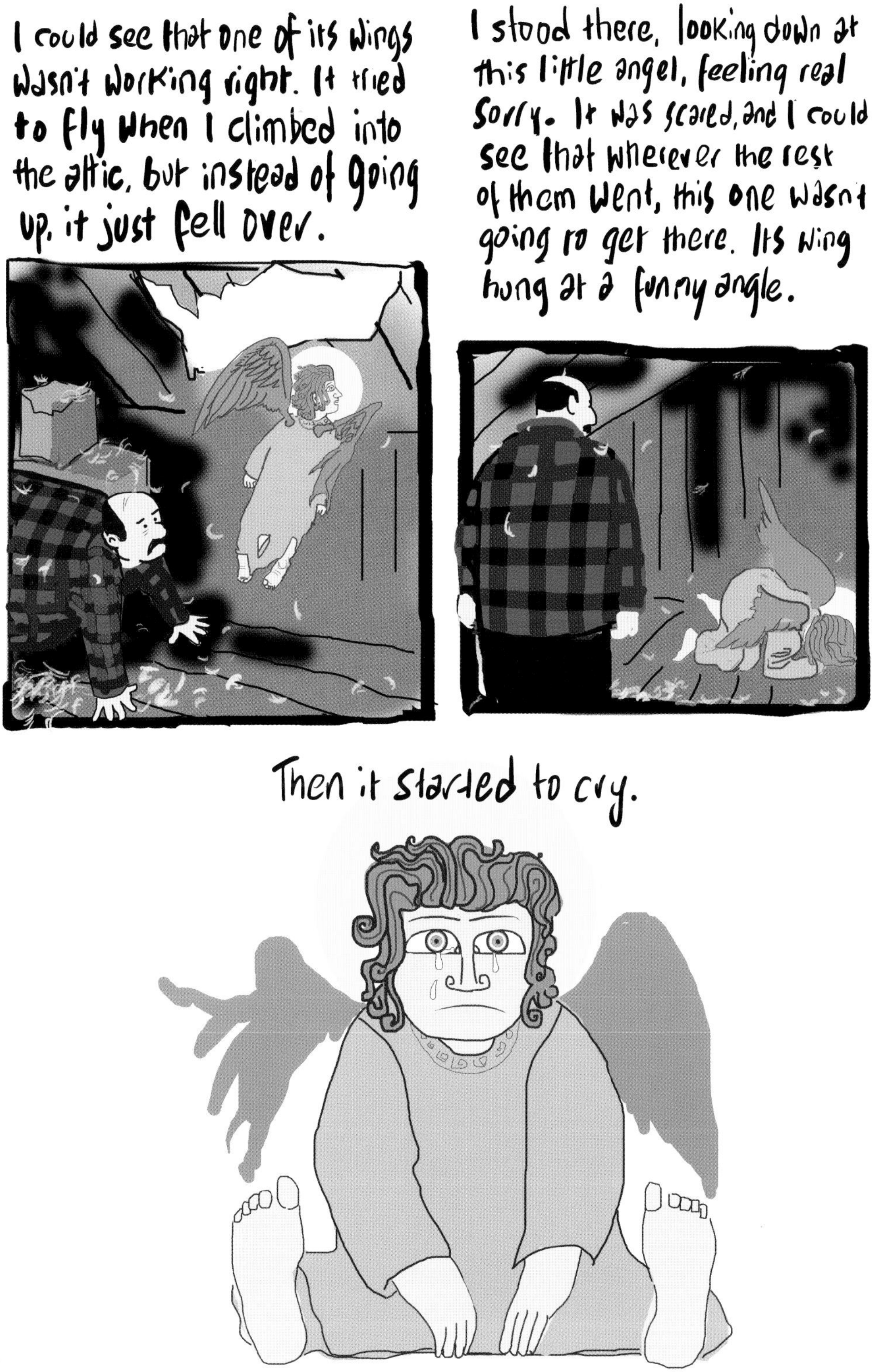
I could see that one of its wings wasn't working right. It tried to fly when I climbed into the attic, but instead of going up, it just fell over.
I stood there, looking down at this little angel, feeling real sorry. It was scared, and I could see that wherever the rest of them went, this one wasn't going to get there. Its wing hung at a funny angle.
Then it started to cry.

Well, you can probably guess the rest. I pulled the angel out from behind the rowing machine, real careful, and brought it downstairs.

I fixed up the spare bedroom for it. and, you know, it makes a real nice pet.

It likes to sing, and even though it can't fly, it likes to go out in the back yard and flap its wings a little.

When it sees wild angels, it cries and holds out its hands, but they always fly right by.

So I guess it's mine now. You might think it's funny, but I've gotten real fond of the little thing. And that angel-proofing the exterminators put in must really work, because I haven't had any more problems with angels in the attic. Now I got squirrels.

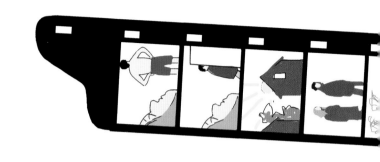
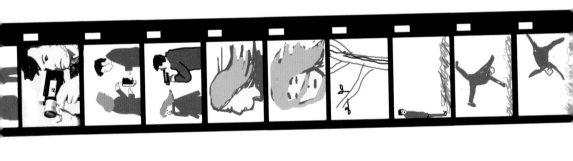
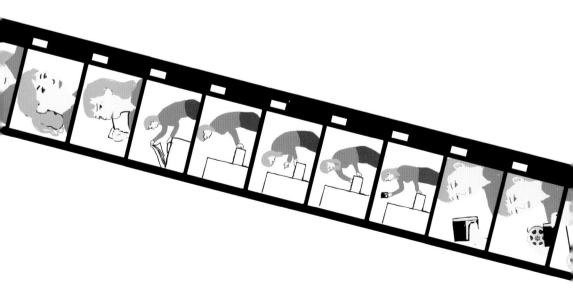

MORGAN
CAMERA

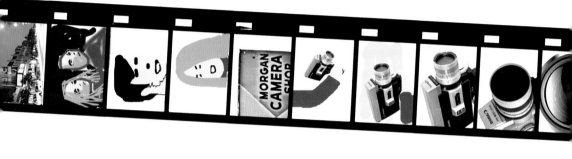

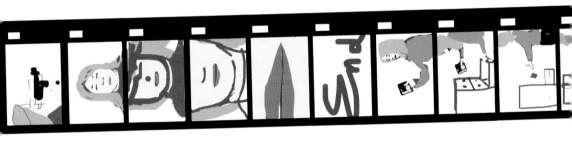

AT THE MOVIES

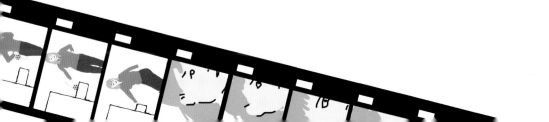

It was the last night. They both knew it was the last night. The night before, lying in bed after making love, he sat up and said, "I think I'd better go now," and she had nodded without looking at him, and he got out of bed and put on his clothes and said, "I'll call you tomorrow," and left.

Now it was the next day, and they were walking down Western Avenue beside a park she didn't know the name of, carrying a Super 8 movie camera. It was seven o'clock in the evening, and the sky was soft and bluer in the east than in the west, which was kind of peach-colored, she thought. They were going to make a movie.

The idea for making a movie had come to them a few weeks earlier; they had gone to the Music Box Theater to see the movie *Dead Man*, and afterward he said, "That was perfect," and she said, "Let's make a movie together," and there was something about the moment, the idea, that made it seem perfectly natural and necessary for them to make a movie even though neither of them had ever made one, so she went to a tiny camera shop on the West Side that sold obsolete equipment, and she bought a small Super 8 camera, which he was now carrying as they walked along the sidewalk without talking, because if either of them said anything, it would end up turning into a conversation about why they weren't going to see each other anymore.

Finally, he said, "Do you know how to work this thing?"

"I think so," she said. "I think you just point it and hold this button down." The camera made a whirring sound. They looked at each other.

"Let's just film anything," he said. "We're just testing. It doesn't matter."

She nodded. He was right; it didn't matter. This was a non-movie, a movie that wasn't going to be for real. He pointed the camera at her, and she looked away.

The movie is three minutes long. The first shot is unsteady. She is looking away, at something far away to the left. She turns her head and looks at the camera, looks as though she is about to cry but doesn't. The next shot is of a tree, a small white-barked tree with only a few leaves on it, even though it is June. Then there is a shot of grass, and then he appears at the edge of the frame, and then he does a cartwheel across the grass, kind of a half-assed cartwheel; he's laughing, and she, holding the camera, is also laughing. The camera lurches, and then the scene shifts abruptly to her face again and zooms in until the whole screen is filled with her lips. And then the movie ends.

When the film came back from the processor, she threw it into a drawer without looking at it. She hadn't seen him since the night they shot it. She didn't expect to see him. It was over. She heard about him from time to time through mutual friends; he had married, had finished his dissertation and moved to Lubbock, Texas, to teach philosophy. After that she didn't hear anything more.

Ten years later, she was rummaging around in the drawer, looking for something else that she thought might be in there, when she came across the little reel of Super 8 film. She unwound a few inches of it and held it up to the window. Tiny frames of her face in profile, ten years ago. She didn't own a projector. She rewound the film onto the reel and thought, not about him (for she had long ago developed the habit of not thinking about him) but about a man whom she had loved before him.

This man had also married. He had met his wife-to-be while standing in line at the Music Box Theater, waiting to see *Dead Man.* She thought about this as she stood there holding the brown plastic reel on her palm. Then she threw the reel of film into the wastebasket, closed the drawer, and went back to what she had been doing.

Copyright, 1887, by Eadweard Muybridge.]

SOME PHASES OF THE CANTER FROM SERIES 44.

Horse "Clinton."

151

MOTION STUDIES: GETTING OUT OF BED

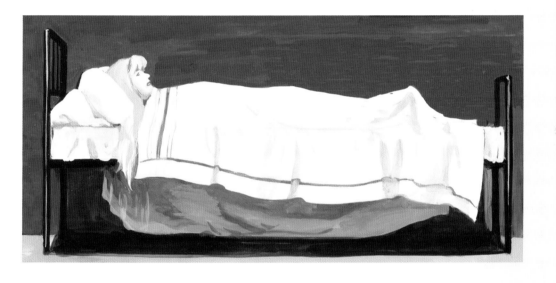

*i*t is ten o'clock in the morning on Friday, October 16, 1885. Blanche Epler is about to get out of bed. The bed is outdoors. It is surrounded by cameras. It is a sunny day but colder even than Philadelphia in October ought to be. Blanche shivers, waiting to peel off the thin sheet, sit up, and get out of the bed. She has thick, blond, waist-length hair and huddles in it for warmth.

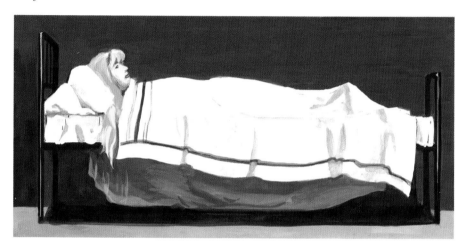

An assistant comes over and pulls it back.

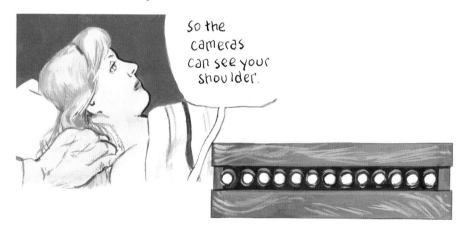

So the cameras can see your shoulder.

They are loading the cameras with dry plates.
There are thirty-six cameras, so it takes some time.

*m*r. Muybridge has explained it to Blanche: Each camera will take one picture. Three cameras will snap at once, from the front, the side, the back.

Twelve sets of three, 1/1,000th of a second. Mr. Muybridge showed her a book . . .

full of horses
running,
men fencing,
birds flying,

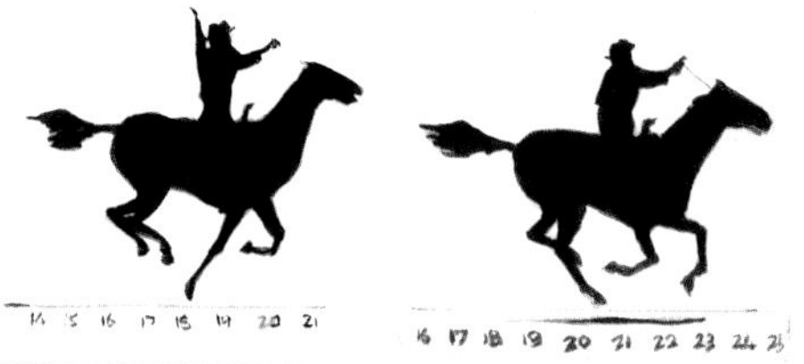

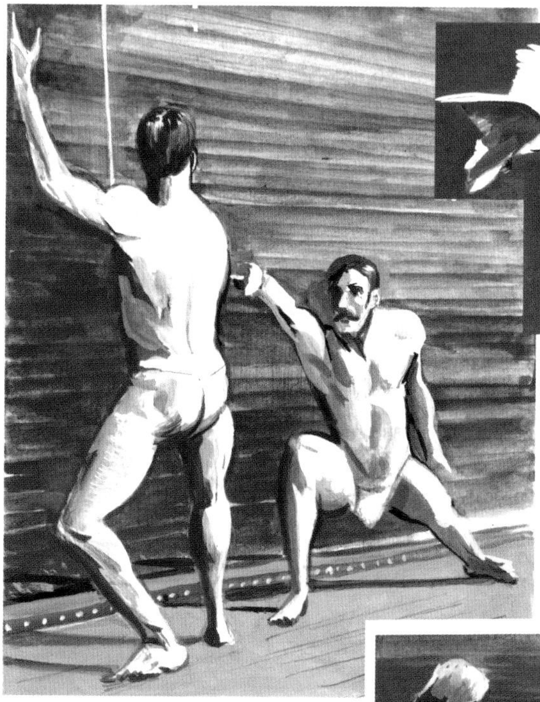

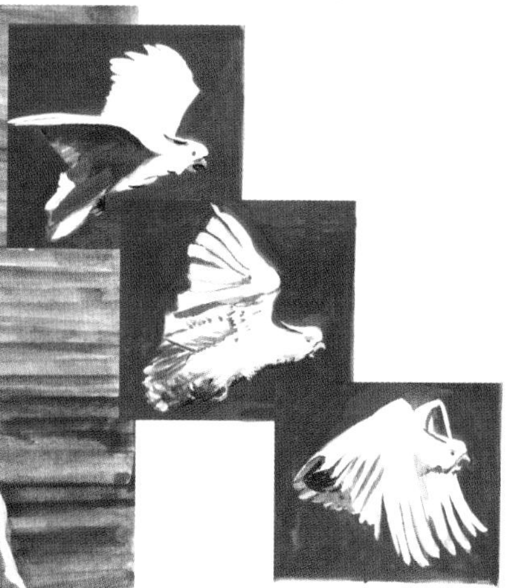

a child splashing water from a pail,
a woman jumping over a chair.

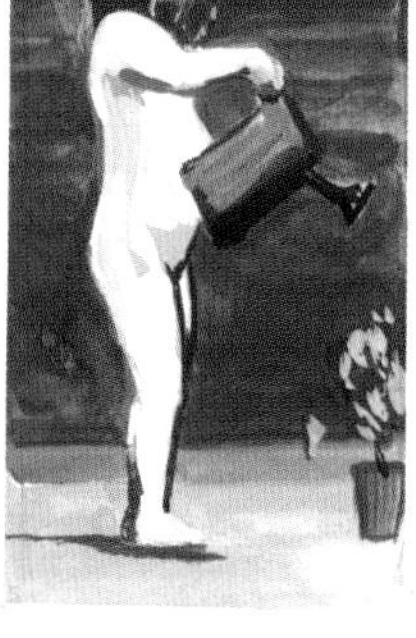

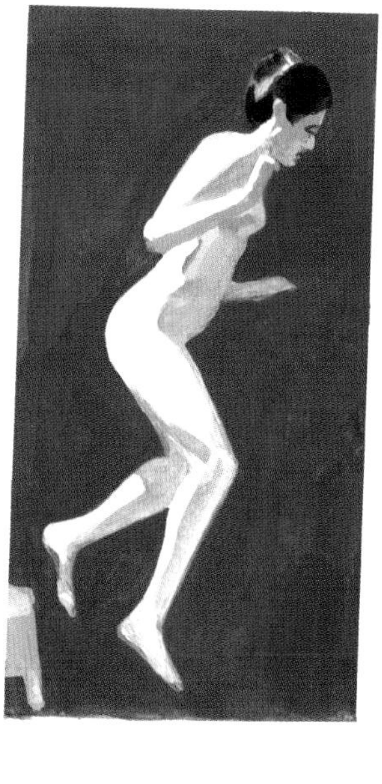

everyone is moving; everyone is perfectly still. Blanche marveled at the stillness, the strangeness.

Who are they?
Why are they
doing that?

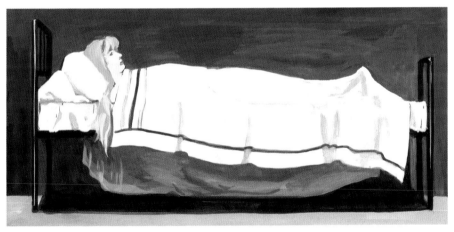

Now Blanche lies on the bed and waits to become a page in the book. She stares at the sky and listens to the mechanical noises the cameras make as the plate holders are inserted.

*S*he can hear horses snorting as they are led past the little enclosure where the bed stands. They are in a yard just off the university's veterinary department. Blanche wonders what the future veterinarians are thinking of her lying naked on the bed. She can see the top windows of a building if she tips her head back. There are a few people gathered at one of them.

Already this morning she has been photographed running, then hopping along the track, draped in a sheet, kneeling on the cold ground, pretending to pray, standing up, carrying a pitcher, and pouring water.

mr. *Muybridge showed her how to pose, then stood behind the cameras, watching. Someone told her he had killed a man, his wife's lover, and the jury acquitted him. Blanche could believe it.*

The photographer is polite, precise, remote. He looks like one of the old-time prophets in the stained-glass windows at St. Boniface's.

At the moment his expression is dissatisfied. He is speaking to Professor Eakins.

b*lanche likes
Professor Eakins.*

*She poses for his life drawing classes.
She likes the way he speaks to the students.*

*She likes the students, too, their shyness at
the beginning of each class, the way they
forget themselves as their drawings progress,
the intensity of their inexperienced perusal
of her body.*

*Blanche thinks some of them might not
have seen a woman naked before; they
seemed so pink and abashed.*

*L*ater in the semester there is always joking; some of the older students often chat with her once she's dressed again.

Blanche is good at posing; she has a talent for holding perfectly still in odd positions, letting her mind prance off into unlikely fancies while maintaining an expression of melancholy or innocence.

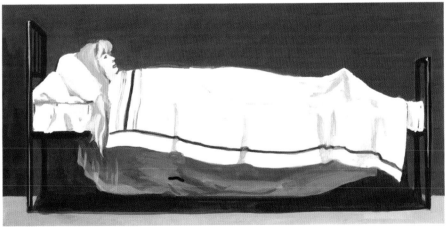

Posing for the students is nothing like posing for the cameras. The cameras want her to move, want to capture her and multiply her.

*t*he cameras are insects, clicking and rubbing their parts together. The cameras are science.

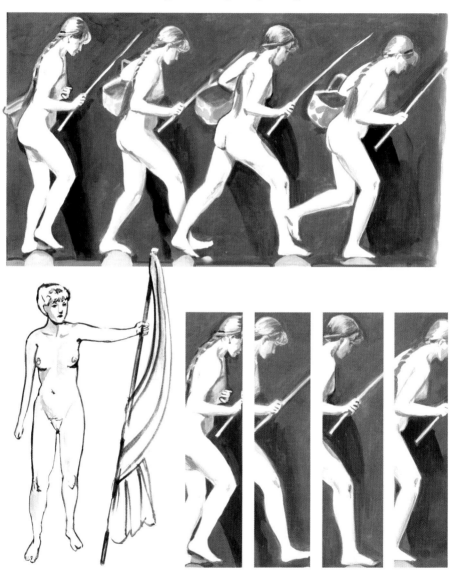

The students hope to transform her into art. They want to distill her into one timeless image.
But today she is being split into slivers of time.

blanche rubs her gooseflesh arms; it's like waiting for Luke to come to bed.

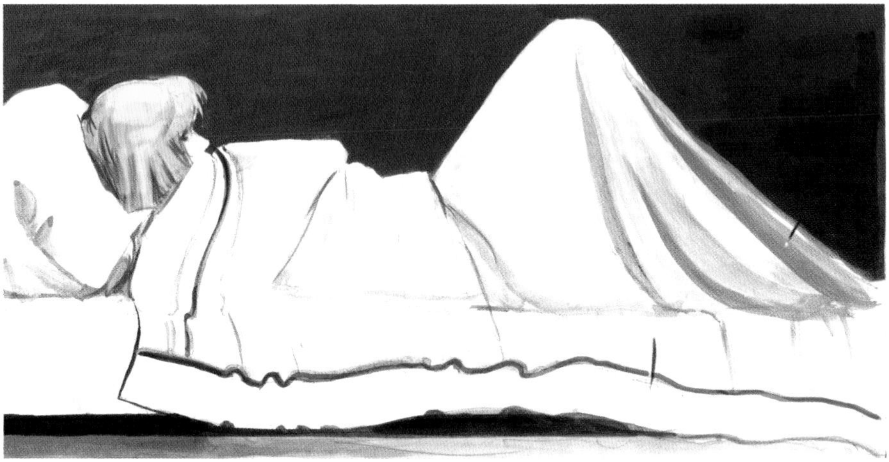

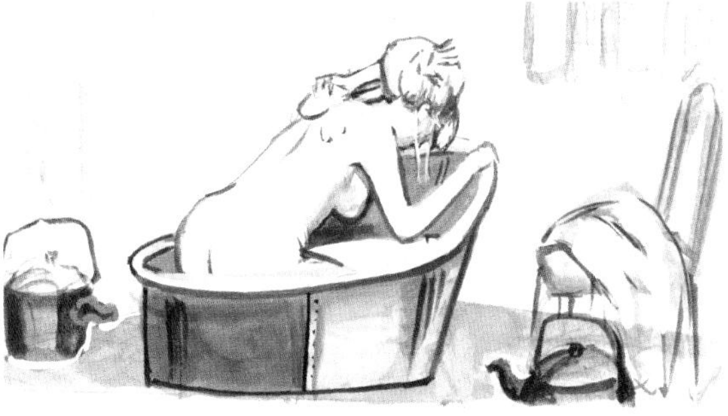

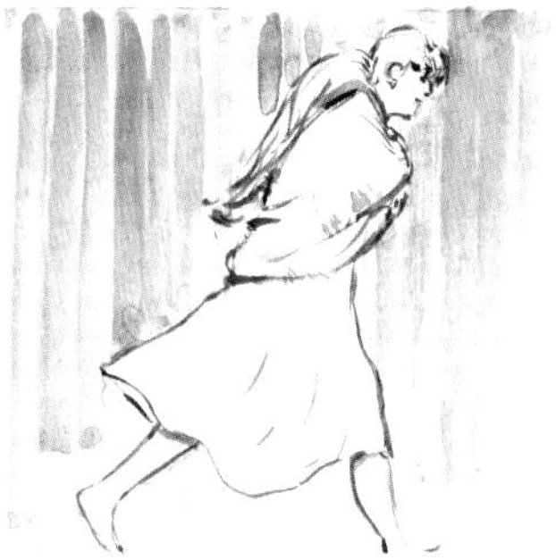

He always lets her bathe first; every Saturday night she heats the water and pours it into the galvanized hip bath. She gets into it as soon as she dares so that it will still be warm for Luke. As she dries herself, she runs down the hall and hops into bed immediately so no heat will be lost and the bed will be warm when Luke comes.

Now she tries to imagine the delicious heat of the bed, tries to warm herself thinking of Luke. They live in a single room on the top floor of a boarding house on Chestnut Street. It's cold there, too. They have stuffed the leaky window with rags, but she still feels the draft.

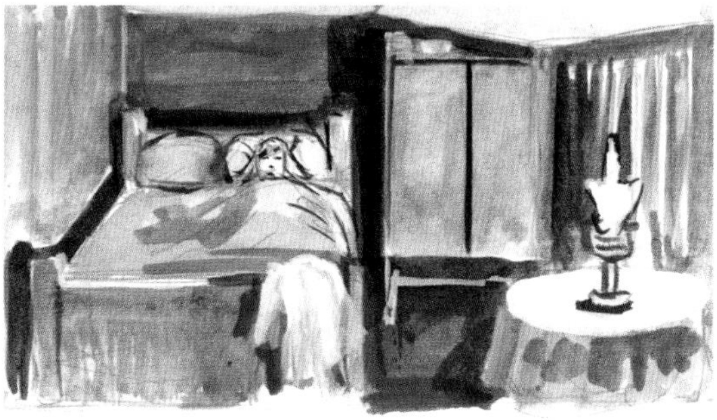

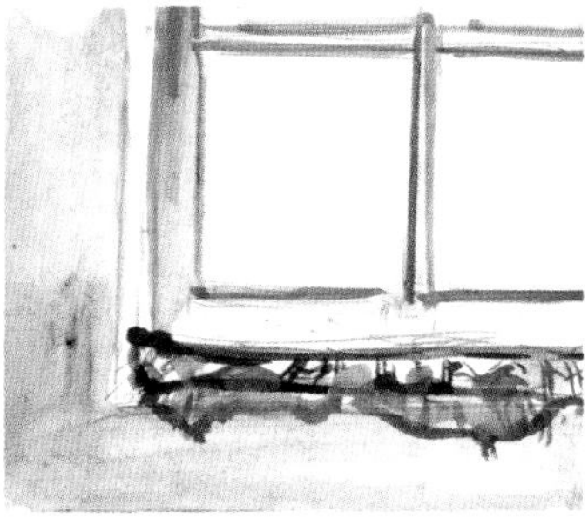

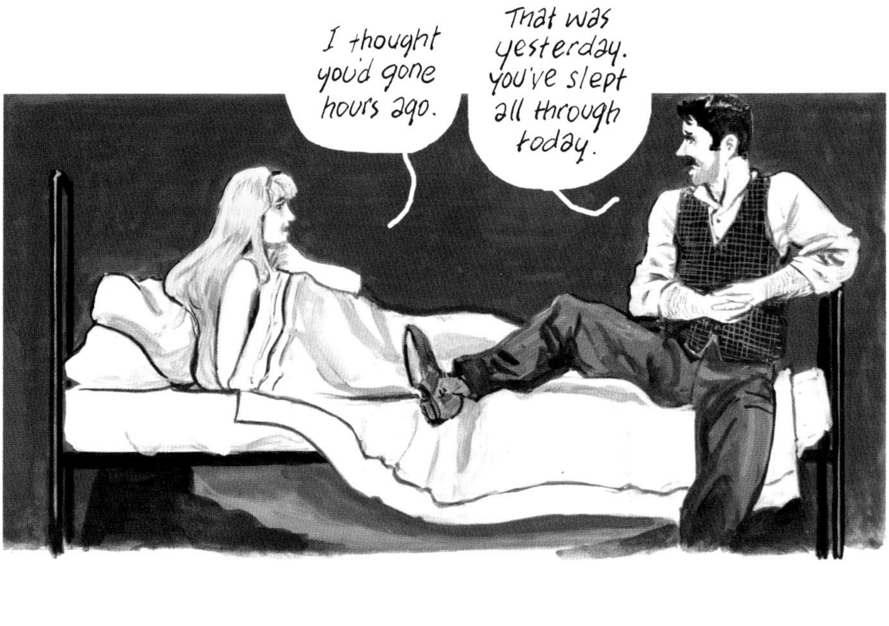
I thought you'd gone hours ago.
That was yesterday. You've slept all through today.

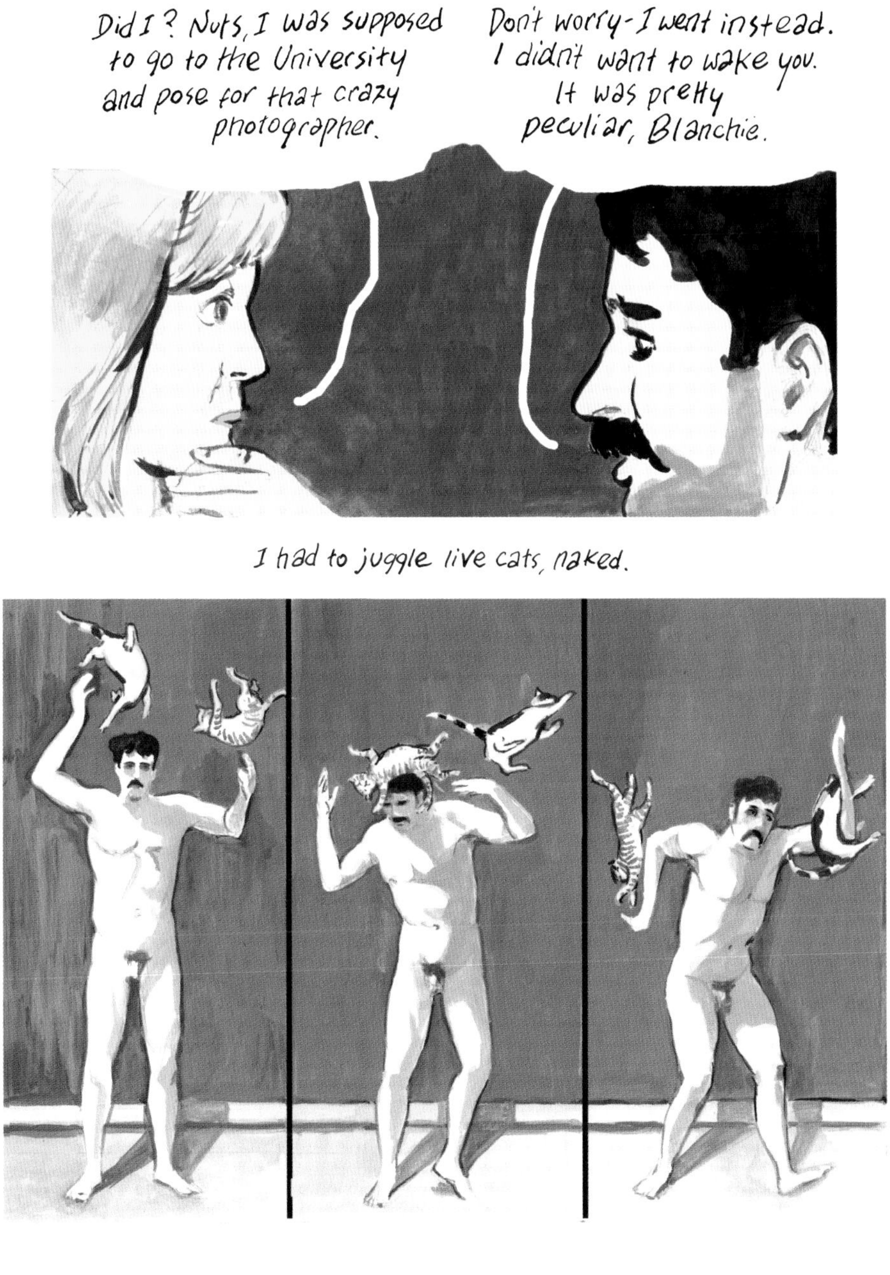
Did I? Nuts, I was supposed to go to the University and pose for that crazy photographer.
Don't worry - I went instead. I didn't want to wake you. It was pretty peculiar, Blanchie.
I had to juggle live cats, naked.

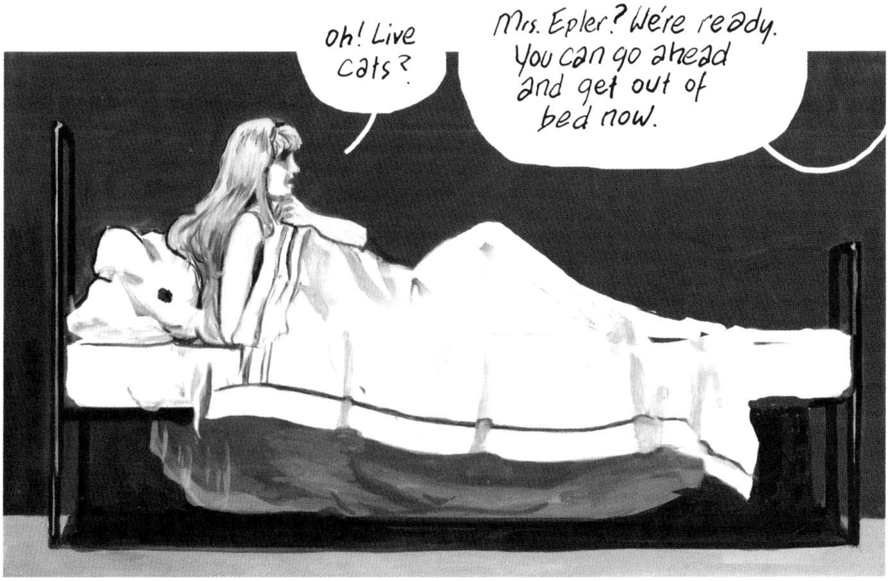
Oh! Live cats?
Mrs. Epler? We're ready. You can go ahead and get out of bed now.

*b*lanche Epler gets out of bed.

*t*hirty-six
camera shutters
open and close . . .

capturing thirty-six
tiny Blanches
in silver . . .

her motion
dissected into stillness,
preserved for always.

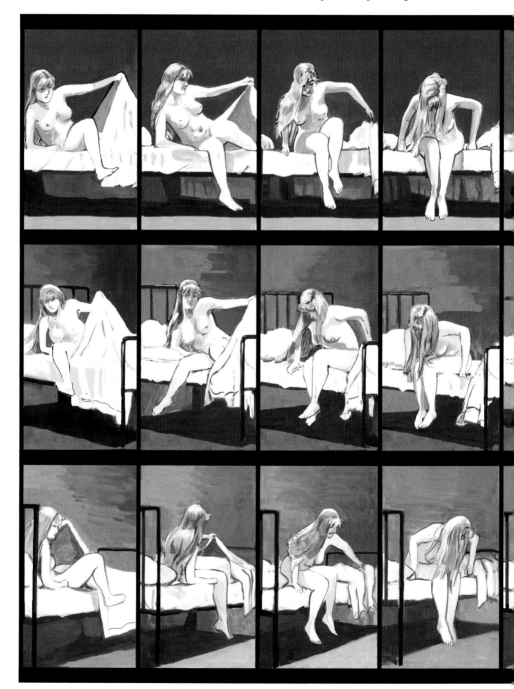

Blanche is cold.
Blanche is
sleepy.

Blanche
is getting
out of bed . . .

again,
always,
again.

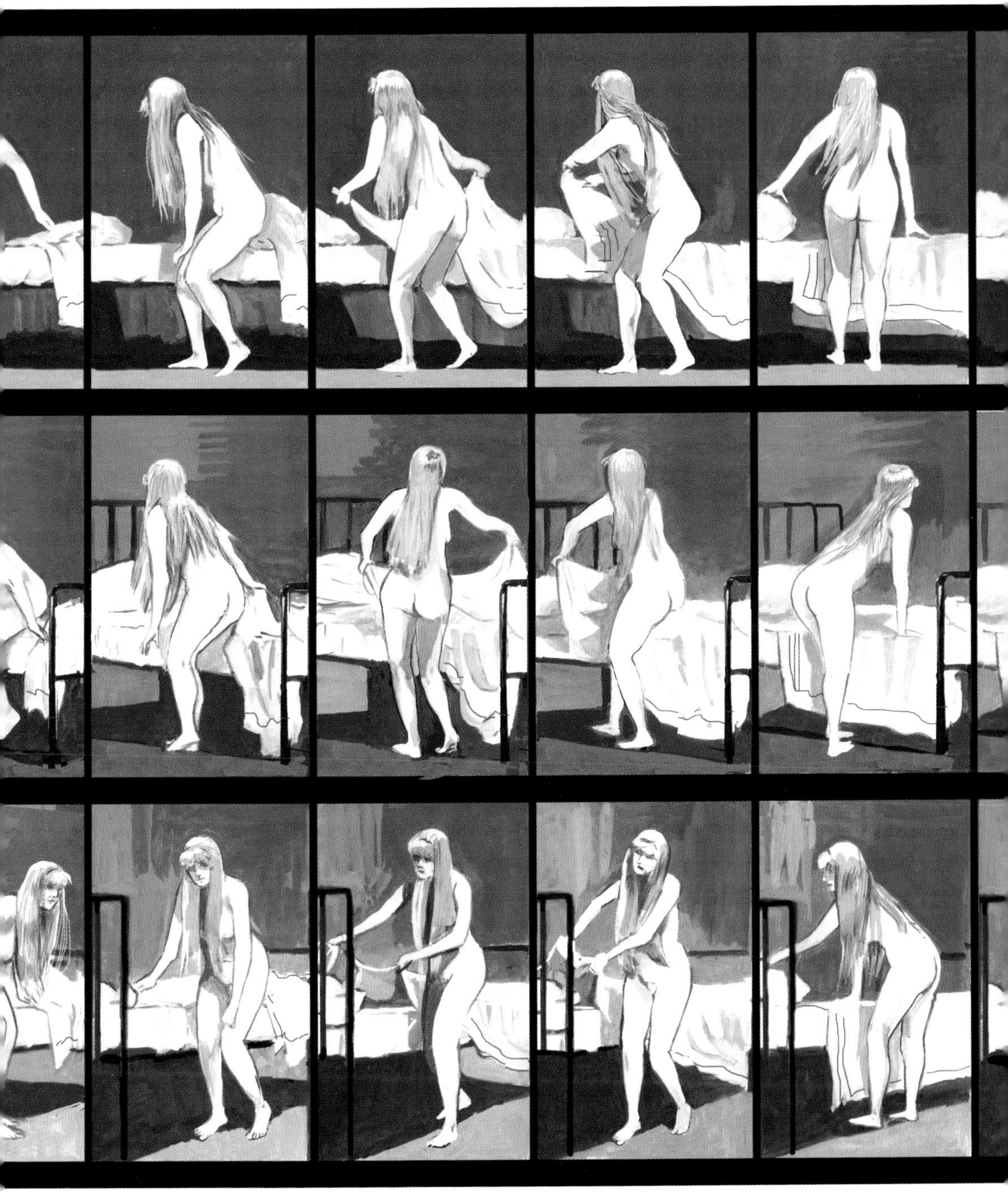

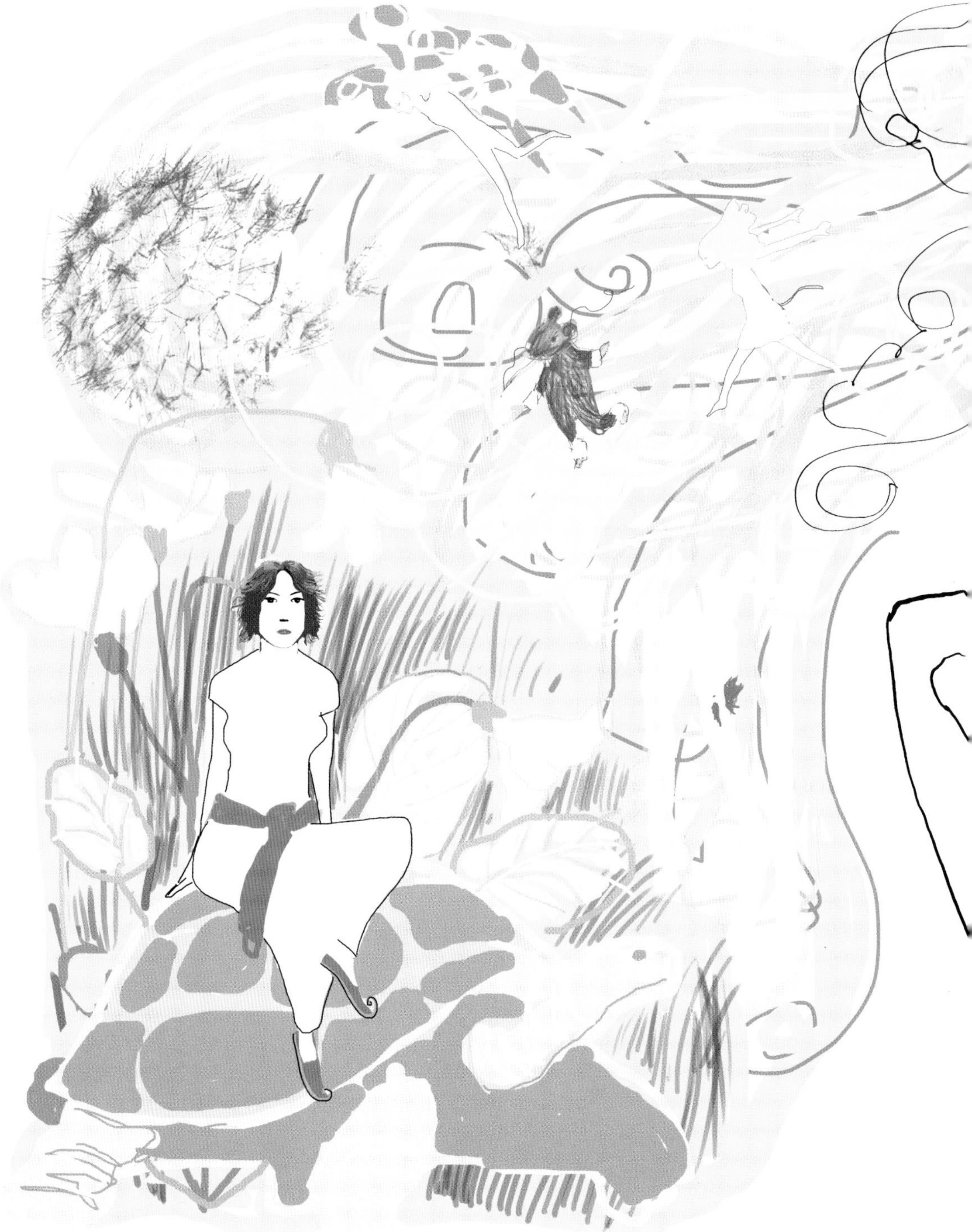

The Wrong Fairy

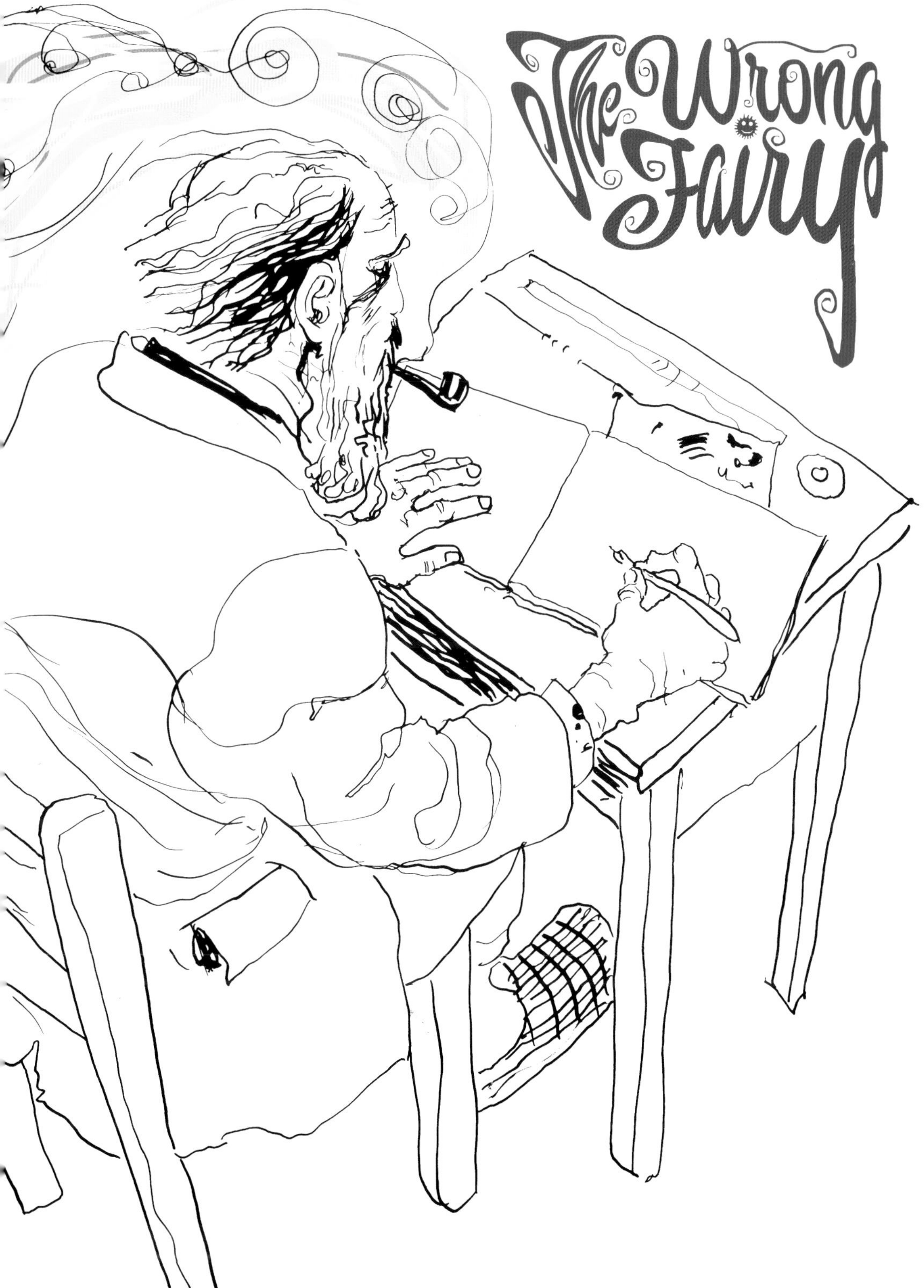

The man sat on the bed and looked about him. There was a washstand, a pink china bowl with its chipped pitcher, a wing chair by the small barred window, a worn carpet, a small bookcase, a desk, an ashtray, a wastebasket, a wardrobe, and a lamp. The bed had whitewashed iron fittings, like a servant's. His own things were piled in a heap at the foot of the bed, his clothing and his painting materials, his books and his pipe. All he needed was there except the bottle, the most important thing.

"You're trying to kill me," the man said to his son. His son stood in front of the door, as though to prevent the man from leaving, or perhaps in order to slip away more efficiently.

His son was a substantial young man with an impressive moustache. He looked prosperous, even sleek, but also very unhappy. "No, Father," he replied. "We're trying to help you." He didn't sigh, though he wanted to.

The man appeared much older than he actually was, and this was certainly because of the drink. The drink had brought him here, had compelled his family to commit him to the care of this dreadful place. Now he was here, and they were going to keep him from drinking. He groaned.

"You can't imagine."

"I can," his son said rather grimly. "And you mustn't try to escape again. We were lucky to find you a place here. Foudoun won't have you back after the way you behaved."

"Where am I, then?"

"Montrose Royal Lunatic Asylum. They call it Sunnyside; there used to be a farm of that name on the property."

"A lunatic asylum?" He felt faint. "Is everyone here insane?"

"No, the staff are very sane indeed. And the patients look mild enough. You've got a private room—no one will bother you here."

The man stared at his son. "Will you ask your mother to come and visit me?"

The son shook his head. "Better not."

The man stood up, and the room reeled. His son steadied him, helped him back to the bed. It was a long time since he had been so physically near his son. He gripped his son's arm and felt him recoil slightly, involuntarily.

"Please," he said.

"Father—" his son began to reply.

Someone knocked on the door and then opened it. The son straightened and stepped away from his father. The matron looked in at them impassively. "Your driver was asking if you'll be much longer, Dr. Doyle?"

"Tell him I'll be down in a few minutes, Mrs. Brewster."

The matron continued to stand there.

"Give my love to the girls. And Mary," the man said with an effort at a smile, conscious of the matron's gaze. His son said, "I will," and "Be well, Father." Then he embraced the man and stepped through the door after the matron. The key turned in the lock. The man lay back on the bed and waited.

The horrors were upon him. He was infested by insects that marched across the underside of his skin like directionless armies. He could feel each tiny foot as it touched each nerve. He was hot, hotter, he was going to burst into flames. *Water,* he thought he said, but no intelligible word came out. Every sound in that unfamiliar place was amplified. Footsteps in the hall, cool wet cloths wrung into the basin, the tap of metal against glass. People stood by his bed and whispered. Someone said, ". . . seizures." They put something cold and hard in his mouth, and they restrained him. The enormous plant-men he called Crawlers massed at the edge of his vision, their etiolated limbs waving and gesturing at him. Great storms possessed him, then blackness. Nurses came and went, sunlight crept into the room, and then it was night. He thought he was at home. His family sat at the table eating oyster soup. His daughter Ida seemed about to recognize him, but then her eyes slid across him and fixed on her mother. He spoke to each of his children in turn, and in turn all nine of them ignored him. He wept. Later he stood on a stony beach and saw birds, small and massed at the horizon, multitudes of birds, all kinds, flying toward him slowly. As they came close, he saw that it was a host of angels and that one among them was Death itself, his own Death, red and magnificent. "Take me," he said. He closed his eyes, lifted his arms, and waited. Nothing happened.

He opened his eyes. The beach was empty and quite silent, the waves rolled and the wind blew without a sound.

"I have been watching for you," a lady said.

He looked about him but saw no one.

"Here I am," she said. He turned. A lady stood near him. She was young but regarded him with a serious, even severe expression. Her short brown hair was loose and cut a bit wildly, as though she had been recently ill. She wore a white tunic, and her arms and feet were bare.

"Aren't you cold?" he asked her. He was shivering, himself. He noticed that there was a tortoise the size of a hackney cab standing near the lady. It was looking at her with adoration and nodding gently.

"No, I'm not cold at all—it's you, you've got the chills." The lady snapped her fingers, and the wind died. He felt better at once.

"Charles Altamont Doyle?" she asked.

"Yes," he replied, somehow not surprised. "You know my name?"

"Of course. We know a great deal. Everything."

He did not like to think what *everything* might encompass. "And—have I died?"

"No, don't be silly. I sent him away."

"I wanted to die," he said. "I was quite ready."

"The queen prefers that you live. She enjoys your paintings of us, and she wishes you to paint according to her own specifications. She will send you instructions once you have recovered your health."

"Yes," he said, without comprehension. He blushed and wondered how Victoria had heard of his work.

"Not that queen. The real queen," said the lady.

"Of course," he said. He was about to ask the lady who this other queen might be when he heard a loud noise and found himself in his bed at the asylum. A char stood by the fireplace, one hand to her mouth in alarm, the other holding an empty coal scuttle. The door opened, and Mrs. Brewster entered in a fury.

"Milly!" she hissed. "What on earth was that noise? And, oh, dear, look at all this coal all over the floor! Pick it up at once!" She glanced at him, and her expression softened.

"Mr. Doyle, good morning. How are you feeling?"

"Better," he said. He raised his head to look at her, and the room spun around. "Still alive."

"Yes," she said. "We nearly lost you."

"I was sent back," he said. "I'm supposed to make some paintings for the queen." Too late, he realized that he sounded like a lunatic.

Mrs. Brewster was used to this. "Well, let's get you washed, and you shall have some nice beef broth, and then we'll see about those paintings. I'm sure the queen can wait until you're steady on your feet again."

The fits came and went, and his hands trembled so much that sometimes he could not hold a spoon. But his health did improve, and on a good warm day he could sit on a bench in the sun on the grounds; he could sit in the common room and watch the other inmates watching him. He studied the habits of the staff. He adapted himself to Sunnyside's routines. Some of the other patients were alcoholics like himself, and of these he made friends with two Irishmen and talked politics happily with them for hours. Time passed slowly at Sunnyside.

Weeks went by before he attempted to draw. The nurse had laid out his watercolours, pencils, sketchbook, and brushes neatly on the desk, as though he might perform surgery with them. He noticed that they had taken away the little knife he used to sharpen his pencils.

He wrote his name and the date, 8 March 1889, on the first page. On the second page he made a drawing of the lady he had met on the beach. He sketched the huge tortoise behind her, roughed in the waves and the shore.

"That's not a very good likeness," the lady said.

He turned to find her sitting in the wing chair looking prim.

"How did you get in here?" he asked. The door was kept locked.

She smiled. "I have a knack." She looked around. "It's rather shabby, isn't it?"

He shrugged. "It's not as grim as some places I've been."

"No," she said. "That's true." She was silent for a long while. He waited politely, unsure what hospitality he should offer. At last she said, "Are you ready to take up your position at court?"

"I'm sorry," he said, "but I don't understand. I'm not allowed to leave."

"Oh, pish, you needn't worry. You'll be back before teatime." She stood up and handed him a small branch of fir. "Keep hold of that. And bring your painting things." He gathered the paints and other supplies. The lady clasped his hand, and immediately the room vanished and they were walking very quickly down a long, tiled corridor with a crowd of strangely dressed people.

"Please!" he said. "Please, could we walk more slowly?" He was dizzy and gasping for breath. "Where are we?"

"Paddington Underground station." The lady stopped by an unmarked door. "Here we are. Close your eyes." He did. He felt the lady tug at his dressing gown, and he opened his eyes to find them both standing in a meadow. The ground was damp under his slippers. He felt a fit coming on. "Oh, bother," he heard the lady say, as the storms overtook his brain.

He woke in his bed, trying to remember his dreams. He felt blank. There was a stick in the bed with him. He held it up. A fir branch. Well, he had kept hold of it, at least.

He began drawing every day. He drew heraldry, elves, birds. He drew a giant squirrel holding a screaming baby. He drew people with absurd facial hair, Mrs. Brewster's teakettle, the maids at their work. He drew the lady being menaced by a massive polecat.

"I suppose you think that's amusing," said the lady.

"Yes," he said. "Do you?"

"I don't have much of a sense of humour," she said. "You would do well to remember that."

He nodded.

"How are you feeling?" she asked, almost kindly.

"Not well," he said. The insects-under-the-skin feeling had been troubling him all morning.

"Ah. Then perhaps we should leave our journey till another day."

"If it's not too much trouble . . ." He faltered. "Could I make the paintings for the queen here in my room? I should be glad to paint anything she likes."

"Oh, but she particularly wanted portraits made of all her children."

"How many does she have?"

"Thousands."

"Dear me. That's . . . prodigious. But I'm sure I will be dead before I can make so many portraits."

The lady smiled. "You needn't worry. We can keep you alive for as long as you like. Nearly forever. We are quite long-lived ourselves, and it's no great trick to lend you a little extra."

He thought of his death, which had been so near, so inviting. He wished he could ask the lady to hasten death toward him. But he thought that must be wrong. "Thank you," he told her. "But I don't wish for anything that isn't mine."

"What do you wish for, then? For you must have a reward. The queen would have it so."

He thought carefully. "Perhaps . . . something for my son Arthur? Good luck?"

The lady nodded. "We will watch over him. But for yourself?"

He hesitated. "Do you have any strong drink, at your court?"

The lady laughed. "We have wonderful spirits, much nicer than anything you have had."

He stood and held out his hand. "Lead me there, and let me have a drink or two, and I'll paint all Her Majesty's children."

"Done," said the lady. He gathered up his painting things, and she gave him another fir branch. Then she compressed him until he was seven inches tall, and she put him in her pocket. He felt marsupial, but it was much more comfortable than going along on foot. They rushed through Paddington and across the meadow. The lady opened a hole in the ground, and they made their way through narrow caves. She stopped, took him out of her pocket, and said, "Now you have to walk." She made herself seven inches tall so they were again the same height. The caves opened into caverns. Light was always just ahead; he could not see the source.

They came to a room that had a table laid for a feast. "Stop and rest," said the lady. "And have your drink." She poured a dark, syrupy liquid into a glass. He drank it and felt restored; he felt better than he had in many years. "One more?" She refilled his glass, and he drank up. His brain seemed to heal. The fog lifted. He grinned at the lady, and she smiled back. "Now, here we are," she said, and she led him into the next room.

The room was enormous. He could see the ceiling but not the walls. There were a great many things in the room, too many for him to make sense of at first. When he looked carefully, he could see piles of things. Each thing was spherical, illuminated—each one was in motion. He drew near one pile and looked into a sphere. Some children were building a snowman. They were in a city. A large shiny vehicle passed by the children, moving under its own power, like a train. One of the children threw a snowball at it. In another sphere there was a war going on, something exploded, and he turned away quickly. Lovers embraced in strange clean white bedrooms. Water gushed from pipes into bathtubs; no servants had to carry the water. Bodies were stacked naked in mass graves. Machines. Murder. Magic. He saw things he had no words for.

He turned to the lady, who was standing in an empty space looking depressed. "How do you like it?" she asked him.

"It's overwhelming," he said. "What is it?"

"The queen's children. The future."

"This? I thought . . . I imagined that fairies were . . ."

"Small and pretty with little gauzy wings?" The lady shook her head. "I'm sure we were, once upon a time. The queen is nostalgic, and she likes to think of her children the way we used to be. She thought perhaps you would be able to see us that way. She hoped you might reimagine us."

"For that, you need a genius. Or a lunatic. I'm only an artist and a drunkard."

The lady looked at him carefully. "At least you're honest about it," she said. She held out her hand. He took it, and they began the long walk through the caves.

Back at Sunnyside he applied himself to his task. He filled the sketchbook with incorrect, out-of-date fairies. He drew five fairies riding on the back of a pheasant, a host of fairies flying through the night sky. Fairies feasting, frolicking, courting, and scheming. The lady came whenever he ran out of paper. She peeled each fairy off the page and tucked it into her pocket. "How many more?" he asked her. "Lots and lots," she always said.

One day she pocketed the last fairy. She leaned over him and took his pen in her hand. "Here is a drawing for you," she said. In his own style she drew a full-length portrait of him, standing in profile with one hand outstretched in greeting. Facing him she drew his death. They shook hands.

Charles Doyle smiled. He slumped forward; his death was a simple, quiet one. Under the drawing the lady wrote *Well met.* She laid down the pen and left the room.

Digging up the Cat

For my father, Larry Niffenegger

It's a lovely Sunday afternoon in late October, just after lunch, when Dad and I decide it is time to dig up my cat. We've been meaning to do it for a while, but other chores always seemed more pressing, and if we don't do it now, the ground is going to freeze again and we'll have to wait till spring.

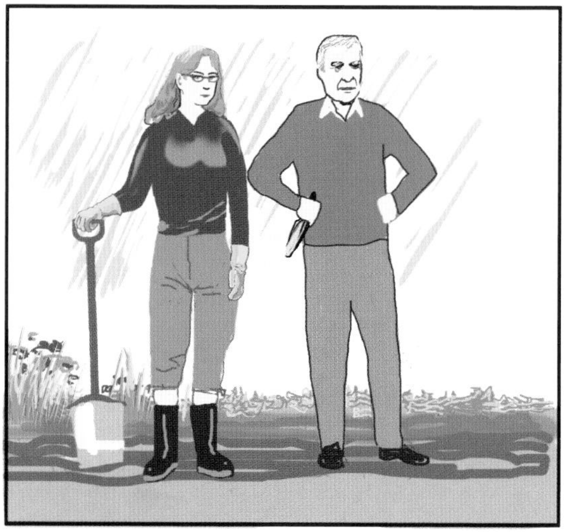

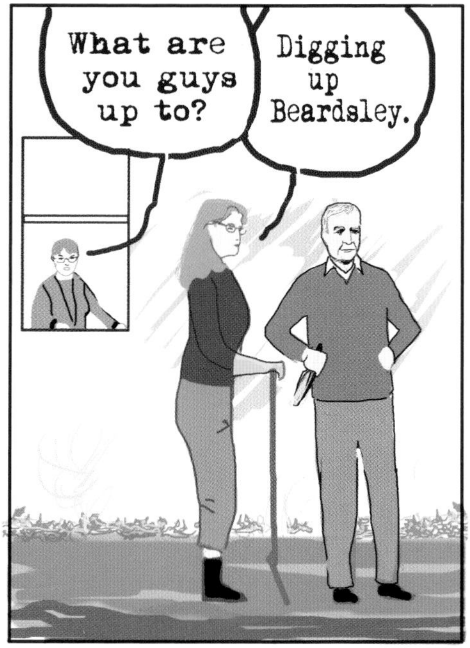
What are you guys up to?
Digging up Beardsley.

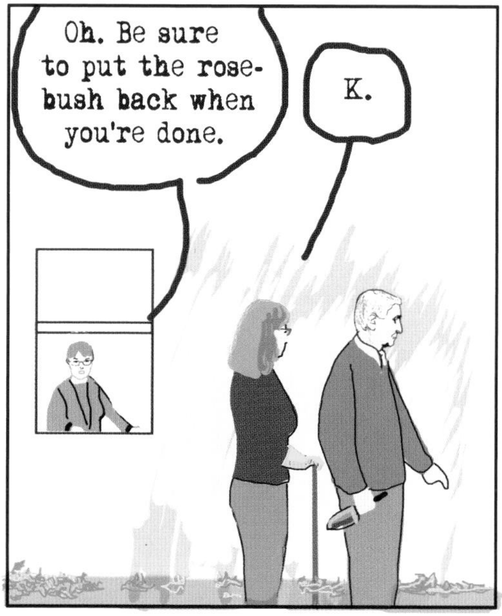
Oh. Be sure to put the rose-bush back when you're done.
K.

Beardsley has been in the ground for almost exactly seven years. We buried him at dusk on an October day that was warmer and softer than this one. We put him in a pine box I had painted electric blue. It was sad; Beardsley dropped dead at the age of six, for no good reason that I could see. Now we are digging him up.

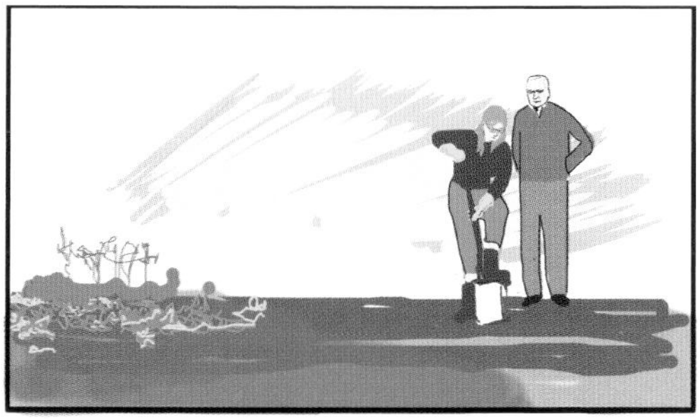

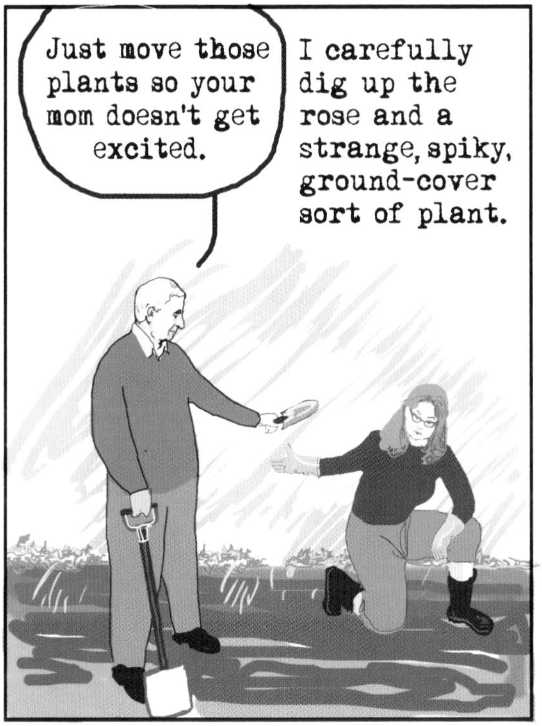
Just move those plants so your mom doesn't get excited.
I carefully dig up the rose and a strange, spiky, ground-cover sort of plant.

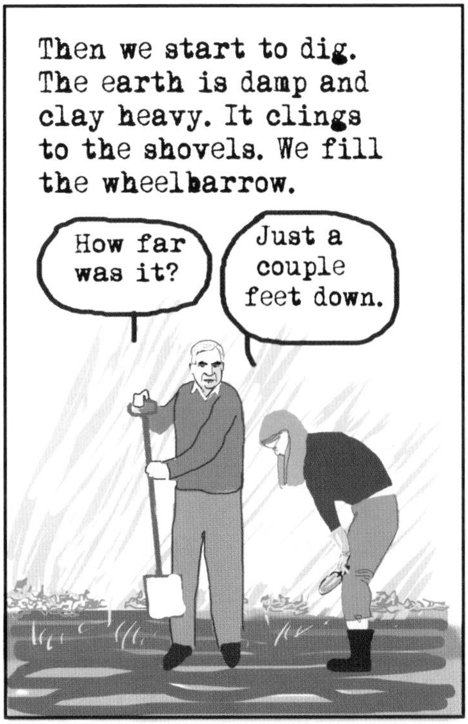
Then we start to dig. The earth is damp and clay heavy. It clings to the shovels. We fill the wheelbarrow.
How far was it?
Just a couple feet down.

We get down to the box, find the edges of it, dig around it, ease it up, lift it out, and lay it on the grass. It's covered with dirt, and one side of the box has caved in a bit. I get soapy water and a rag and wipe off the box.

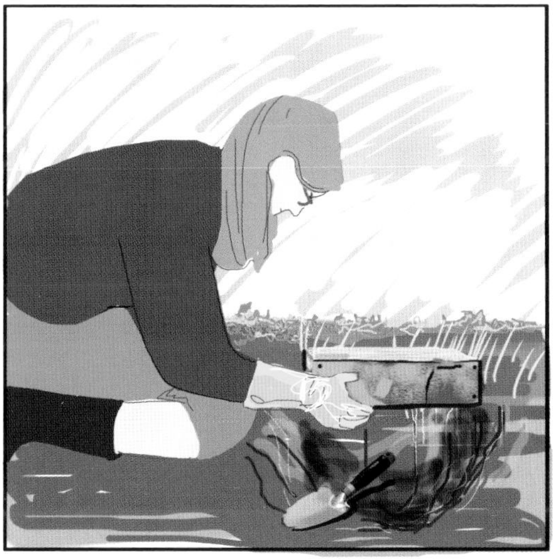

We are digging up my cat because his sister, Jane, has died. Actually, Jane died last December. Since the ground was frozen under two feet of snow, I wrapped Jane carefully in plastic and placed her gently in my freezer, where she has resided ever since.

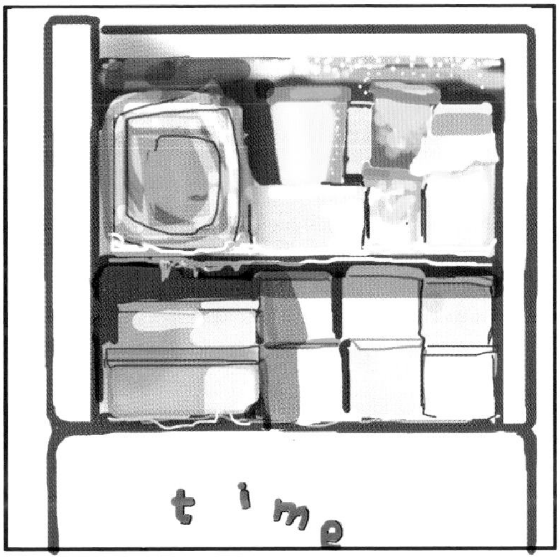
time

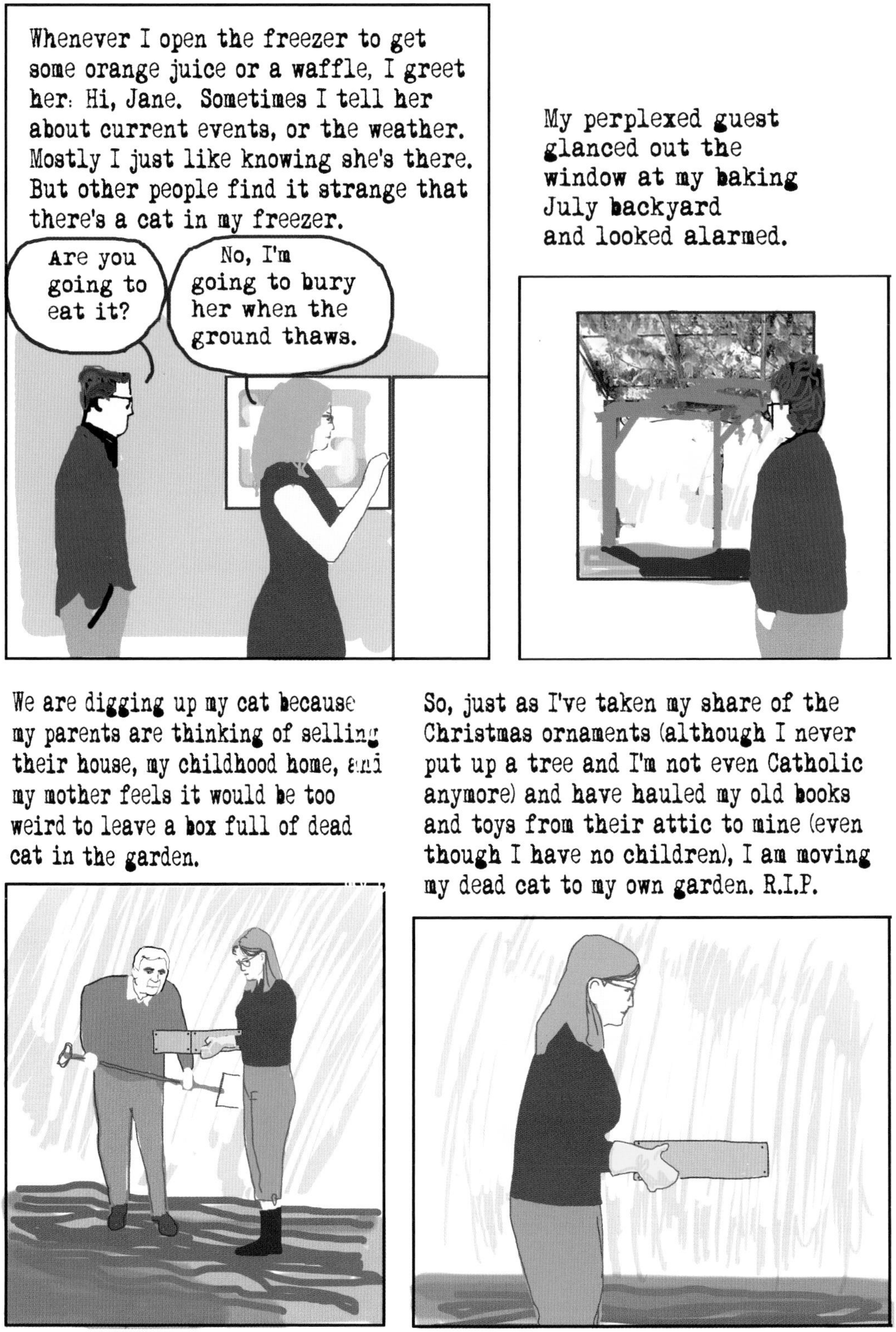
Whenever I open the freezer to get some orange juice or a waffle, I greet her: Hi, Jane. Sometimes I tell her about current events, or the weather. Mostly I just like knowing she's there. But other people find it strange that there's a cat in my freezer.
Are you going to eat it?
No, I'm going to bury her when the ground thaws.
My perplexed guest glanced out the window at my baking July backyard and looked alarmed.
We are digging up my cat because my parents are thinking of selling their house, my childhood home, and my mother feels it would be too weird to leave a box full of dead cat in the garden.
So, just as I've taken my share of the Christmas ornaments (although I never put up a tree and I'm not even Catholic anymore) and have hauled my old books and toys from their attic to mine (even though I have no children), I am moving my dead cat to my own garden. R.I.P.

Dad has filled up the hole and comes over to where I'm kneeling on the lawn next to the box.

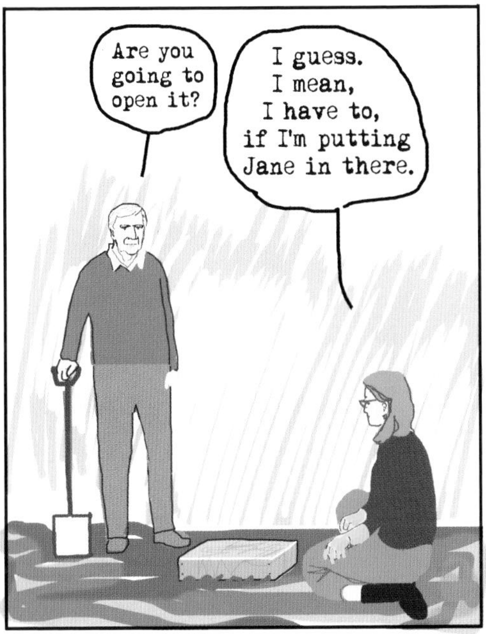
Are you going to open it?
I guess. I mean, I have to, if I'm putting Jane in there.

He continues to stand there. I open the box. Inside is a beautiful, delicate cat skull, brown and nestled in brown sludge amidst bones of many intricate shapes. A jigsaw puzzle that was a cat. Tiny white maggots busy themselves over burst parchment skin fragments. I close the lid.

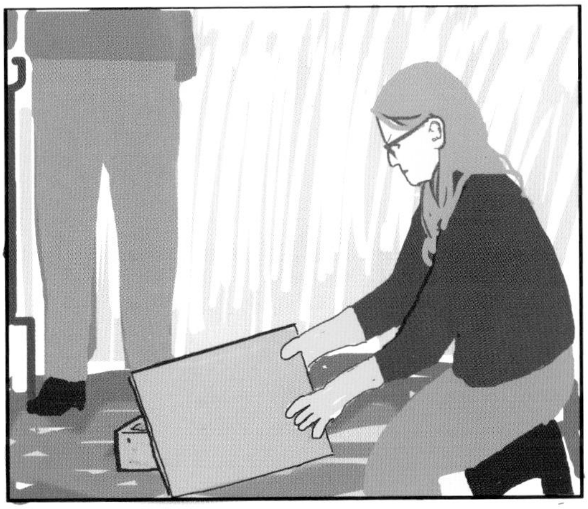

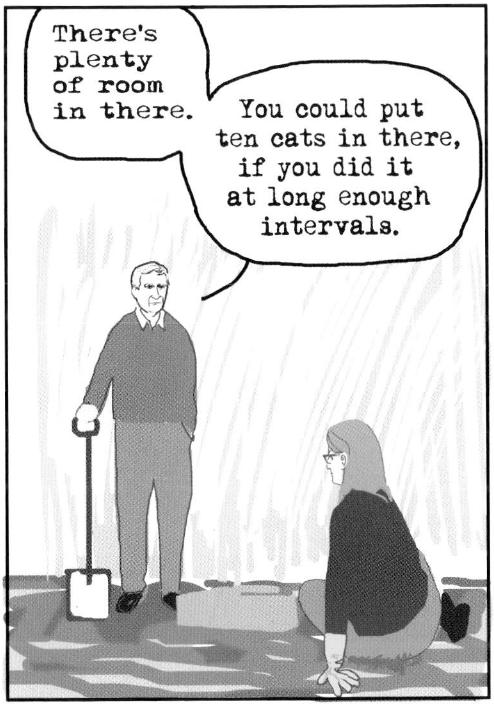
There's plenty of room in there.
You could put ten cats in there, if you did it at long enough intervals.

Ten cats at seven-year intervals equals seventy years' worth of cats. That should be enough. That ought to cover it.

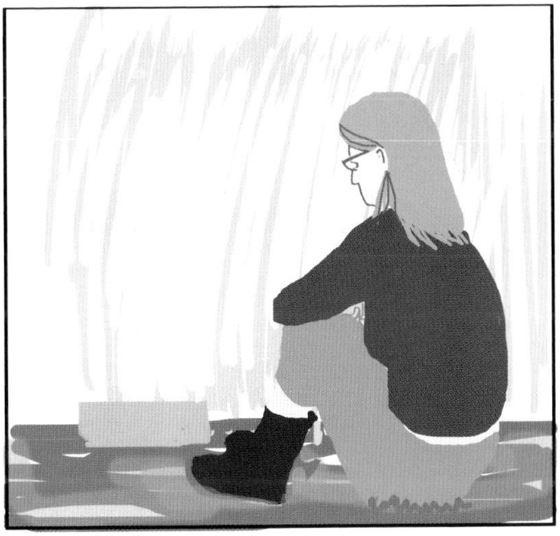

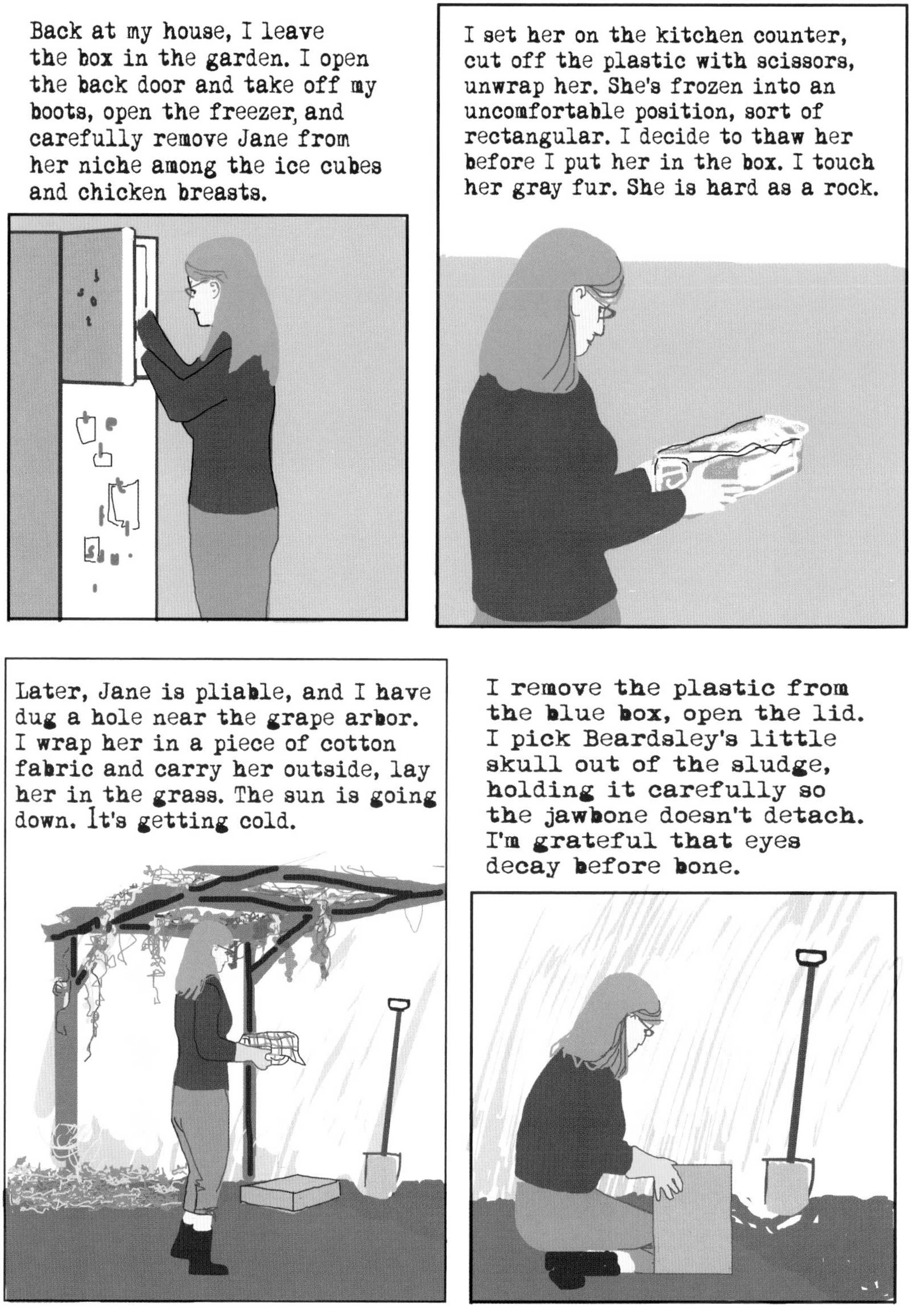
Back at my house, I leave the box in the garden. I open the back door and take off my boots, open the freezer, and carefully remove Jane from her niche among the ice cubes and chicken breasts.
I set her on the kitchen counter, cut off the plastic with scissors, unwrap her. She's frozen into an uncomfortable position, sort of rectangular. I decide to thaw her before I put her in the box. I touch her gray fur. She is hard as a rock.
Later, Jane is pliable, and I have dug a hole near the grape arbor. I wrap her in a piece of cotton fabric and carry her outside, lay her in the grass. The sun is going down. It's getting cold.
I remove the plastic from the blue box, open the lid. I pick Beardsley's little skull out of the sludge, holding it carefully so the jawbone doesn't detach. I'm grateful that eyes decay before bone.

I replace his skull in a corner of the box and place Jane next to the skull. She is heavy, like a fur-covered IV bag of blood. I tell her I will miss seeing her in the freezer.

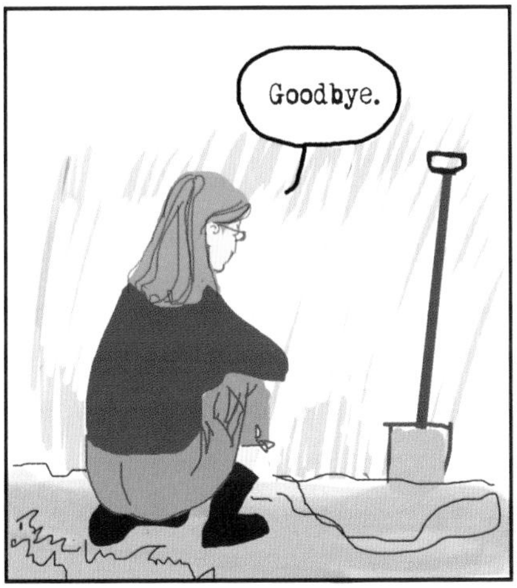
Goodbye.

As I shovel earth over the cats I have a sense of déjà vu. Perhaps it's a presentiment of all the cats to come, all the things and people I will lose. In the garden everything is brown, and the grape leaves rattle above my head as I shovel.

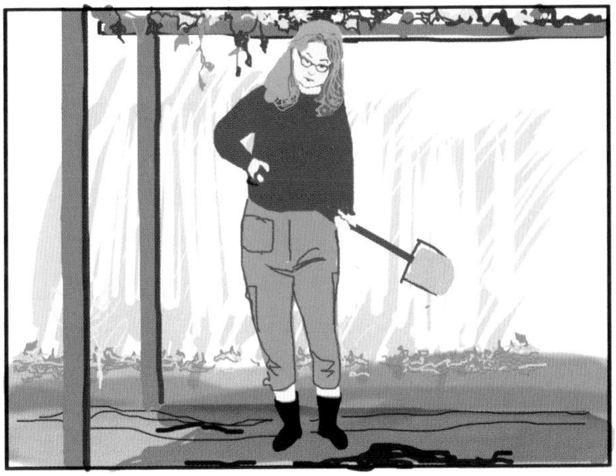

That evening I call home to tell Dad about it, that feeling I'm having trouble putting a name to.

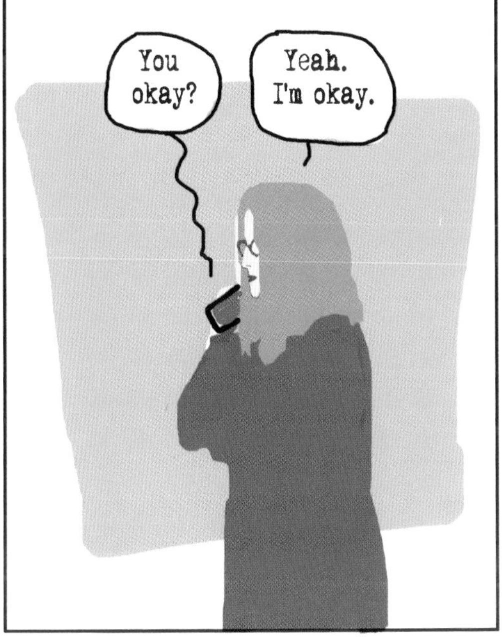
You okay?
Yeah. I'm okay.

After a while, it will be true.

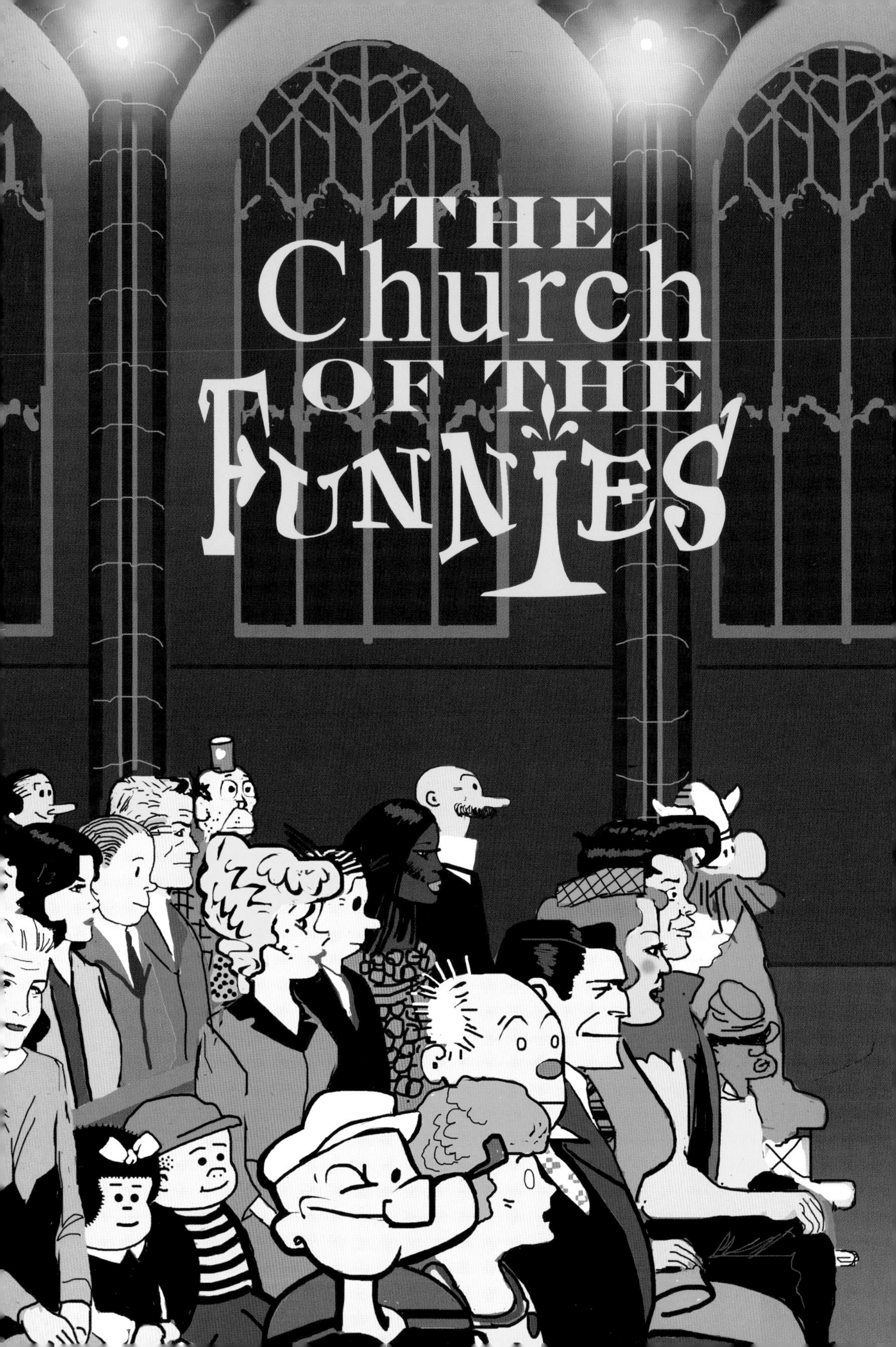
THE
Church
OF THE
FUNNIES

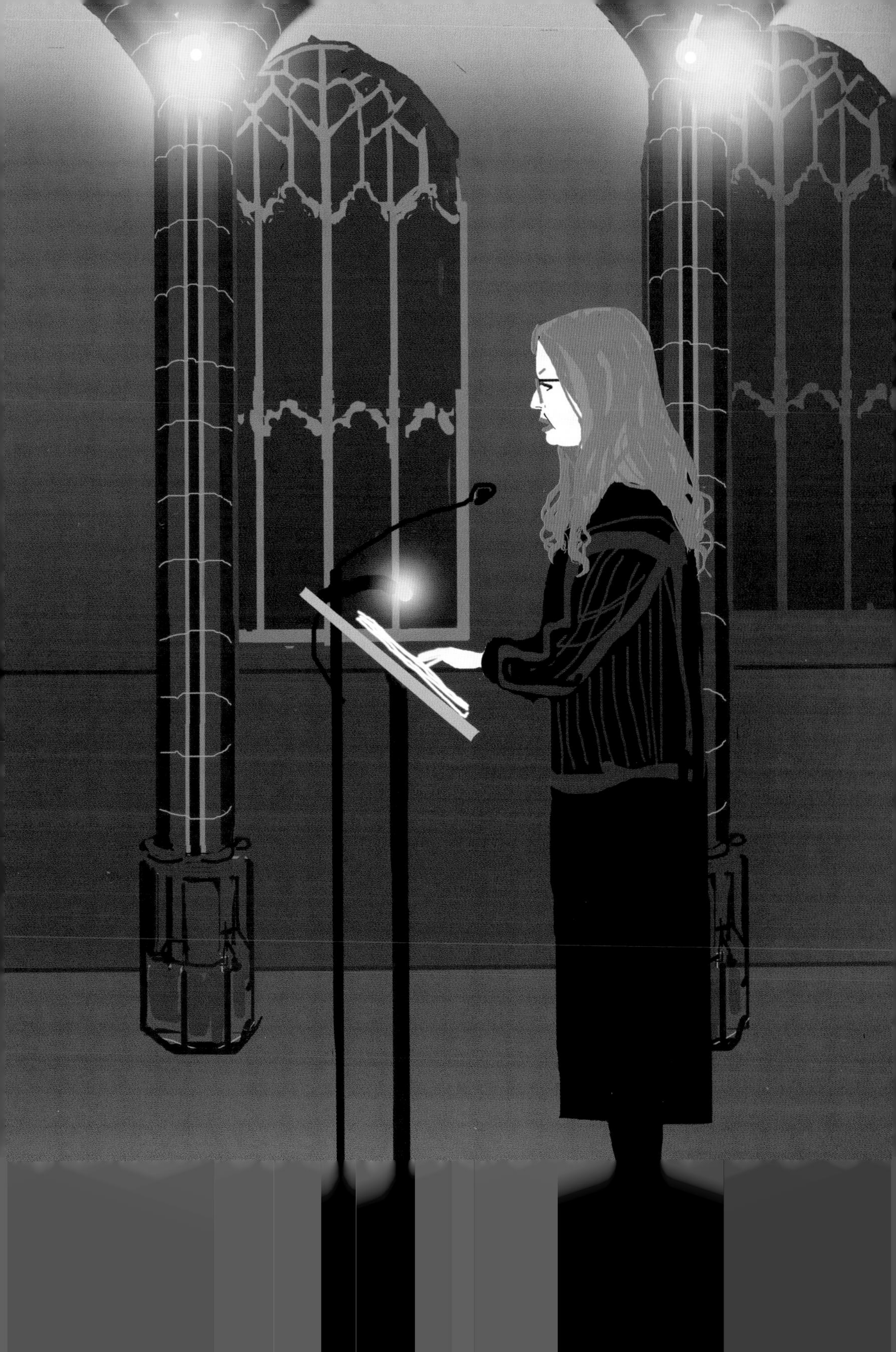

THE
Gaeia Manchester Sermon

I am an inappropriate person to be giving a sermon. I have spent thirty-six years of my life avoiding sermons. I might even be allergic to sermons; they make me itch. So when offered the chance to come and sermonize to you tonight, I hesitated. I usually avoid the Bible, as it has been my experience that if someone is quoting the Bible at me, I'm about to get mad. But then I remembered the Church of the Funnies, and I was tempted into coming here and doing a little proselytizing.

When I was small, my mother used to make me and my sisters all presentable every Sunday morning and then haul us off to church. On our way out the door, we were usually treated to the sight of my dad lying on the living room sofa with the newspaper spread comfortably around him, reading the Sunday comics. One Sunday I said to my mom, "Why doesn't Dad have to come to church with us?" And my dad, overhearing me, replied, "I don't belong to your

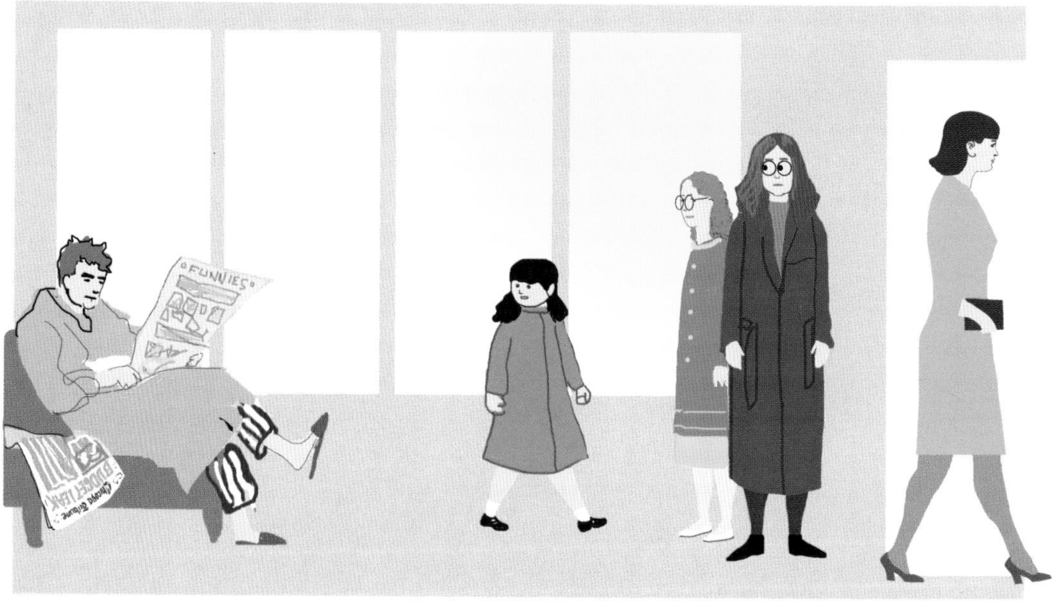
FUNNIES

church." Which was quite true; we were Catholic, and my dad was First Congregational, a sort of Protestant. I said, "What church do you belong to? Why aren't you in church?" And my dad replied, "I belong to the Church of the Funnies."

Now, at the time I thought, *Ha-ha, Dad,* and skulked off to church. But it stayed with me, this notion of the Church of the Funnies. And it grew. What began in my mind as a bunch of Peanuts characters sitting in the pew next to me evolved. And now the Church of the Funnies is a big church, a megachurch, and in my mind it encompasses not only comics of every sort but also all of Art. The Church of the Funnies has room for Snoopy, children's drawings, the Rothko Chapel, the Sistine ceiling, every Dickens character, Bugs Bunny cartoons, all the books in all the libraries in all the languages, all the art lost in wars, the art not yet made by artists not yet born. Make a doodle on a bar mat in a pub just before last call, and you are making a sacred offering in the Church of the Funnies. Its parishioners are a varied bunch, but I imagine us as anyone who looks for solace or inspiration in art, anyone who asks the big questions and tries to use art to find the answers.

In second grade, as we prepared for First Communion, I remember my teacher explaining the Commandments; the Second Commandment was given as: "You shall not take the name of the Lord your God in vain." And I was fine with that—I was a child of the American Midwest, and we were, mostly, very polite kids. But when I encountered the text in the Bible a few years later, part of it read: "Thou shalt not make unto thee any graven image, or any likeness *of any thing* that *is* in heaven above, or that *is* in the earth beneath, or that *is* in the water under the earth." Whoa. Wait a minute. This is Exodus 20:4. For me it was the beginning of doubt.

My teachers said it was supposed to mean: *Hey! Don't worship any statues or images of other gods! The real, One True God is formless, and you can't make a picture of Him anyway, so forget it.* But as a little Catholic I was surrounded by images of God, Jesus, Mary, little white doves that were supposed to mean the Holy Spirit, various saints with their various body parts chopped off and on display. When I was a child, I was quite devout. I would make shrines in my bedroom, conglomerations of holy cards and flowers, dolls, suitcases, and things like buttons and shells that just looked pretty. Also occasionally my gerbils were allowed to investigate the shrines, because, heck, why not? I didn't understand how to reconcile the crucifix that hung in every classroom of my school with the No Graven Images policy. I couldn't wrap my tiny brain around the concept of a symbol: This isn't the thing; it's just here to remind you of the thing. The imaginary was very real to me. Jesus, the Easter Bunny, Peter Pan, Narnia, Moses, St. Joan of Arc, Paddington Bear: all equally invisible, all equally real. Though I have to admit that it was Santa who loomed largest in my celestial hierarchy. In art school I once saw some graffiti that said it well: "Jesus saves, but Santa gives." I didn't want to annoy anybody, so I prayed to everybody who might be listening.

"Thou shalt not make unto thee any graven image, or any likeness *of any thing* that *is* in heaven above, or that *is* in the earth beneath, or that *is* in the water under the earth." What can I say about that except: Too late. We've already made millions and millions of images. We have made images on cave walls of horses and bison and of our own hands. We have made small ladies with enormous bosoms and bottoms out of stone, clay, and bone in the hopes of fertility. We have made statues of so many gods and goddesses, paintings of the

Madonna and baby Jesus, portraits of saints, woodcuts of geishas and samurai, murals of famous communists, gigantic Buddhas carved into hillsides, presidents' heads carved out of mountains, bazillions of selfies on millions of phones, billboards of movie stars, movies of dancing penguins, an eight-hour film of the Empire State Building, television commercials for sneakers and electric cars and politicians and breakfast cereal. We have made photographs of the earth from outer space. We have made scans of our own brains while we are thinking about sex, ultrasounds of fetuses, footprints of newborn babies. We have made countless videos of cats behaving foolishly. We have attempted to photograph ghosts. We take digital photos of ourselves standing in front of famous paintings.

John Lennon once got into trouble by suggesting that the Beatles were more popular than Jesus. I am going to live dangerously here in front of you in this incredibly impressive church by asserting that some of us believe in Art more than we believe in God.

I managed to leave the Catholic Church when I was fifteen. I made a deal with my mom: I would read the Bible, and I didn't have to go to church anymore. The problem with this bargain was that reading the Bible only fed my fury with the whole idea of God and authority in general. The Old Testament is full of injustice, arbitrary behavior, patriarchal assumptions, and all-purpose insanity. It presents God as the Supernatural Toddler, having tantrums about every little thing, and also as the Ultimate Bad Dad, handing out punishments out of all proportion to the sins of the hapless humans. Raining frogs, plagues of locusts. Slaughters of innocents. Ladies turned to pillars of salt; the whole world wiped out in forty days and forty nights of rain. Jeepers. The Bible read as though God was a gleefully sadistic author intent on chastising his characters for no reason except his own amusement. I put down the Good Book, confused. On the radio Elvis Costello sang "(What's So Funny 'Bout) Peace, Love, and Understanding." I went back to reading, slogging toward the virgin birth, the babe in the manger. I needed a God who made sense to me, and I could not find Him in these pages.

I did eventually join the Church of the Funnies: I became an artist. My application essay for art school was about my desire to become an Art Nun. This had nothing to do with poverty or celibacy; it was about devotion. I was trying to express my willingness to devote my life to Art, to forsake all other pursuits and to be a ruthless dreamer, a bride of Art. I was ready to serve, and the thing I wanted to serve was the mystery, the beauty, the deep transcendence I experienced with certain works of art. I was looking for the communion of souls in the museum, in the library, on the radio, and finding it there more often than not.

One day in art school, in 1982 or so, a professor handed me a Xerox of a speech by Jacques Barzun. It was called "The Rise of Art as Religion," and the central idea—that art has taken the place of religion in our daily lives, that art is occupying the void left by our retreat from God—made a lot of sense to me. He wrote it in 1973 as one of a series of talks he gave that were published under the title *The Use and Abuse of Art*. To me, a nineteen-year-old art student, the idea that art could be useful was startling; I had been brought up on "art for art's sake," and it had never occurred to me to ask what art is for. Why do we make art? What is it supposed to do?

Those beautiful drawings on the walls of the caves are surely not the earliest things humans made, but they are what we have now, they have survived all this time, and time has not deprived them of their power—time has only added to their mystery. In a young world, when there were not many man-made things, these drawings must have thrilled everyone who saw them. Someone stood there, all those years ago, with a burnt stick in his or her small hand, and made a picture. This may have had to do with their religion, but I imagine that when the artist stood back and looked at the finished drawing, that artist felt the same way artists always feel at that moment: joy and disappointment. It's good, but it isn't as good as the thing we meant to make. The thing we cannot quite achieve leads us to make the next thing, and the next after that. We make things to find out what they are, what they can be, what they might mean. We make things to keep us company in the world. We make things to show them to other people, because we want them to understand.

The thing that makes us want God is the same thing that makes us want Art—we want meaning. We want there to be more than meets the eye.

God is an attempt at an explanation for the universe. Art is not an explanation. Art is a question that is permanently unanswered.

Art is like the little red laser dot being chased by Claudine, my cat: It's uncatchable, and if you do catch it, it disappears. And God is like that, too. Elusive, maybe nonexistent, though others have attested to His reality.

Shortly after I graduated from art school, I was having lunch with my mother in a Chinese restaurant when she told me that she was leaving the Catholic Church. I was surprised, but it made sense. She had been doing a lot of reading, some Joseph Campbell, some books about American Indians, books about Buddhism. She didn't like the way the church treated women; she had quietly observed a lot of contradictions and worrisome ideas being advocated by the church, and she had decided she was done with that.

A few weeks later I found a letter in our laundry room; my mom had accidently or on purpose left it there, so I read it. It was from the pastor of our church. It said he was sorry she was leaving, but perhaps she would change her mind and come back, so could she please continue tithing the same amount of money she had been giving before? It was perhaps the most cringe-worthy letter I have ever read before or since. Even though I had deserted Catholicism, I still wanted it to be above everyday things like money. I wanted the church to be holy and pure, and it persisted in being a human thing, full of human inconsistencies. And maybe I love it and hate it all the more for that.

In the Church of the Funnies the sins are different from the sins in the Ten Commandments. Hardly anybody in the Church of the Funnies seems to mind a little mild blasphemy, and making graven images of everything heavenly and earthly and under the sea is no problem at all. The seven deadly sins of art are: Unoriginality, Dishonesty, Censorship, Banality, Sentimentality, Egotism, and Selling Out. You can see that these somewhat correspond to the originals (which are Lust, Envy, Sloth, Wrath, Gluttony, Greed, and Pride, in case you need a quick review). The virtues of art are: Humility, Patience, Originality, Openness, Generosity, Diligence, and Gratitude.

You might have noticed that this Church of the Funnies, this religion of Art, does not require genius or even talent. We all aspire toward quality. We all do our best. Whether we are artists, trying to create, or audience members, trying to understand, we bring our virtuous Openness and Diligence to the task, and we are Generous and Grateful if we manage to connect with the art, or each other. We accept any hints we may receive about the nature of the universe with Humility. We try not to Sell Out on the way to serving the mysterious Church of the Funnies, or God, or Santa, or whoever might be listening.

The other day I called my mom because I wanted to run this sermon by her, to make sure she didn't mind my telling the world about her spiritual concerns. My mother is also an artist, so she knew what I meant about this Church of the Funnies business. She's a quilter and a fiber artist, and she knows that feeling, when you open yourself out to the nothingness, and then there is something, an idea, that wasn't there a moment ago, but now it seems to have been just waiting for you to ask. Some people have called this divine inspiration, to be breathed upon by the gods. My mom surprised me by saying that she and my dad had talked this over, inspiration and creation and all of it, the whole shebang, and that they'd agreed: Everything is connected. It doesn't matter if you call it God or Art or the Funnies or a cat chasing an uncatchable red laser dot. Mom said that she and Dad had always liked the idea of the Force in the *Star Wars* movies. Yes, I said, I'm sure a lot of people feel the same about that. We both paused, because it felt a little weird to be discussing heavy philosophical ideas in *Star Wars* jargon, but there it is: Everything is connected. May the Force be with you. Amen.

Backwards in Seville

Helene stood at the front railing on the upper deck in the dark, watching as the ship maneuvered at a funny angle too close to a low stone bridge. A few people stood near her, all watching quietly as the crew worked on the deck below them. The band was playing Ellington at the other end of the ship; couples would be dancing neatly, persistently. In the cabins below most of the passengers were asleep.

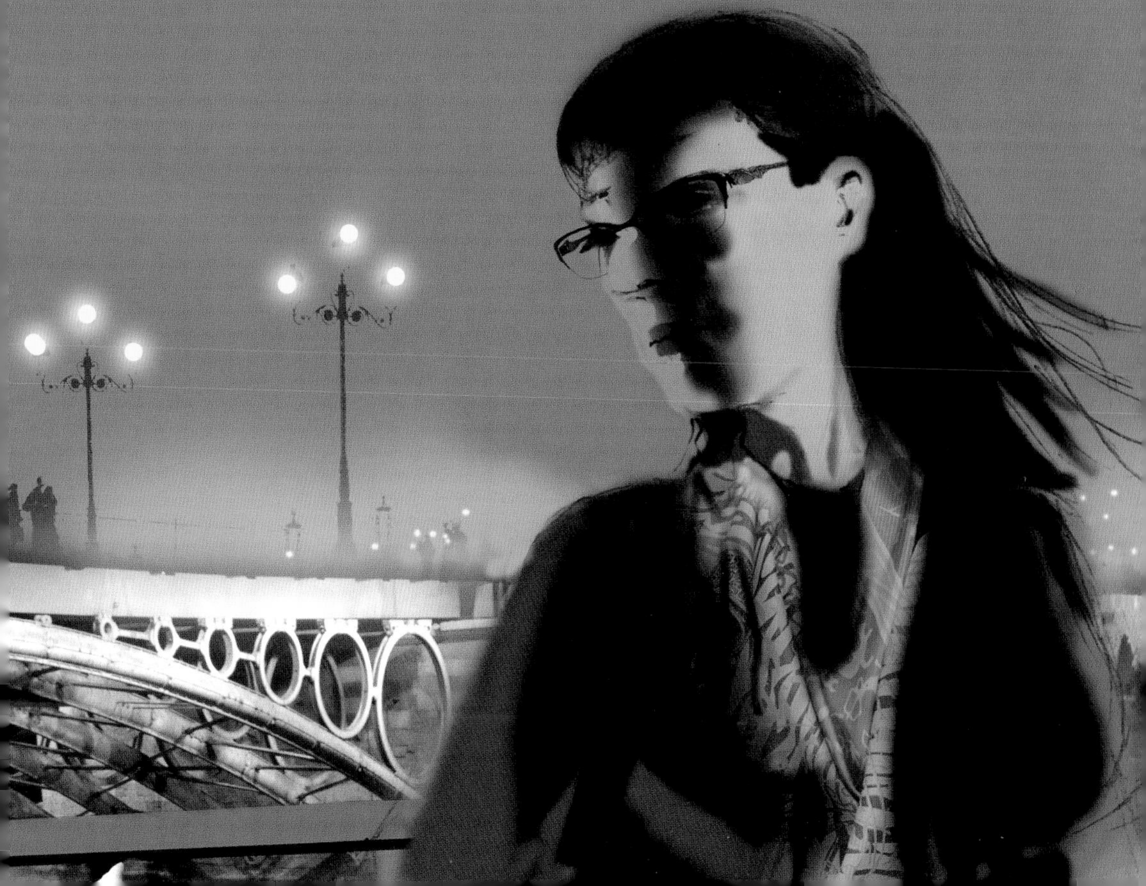

Helene's father, Lewis, had been sleeping when she left their cabin, his face collapsed without the dentures, his mouth open, snoring. In sleep he frightened her. *Let him wake up tomorrow*, she prayed every night, though she was not religious. *Don't take him from me yet*.

The *Persephone* wasn't very large for a cruise ship. There were three hundred passengers and one hundred and fifty crew members. Helene had never been on a cruise before and had braced herself for bingo, seasickness, and enforced camaraderie, though her father kept assuring her it wasn't that kind of cruise.

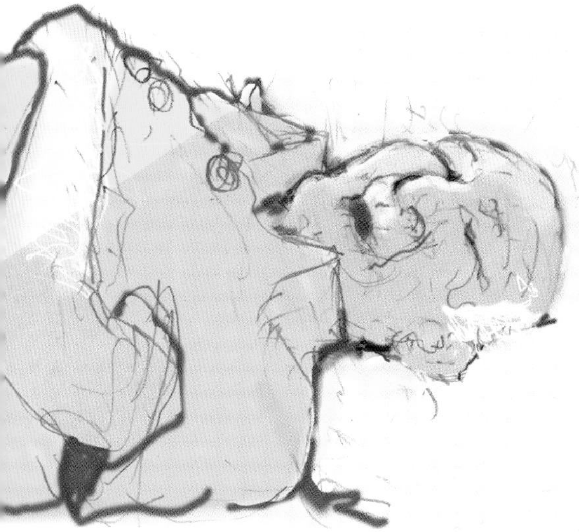

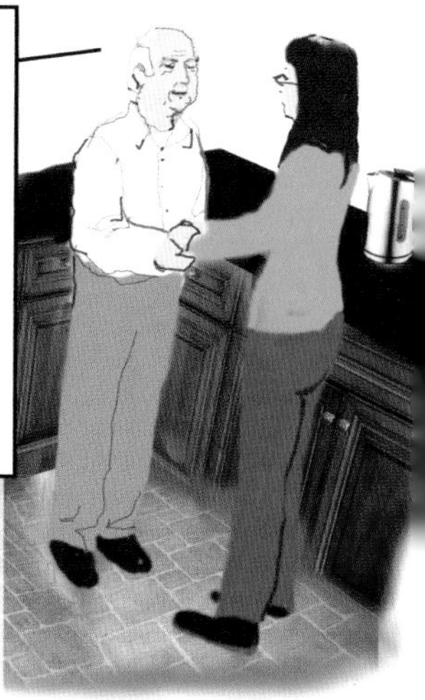
It's low-key, mostly excursions to churches and lectures on Matisse. You've never been to Rome or Barcelona; you'll love it. The Mediterranean is very calm in June. Don't worry so much, Sweet Pea.

She had nodded and smiled. Of course she would love it; he wanted her to love it.

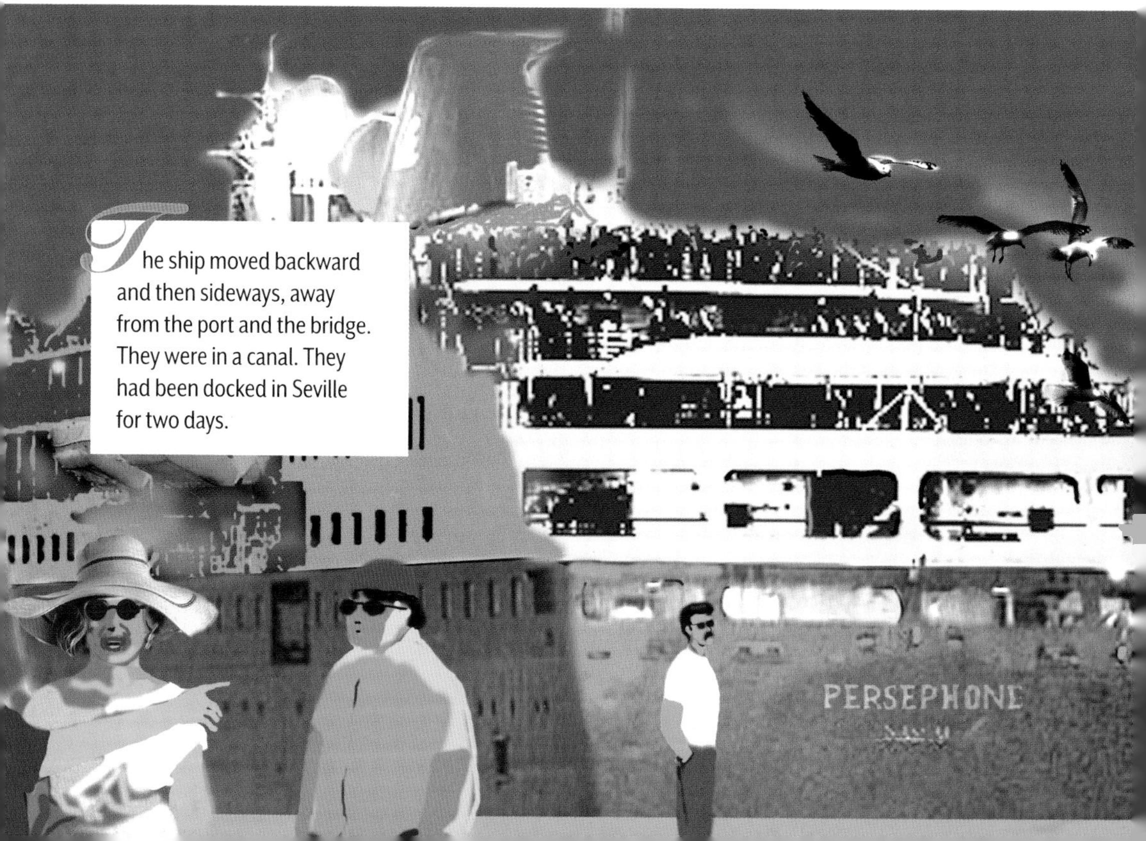
The ship moved backward and then sideways, away from the port and the bridge. They were in a canal. They had been docked in Seville for two days.
PERSEPHONE

In Seville Helene had gone on an excursion to a convent, a very sad convent run by an order called the Poor Clares.

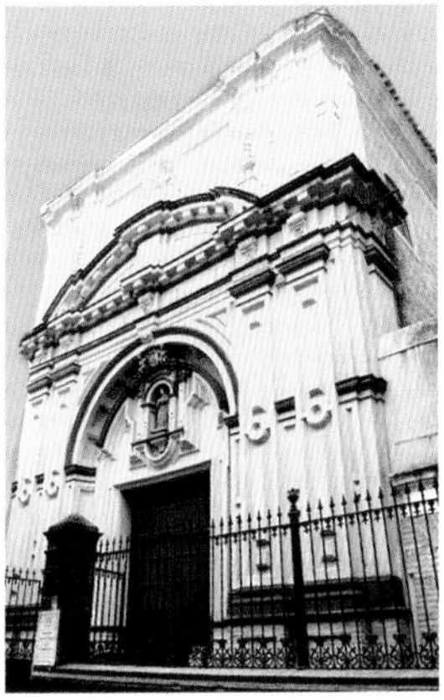

All the nuns were from Africa and had been cloistered until recently, but then the Poor Clares had become too poor, and now they sold baked goods and let tourists come inside for a few euros each.

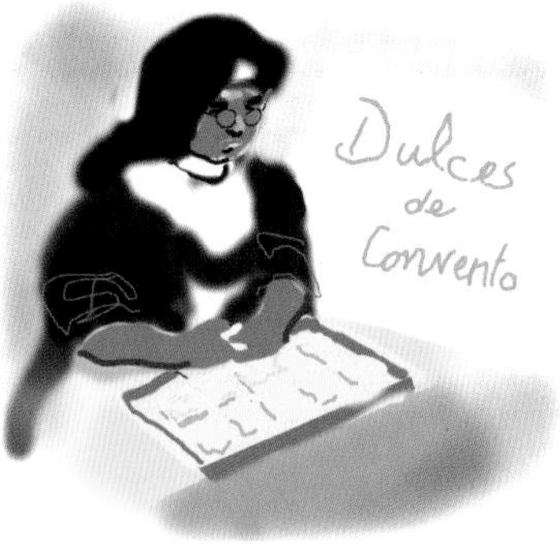
Dulces de Convento

Helene felt bad for them. She thought of the Sistine Chapel and St. Peter's, which had been her first excursion.

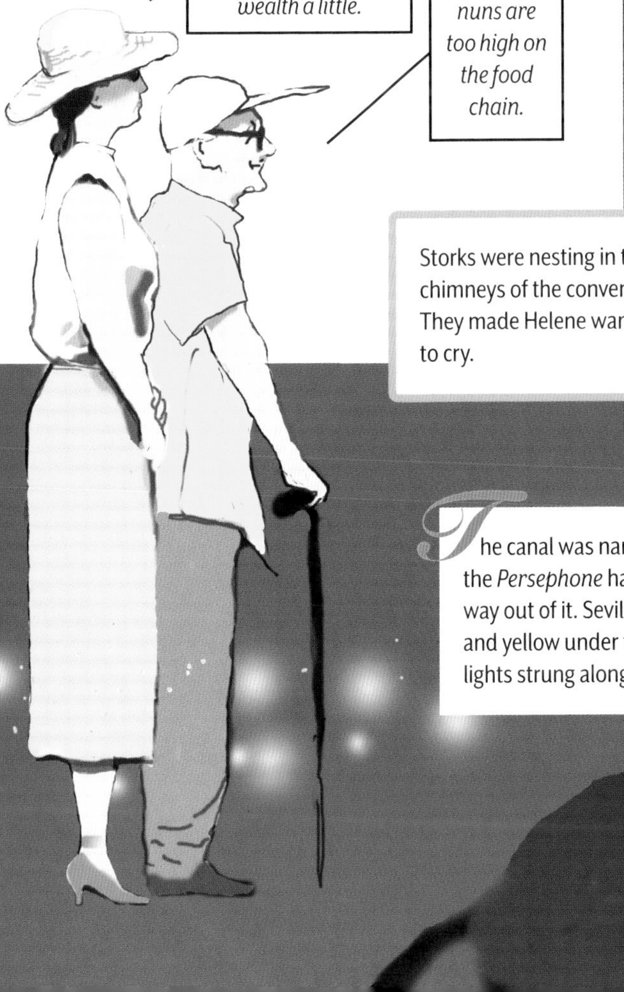
You'd think they could redistribute the wealth a little.
I don't imagine nuns are too high on the food chain.

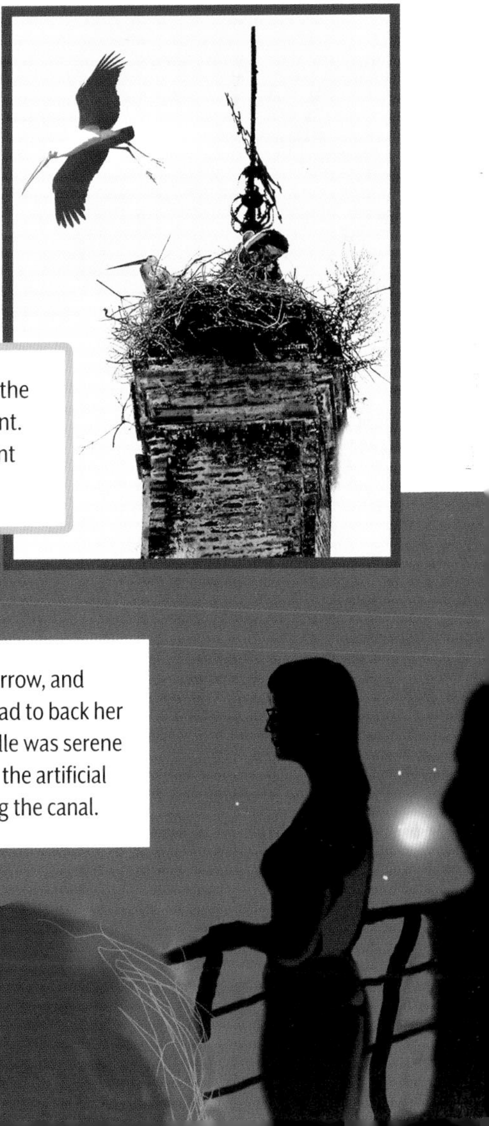

Storks were nesting in the chimneys of the convent. They made Helene want to cry.

The canal was narrow, and the *Persephone* had to back her way out of it. Seville was serene and yellow under the artificial lights strung along the canal.

Seville receded. Helene tried to remember where they were headed . . . Lisbon. Then home: They would fly to London and then back to Chicago.

Lewis had been tired before they began the trip. She realized that he should have had a wheelchair, her heart sinking as she remembered that he always refused to use a wheelchair.

She screwed up her courage and asked him anyway and was surprised when he nodded, still breathing heavily. Helene didn't travel much, but Lewis always had so it was all familiar to him.

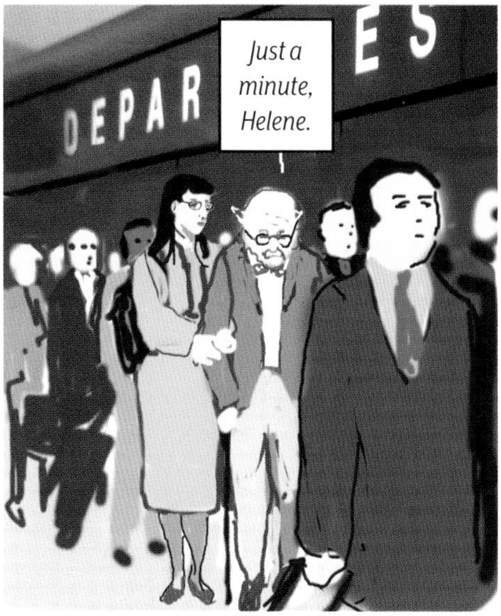
DEPAR ES
Just a minute, Helene.

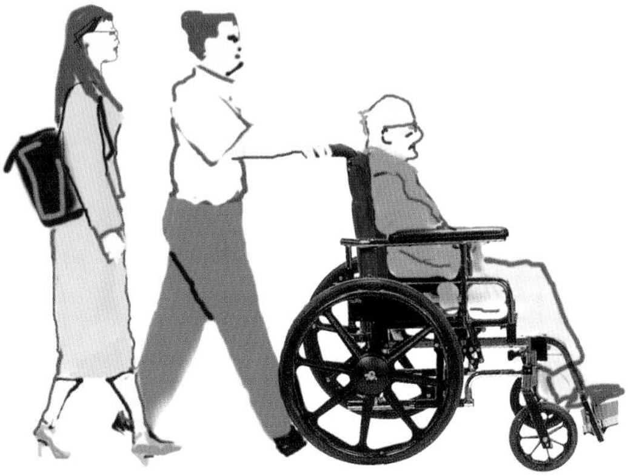

She watched her father sit, chin sunk into chest, and she finally admitted to herself that he was terribly old. *When did this happen?*

He was always fine, and now . . . Her mother had died in February. It was her mother's place Helene occupied here on the ship. She slept in the narrow bed her mother should have slept in, ate the bland food her mother would have eaten.

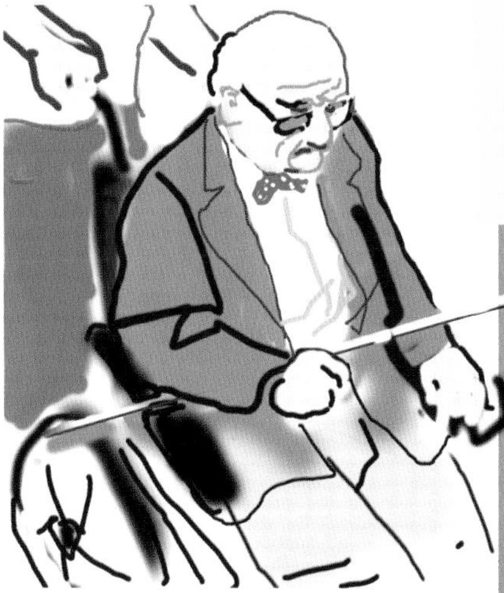

Lewis accepted Nora's absence with grace; he might say, "Your mother would have liked that," or "Your mother always did this," but he never made Helene feel that he would have preferred his wife's company to hers.

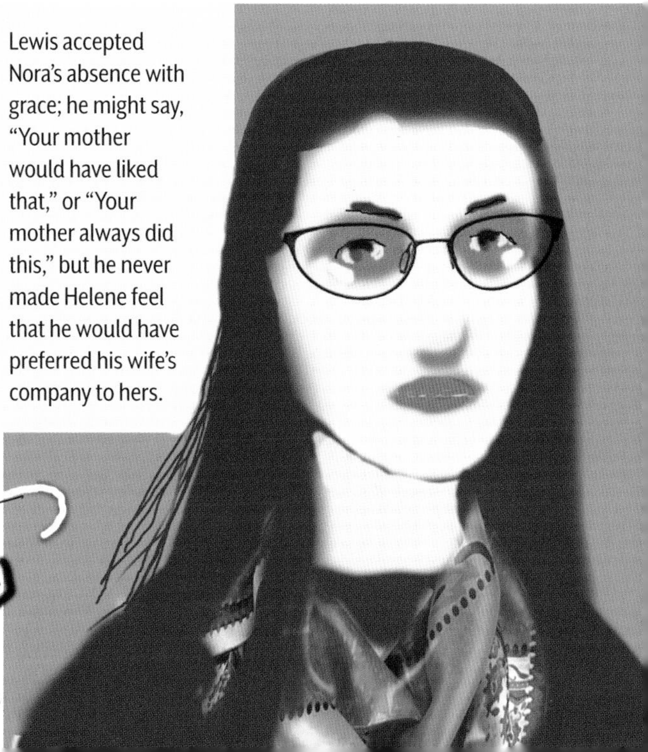

When Helene was small, she had stolen her mother's lipstick and gone down to breakfast with scarlet lips. Her parents had smiled at each other and pretended not to notice as she left lip prints on her juice glass.

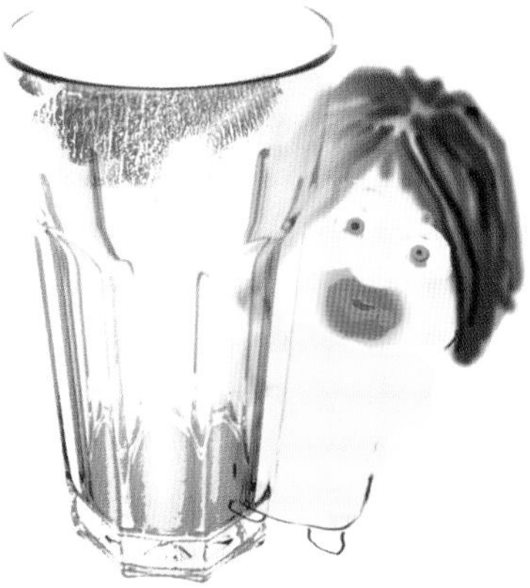

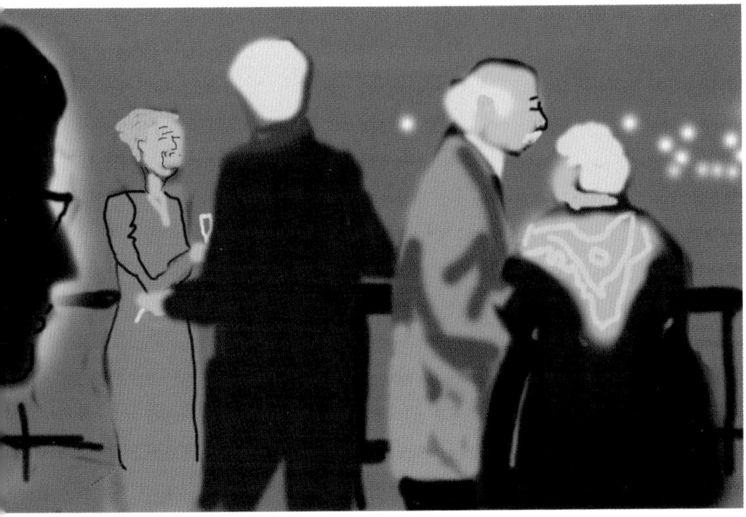

Helene was forty-five years old, by far the youngest passenger on the ship. The other passengers at the rail were all in pairs. They were white-haired and bent but exceedingly compatible, each husband inclining toward his wife when she spoke quietly into his ear, all of them dressed for dinner with care, all leaning on the rail for support with a glass of wine or a cocktail clutched in one hand.

Helene thought of Evan. *Is that what we would have looked like in forty years?*

She had met Evan when she was twenty-eight and he was thirty-six. He'd always seemed on the verge of marrying her; she was patient.

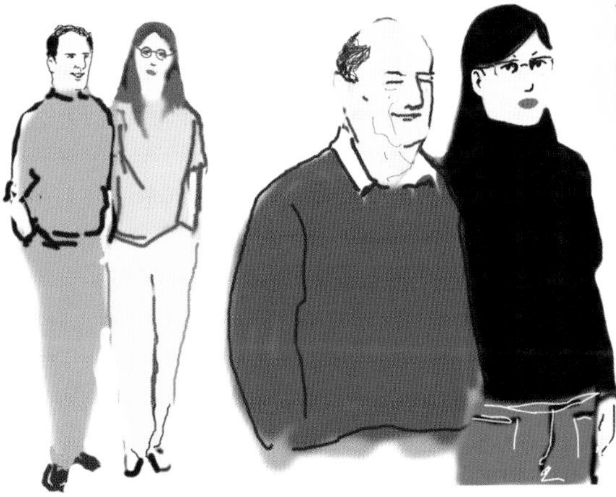

When he broke up with her fourteen years later and married a girl half her age, she understood that she'd been gullible and that he was a jerk, but, oh, well, and so she had lapsed into a quiet, permanent rage.

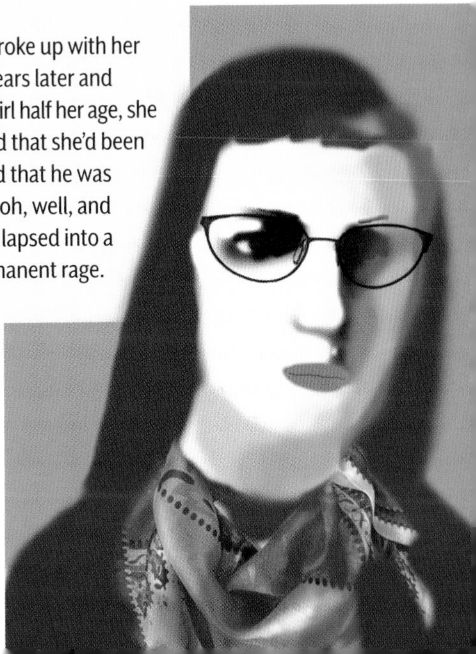

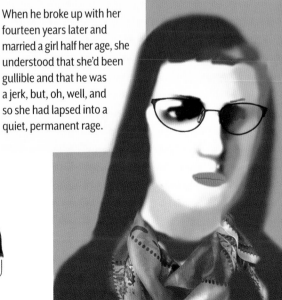

It would be nice to have a drink, but lethargy kept her at the railing. The canal unspooled backwards, around the ship. It gave Helene the feeling that time was reversing, that things might be undone. *Daddy wouldn't be old, Mom wouldn't have died, Evan would come back, and we'd have kids; it would all be different, I would change everything. I would change.*

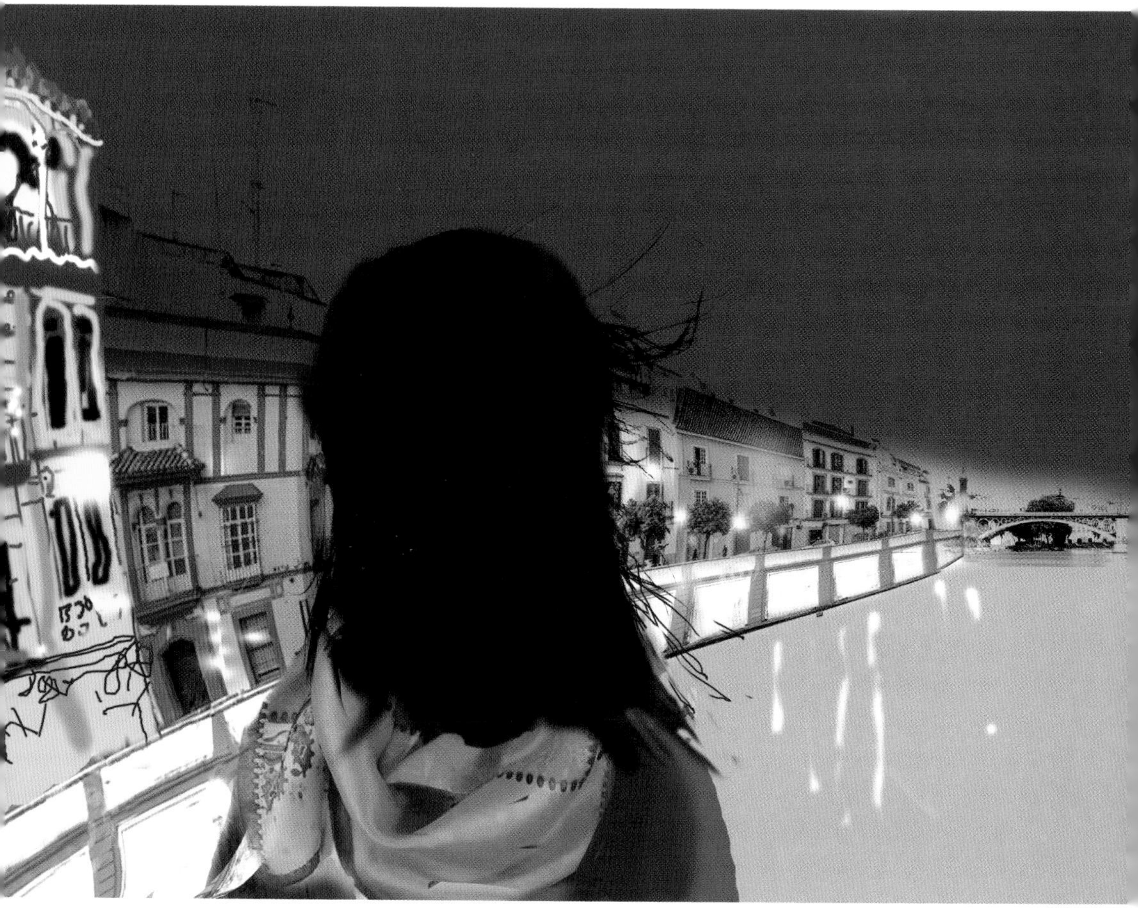

Trees and houses came from behind her; little boats began to appear in the water as the canal widened. Soon they would turn the ship and sail forward. Everything flowed away into the distance and the darkness.

One of the women at the rail dropped her cane, and her husband bent painfully and retrieved it for her. *How he cares for her*, Helene thought. *No one takes care of me; it's always me taking care of somebody*. When she was a child, she had been very timid, scared of strangers, thunder, the poodle next door, escalators, anything new or loud, anything that moved, pretty much. Her mother had kept her close, kissed her on the tip of her ear, whispered encouragement.

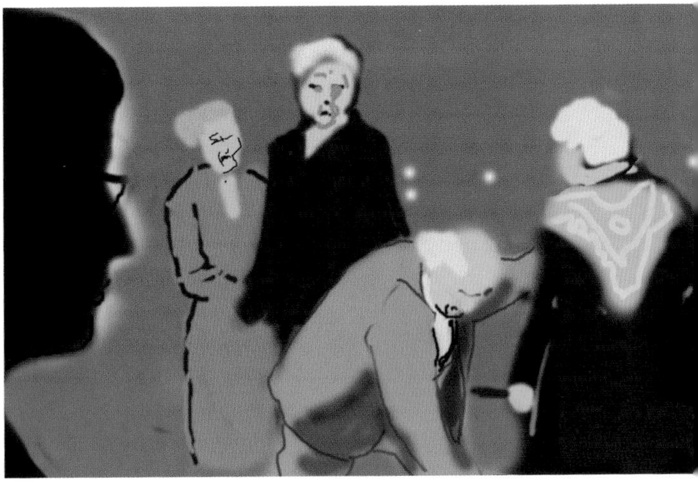

Her father had bought her funny presents, a tiny silk umbrella from Paris,

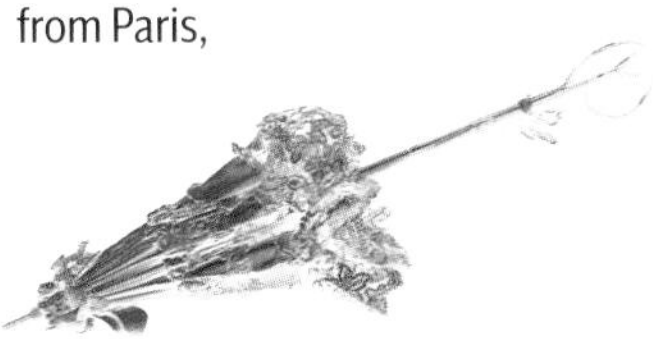

a tin of green tea from Kyoto.

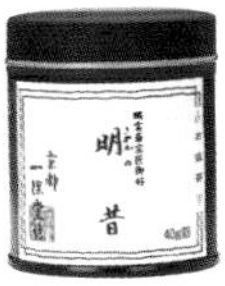

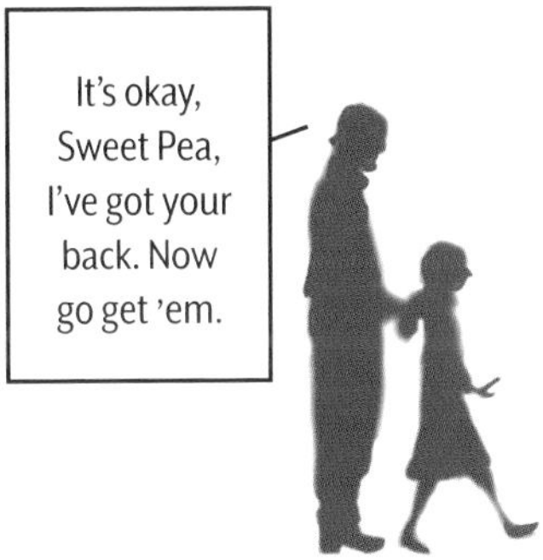
It's okay, Sweet Pea, I've got your back. Now go get 'em.

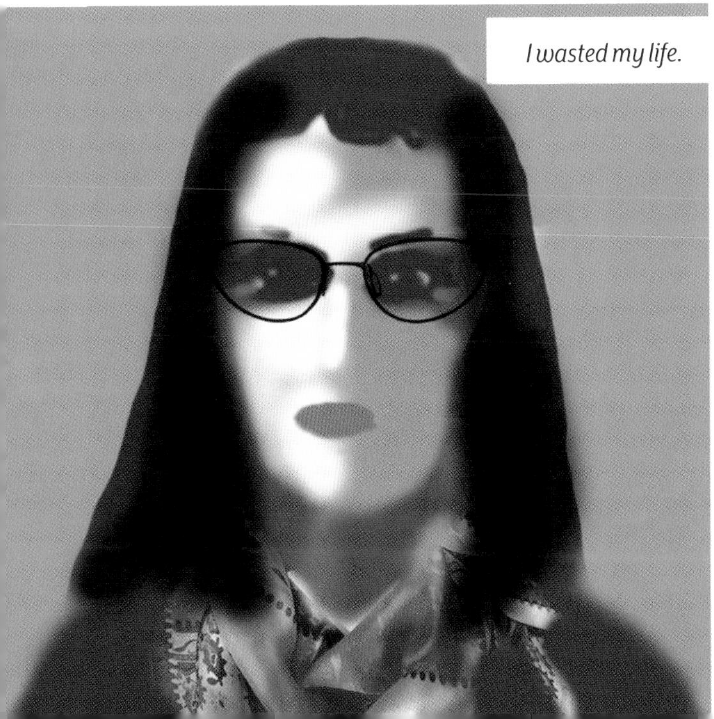
I wasted my life.

She imagined the Poor Clares, tucked into their neat beds in their cloister, secure in the night, in belief. *How good it must be to believe*. Lewis and Nora were indifferent to religion. When Helene was nine, she had asked about God. Lewis had taken her to synagogue, and Nora had taken her to church, once each, and they had asked very carefully if she wanted to go back, and she'd said no thank you, sensing their lack of enthusiasm.

Now Helene wondered what her father believed, now when he was so close to death, when death had already claimed her mother. He was never afraid. He'd watched the couples dancing tonight with a smile.

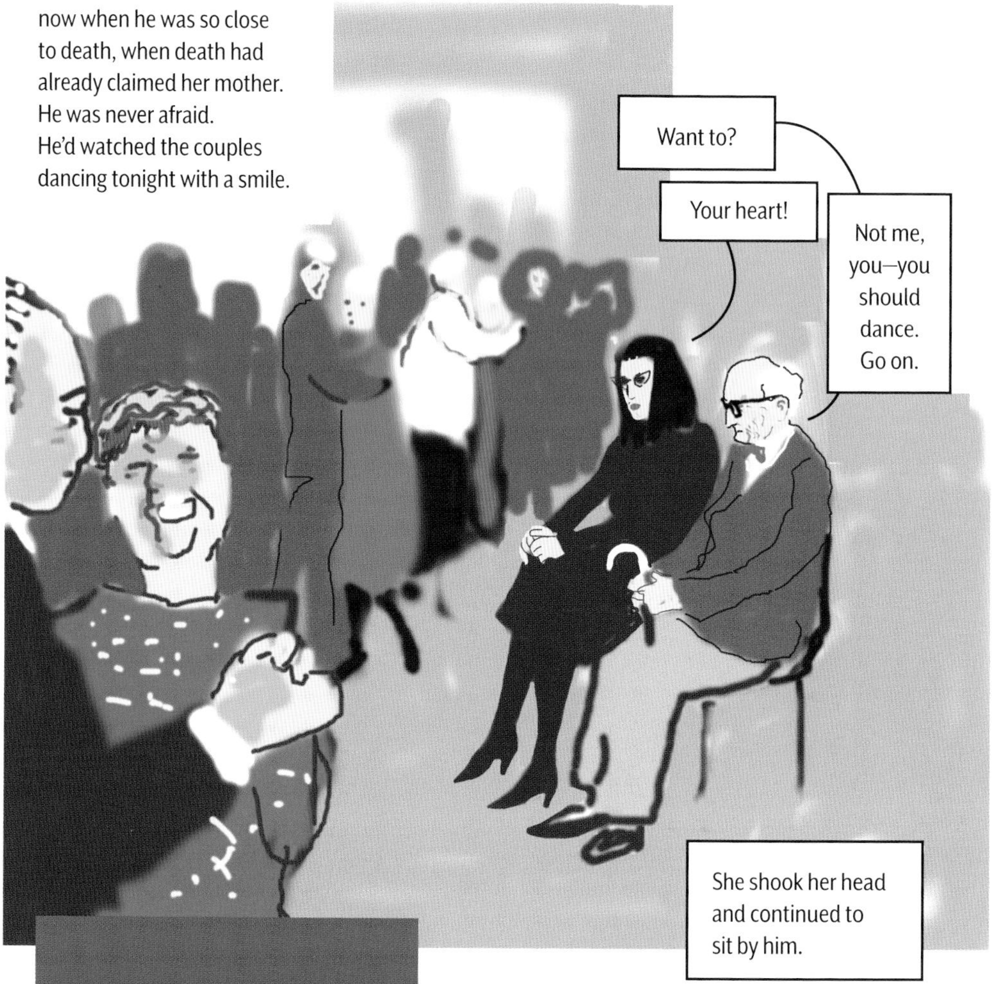
Want to?
Your heart!
Not me, you—you should dance. Go on.
She shook her head and continued to sit by him.

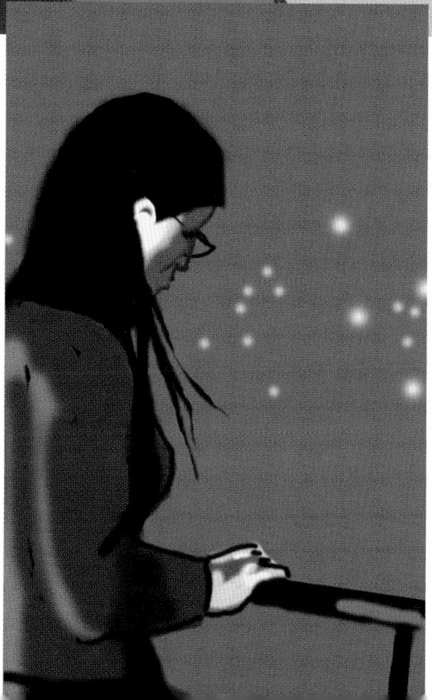

Helene looked over the railing. The water was down there somewhere; she could hear it churning. The first day they were on the ship, there had been a muster of all the passengers. They had been instructed in how to use their life jackets and where to gather if the alarm sounded. They had been told never to even think of diving off the ship; it was a long way down, you could break your neck, you could drown. Sharks could eat you. You might never be found.

I wish I could give the rest of it to him, Helene thought. *Daddy would know what to do with another half a life. To me it's just a burden.* Helene closed her eyes and tried to pray. She opened her eyes and felt foolish.

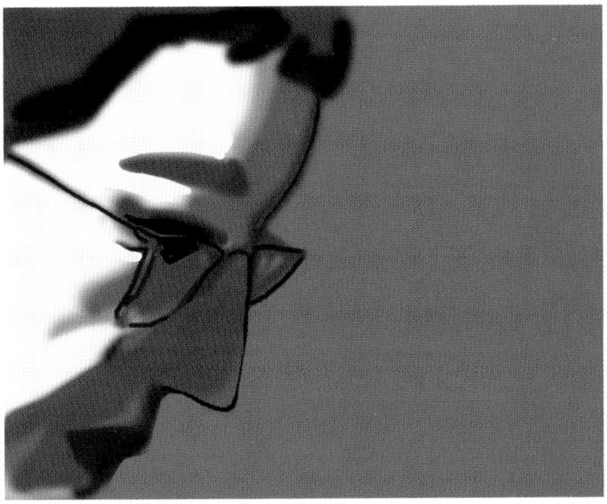

The canal was wide enough now, and the ship began to turn. The world revolved around Helene, and she saw the way ahead. They were about to pass under an enormous bridge.

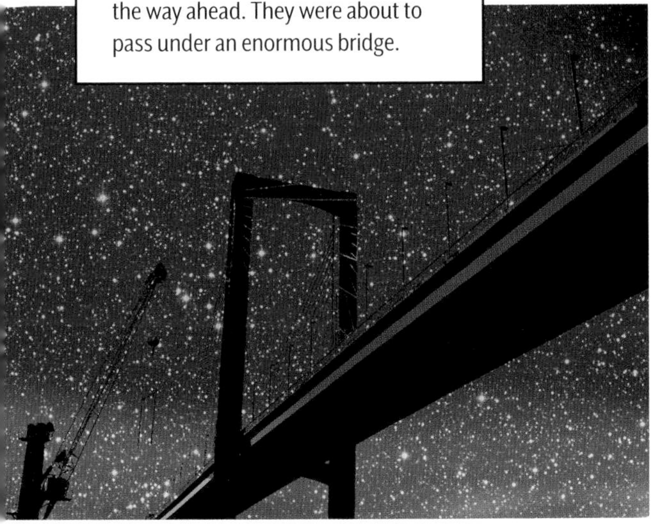

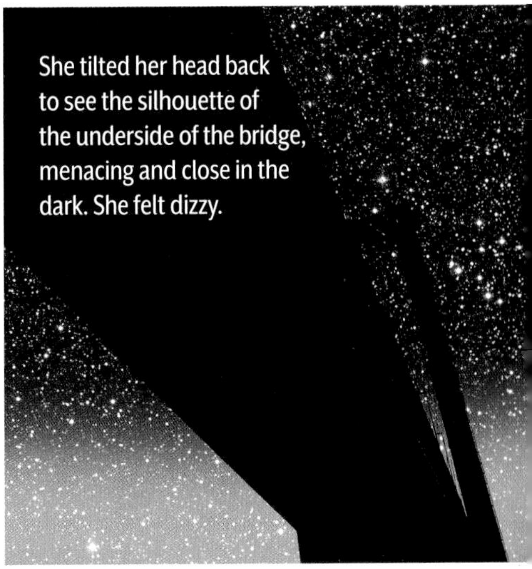
She tilted her head back to see the silhouette of the underside of the bridge, menacing and close in the dark. She felt dizzy.

She looked down and saw her hands on the railing, hands suddenly unfamiliar, knobby-knuckled and spotted. *Oh!* she thought, *is it really that easy?*

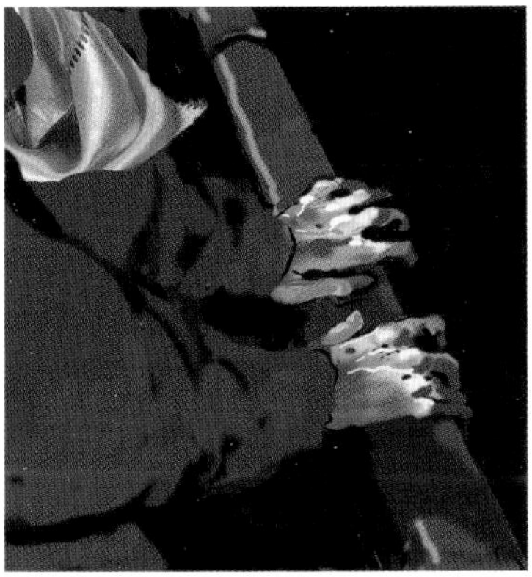

She put her hands to her soft, wrinkled face, looked down at her now-loose clothing. Her heart pounded, her vision blurred. Aches and pains beset her. The sounds of the world were suddenly muted. The ship sailed on as before.

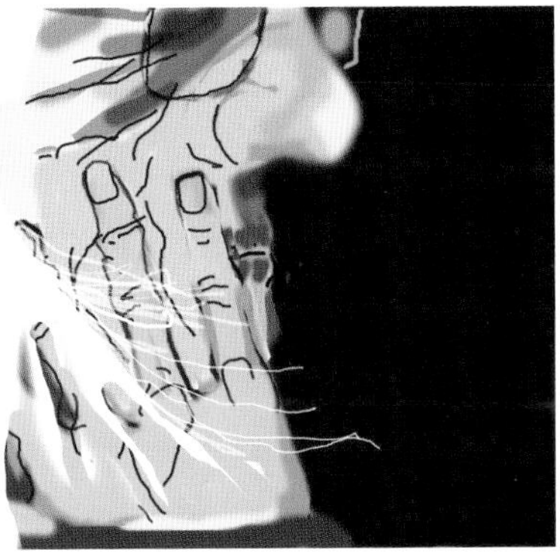

Helene began to creep along the railing, back to the cabin, joyously certain of what she would find there.

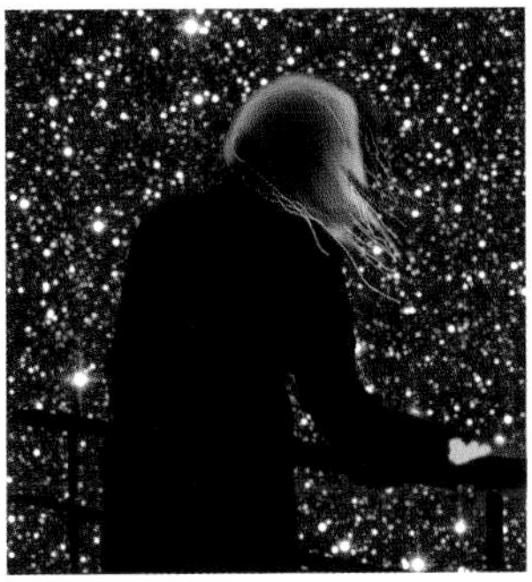

end

Acknowledgments

Thanks and credit where credit is due:

We would like to thank Ken Gerleve for coloring two stories, *The Composite Boyfriend* and *RoseRed-SnowRidingBeautyShoesHoodSleepingWhite*, and for providing invaluable assistance every step of the way.

Thanks to Joseph Regal, Tamar Brazis, Dan Franklin, Sara Corbett.

Thanks to Patricia Niffenegger and Beth Niffenegger for finding old *Reader's Digest* Condensed Books (books so unwanted that no bookshops keep them).

And thanks to Hayley Campbell for introducing us to each other in the first place: This book wouldn't exist without you.

Publishing History

Some of these stories have been previously published in their original (text-only) form. Two of them, "Thursdays, Six to Eight p.m." and "Backwards in Seville," have been published as comics before but are revised here for maximum effect.

THURSDAYS, SIX TO EIGHT P.M.

This comic is an expanded version of our first joint effort. It was originally published in April 2014 in the *Guardian Weekend*'s feature *Novelists Do Comics* to mark the opening of the British Library's exhibition of British comics.

THE COMPOSITE BOYFRIEND

This story first appeared in the anthology *Mr. Wrong: Real-Life Stories About the Men We Used to Love,* edited by Harriet Brown. New York: Ballantine Books, 2007.

ROSEREDSNOWRIDINGBEAUTYSHOESHOODSLEEPINGWHITE

This fairy tale was written for the December 2014 issue of British *Elle*, an issue devoted to feminism. The prompt was a photograph by Bjarne Jonasson.

SECRET LIFE, WITH CATS

A slightly different version of this story was serialized in the *Chicago Tribune* in October 2006 with art by Audrey. This version was recently included in *Ghostly*, a collection of ghost stories Audrey edited. New York: Scribner, 2015; London: Jonathan Cape, 2015.

THE RUIN OF GRANT LOWERY

This was written for the *Guardian*'s twenty-first-century fairy-tale feature "Once Upon a Time . . . ," published November 10, 2007.

GIRL ON A ROOF

This was written for *Four Letter Word: Invented Correspondence from the Edge of Modern Romance* (eds. Joshua Knelman, Rosalind Porter). New York: Free Press, 2008.

JAKOB WYWIALOWSKI AND THE ANGELS

This piece originally appeared as a holiday story on Amazon's home page in December 2003.

AT THE MOVIES

This was written in 2005 as a performance piece and has not been previously published. It was performed for Jeff Abell's Sound Images class.

MOTION STUDIES: GETTING OUT OF BED

This was written as a performance piece and was performed at the Museum of Contemporary Art in Chicago in October 2007 with the writing group Text III. It has not been previously published.

THE WRONG FAIRY

This was first published in the anthology *Magic: An Anthology of the Esoteric and Arcane* (ed. Jonathan Oliver). Oxford, UK: Solaris, 2012. "The Wrong Fairy" was inspired by *The Doyle Diary: The Last Great Conan Doyle Mystery—With a Holmesian Investigation into the Strange and Curious Case of Charles Altamont Doyle* (Charles Altamont Doyle, introduction by Michael Baker). New York: Paddington Press, 1978.

DIGGING UP THE CAT

This piece was written in 2006 and has not been previously published.

THE CHURCH OF THE FUNNIES

This was written and given as the Gaeia Manchester Sermon in

October 2014 for the Manchester Literary Festival at Manchester Cathedral. Many thanks to Arts Council England and the Manchester City Council.

BACKWARDS IN SEVILLE

This was written for *Shadow Show: All-New Stories in Celebration of Ray Bradbury,* edited by Sam Weller and Mort Castle. New York: William Morrow, 2012. Our original comics version was first published in *Shadow Show #2*, San Diego: IDW, 2014 and again in *Shadow Show: Stories In Celebration of Ray Bradbury,* San Diego: IDW, 2015.

1 3 5 7 9 10 8 6 4 2

Jonathan Cape, an imprint of Vintage Publishing,
20 Vauxhall Bridge Road,
London SW1V 2SA

Jonathan Cape is part of the Penguin Random House group of companies whose addresses
can be found at global.penguinrandomhouse.com.

Penguin
Random House
UK

Copyright © Audrey Niffenegger & Eddie Campbell 2018

Audrey Niffenegger & Eddie Campbell have asserted their
right to be identified as the authors of this Work
in accordance with the Copyright, Designs and Patents Act 1988

First published in the United Kingdom by Jonathan Cape in 2018

penguin.co.uk/vintage

A CIP catalogue record for this book is available from the British Library

ISBN 9781911214236

Printed and bound in China